Political Engagement and Popular Print in Spanish Naples (1503–1707)

Library of the Written Word

VOLUME 130

The Handpress World

Editors-in-Chief

Andrew Pettegree (*University of St Andrews*)
Arthur der Weduwen (*University of St Andrews*)

Editorial Board

Ann Blair (*Harvard University*)
Falk Eisermann (*Staatsbibliothek zu Berlin – Preußischer Kulturbesitz*)
Shanti Graheli (*University of Glasgow*)
Earle Havens (*Johns Hopkins University*)
Ian Maclean (*All Souls College, Oxford*)
Alicia Montoya (*Radboud University*)
Angela Nuovo (*University of Milan*)
Helen Smith (*University of York*)
Mark Towsey (*University of Liverpool*)
Malcolm Walsby (*ENSSIB, Lyon*)

VOLUME 107

The titles published in this series are listed at *brill.com/lww*

Political Engagement and Popular Print in Spanish Naples (1503–1707)

By

Laura Incollingo

BRILL

LEIDEN | BOSTON

Cover illustration: Engraving of the Vesuvius mid-eruption. From Giovanni Apolloni, *Il Vesuvio Ardente* (Naples: Egidio Longo, 1632). The text in the scroll is Isaia 33:13: "Sentiranno coloro che sono lontani quanto ho fatto, sapranno i vicini qual è la mia forza". ("You who are far away, hear what I have done; you who are near, acknowledge my power"). Naples, Private Collection.

Library of Congress Cataloging-in-Publication Data

Names: Incollingo, Laura, author.
Title: Political engagement and popular print in Spanish Naples (1503–1707) / by Laura Incollingo.
Description: Leiden ; Boston : Brill, 2024. | Series: Library of the written word, 1874–4834 ; volume 130 | Includes bibliographical references and index.
Identifiers: LCCN 2024026421 (print) | LCCN 2024026422 (ebook) | ISBN 9789004549395 (hardback) | ISBN 9789004549401 (ebook)
Subjects: LCSH: Publishers and publishing—Italy—Naples (Kingdom)—History—16th century. | Publishers and publishing—Italy—Naples (Kingdom)—History—17th century. | Printing—Italy—Naples (Kingdom)—History—16th century. | Printing—Italy—Naples (Kingdom)—History—17th century. | Street literature—Italy—Naples (Kingdom)—History and criticism. | Books and reading—Italy—Naples (Kingdom)—History. | Naples (Kingdom)—History—Spanish rule, 1442–1707.
Classification: LCC Z345.3.N37 I53 2024 (print) | LCC Z345.3.N37 (ebook) | DDC 070.50945/709031—dc23/eng/20240819
LC record available at https://lccn.loc.gov/2024026421
LC ebook record available at https://lccn.loc.gov/2024026422

Typeface for the Latin, Greek, and Cyrillic scripts: "Brill". See and download: brill.com/brill-typeface.

ISSN 1874-4834
ISBN 978-90-04-54939-5 (hardback)
ISBN 978-90-04-54940-1 (e-book)
DOI 10.1163/9789004549401

Copyright 2025 by Koninklijke Brill BV, Leiden, The Netherlands.
Koninklijke Brill BV incorporates the imprints Brill, Brill Nijhoff, Brill Schöningh, Brill Fink, Brill mentis, Brill Wageningen Academic, Vandenhoeck & Ruprecht, Böhlau and V&R unipress.
All rights reserved. No part of this publication may be reproduced, translated, stored in a retrieval system, or transmitted in any form or by any means, electronic, mechanical, photocopying, recording or otherwise, without prior written permission from the publisher. Requests for re-use and/or translations must be addressed to Koninklijke Brill BV via brill.com or copyright.com.

This book is printed on acid-free paper and produced in a sustainable manner.

Contents

Acknowledgements   VII
List of Figures, Maps and Charts   VIII
Abbreviations   X

Introduction   1
1   Cheap Print and the Problem of Readership   4
2   A Note on Sources and Terminology   7
3   Popular Culture in Italian Historiography   10
4   Into the Archives   15
5   Aim and Structure of the Book   23

1   Printing in Naples   25
1   An Organization for Booksellers and Printers   26
2   A Thriving Industry   32
3   Laws and Regulations   45
4   Biographical Notes on Notable Printers   54

2   Print and Politics   57
1   Broadsheets, Proclamations and the Communication of the Law   59
2   Newspapers and Propaganda   67
3   The Cost of News   83

3   Print in Times of Crisis   87
1   Masaniello's Revolt   92
2   French Propaganda in the Neapolitan Republic   97
3   The Pamphlet War   109
4   The Spanish Side of the Argument   112

4   Print and Natural Disasters   116
1   The Vesuvius Eruption of 1631   122
2   The Plague of 1656   137

5   Print and Religion   151
1   Religious Censorship   153
2   Printing Religious Books   163
3   A Harmonious Relationship   169
4   Peculiarities of Neapolitan Devotion   174

Conclusions   182

Appendix: People of the Book Trade in Seventeenth-Century
Naples   187
Selected Bibliography   200
Index of Modern Authors   224
Index of Names and Subjects   225

Acknowledgements

It feels very surreal to write these acknowledgements. It is the final touch, the cherry on top. Once these are done, so will be my first – I hope of many – book.

Looking back to the journey that brought me here, I relish in the opportunity to express my deepest gratitude to the many people that help me reached this point.

First and foremost, I want to thank Andrew Pettegree, Arthur der Weduwen and my editor at Brill for giving me this opportunity and believing in my work enough to actually publish it. I want to thank Simon Ditchfield for the stimulating questions and suggestions during my Viva, which helped me turning my dissertation into a book.

I am exceptionally grateful to the archivist and librarians from the various institutions in Naples, Rome, Simancas, Venice and Florence for their assistance in navigating their collections. Without their help, this research would have taken thrice as long. Particularly I want to thank Paola Milone at the Società Napoletana di Storia Patria for always making sure to save a spot for me, Padre Gerardo Imbriani from the Archivio Storico Diocesano for his invaluable insights and Simona Mammana from the National Library of Florence for her kindness in providing me reference material while away from Italy.

I have many friends that I want to thank. Without their support and companionship this book would not exist: Veronica Angeli, Alberto Josè Campillo, Jacob Baxter, Basil Bowdler, Zachary Brookman, Elena Cassi, Francesca Comelli, Barnaby Cullen, Nora Epstein, Jessica Farrell-Jobst, Panos Georgakakis, Hanna de Lange, Jessica Purdy, Simone Ricci, Chelsea Reutcke, Luigi Veneruso, Jacopo Di Vito, Elise Grace Watson, Alexa Zildjian, Maria Zukovs.

And of course the biggest thanks of all goes to my family. To my mother and sister, who encouraged and supported me in every way possible every step of the way. To my family in Naples, Silvana e Piero for housing and feeding me during my archival research, and Paolo, Sabrina, Maria Elena and Natascia for providing much needed distraction, love and laughter and for walking countless times with me among the streets of Naples, looking at churches and street signs.

Thanks to Leonardo Anatrini, my partner and biggest supporter. Thanks for being my sounding board, for listening to my complaints against archival restriction post COVID, for being always there to provide food, love, and support.

Figures, Maps and Charts

Figures

1.1   Street sign   29

2.1   First page of the contract for the newspapers. ASNA, Notai XVII, 531–532. Naples, Archivio di Stato   69

2.2   Neapolitan newspaper. SNSP, SG.B.1. Naples, Biblioteca della Società Napoletana di Storia Patria   71

2.3   Contract between Cavallo and the Real Giurisdizione. ASNA, Notai del Seicento, fs. 531/32, f.398r. Naples, Archivio di Stato   77

3.1   Micco Spadaro (1609–1675), *La rivolta di Masaniello* (post 1647/1660). Naples, Museo di Capodimonte   94

3.2   Broadsheets by Henry of Lorraine, Duke of Guise, SNSP, ms XXIX.E.2 f.11r Naples, Biblioteca della Società Napoletana di Storia Patria   98

3.3   Broadsheets by Henry of Lorraine, Duke of Guise, SNSP, ms XXIX.E.2 f.24r. Naples, Biblioteca della Società Napoletana di Storia Patria   99

3.4   [Anon], *Manifetso ritrovato di mattina affiso in una piazza di Napoli stampato in Aix et risposta* (1648). BNN, Bib. San Martino, ms 253 (ex 244). Naples, Biblioteca Nazionale   111

4.1   Micco Spadaro, Processione di San Gennaro per l'eruzione del 1631 (1656/1660). Naples, Museo di Capodimonte   127

4.2   The constellations in October 1631; the constellations in December 1631. SNSP, Sismica 06.G.15(16). Naples, Biblioteca della Società Napoletana di Storia Patria   130

4.3   The constellations in October 1631; the constellations in December 1631. SNSP, Sismica 06.G.15(16). Naples, Biblioteca della Società Napoletana di Storia Patria   131

4.4   [Giovanni Orlandi], *Nuova, e compita relatione del spaventevole incendio del Monte di Somma detto il Vesuvio* (1632). SNSP, Sismica 49.9. Naples Biblioteca della Società Napoletana di Storia Patria   133

4.5   Micco Spadaro, Largo mercatello durante la peste a Napoli (1656). Naples, Museo di Capodimonte   139

5.1   Forged indulgences attributed to Pope Alexander VI (*c.*1599) ASDN, Sant'Ufficio, 1138. Naples, Archivio Storico Diocesano   159

5.2   Forged indulgences attributed to Pope Alexander VI (*c.*1599) ASDN, Sant'Ufficio, 1138. Naples, Archivio Storico Diocesano   160

5.3   Holy Shroud indulgence (Roma & ristamp. in Napoli, per Nicolò Perrey & per il Maccarano & per Ottavio Beltrano, 1629). Turin, private collection   176

Maps

1.1 Map of Naples city centre as it appears today 27

Charts

2.1 Neapolitan currency equivalence chart 86

Abbreviations

ACDF   Archivio della Congregazione per la Dottrina della Fede
AFBN   Archivio della Fondazione "Banco di Napoli"
AGS   Archivo General de Simancas
ASDN   Archivio Storico Diocesano di Napoli
ASF   Archivio di Stato di Firenze
ASM   Archivio di Stato di Milano
ASMN   Archivio Storico Municipale di Napoli
ASN   Archivio di Stato di Napoli
BNCF   Biblioteca Nazionale Centrale di Firenze
BNN   Biblioteca nazionale di Napoli
SNSP   Società Napoletana di Storia Patria

Introduction

On 16 May 1503, Gonzalo Fernandez de Cordoba (1453–1515) entered the city of Naples at the head of his victorious troops to claim formally the title of Viceroy of Naples, thus inaugurating a period of over two centuries in which Spanish control over Naples took on the form of a Viceroyalty. This came after the Spanish army, led by Gonzalo himself, defeated the French in the Battle of Garigliano (1503), the last act of the Italian Wars as far as the Neapolitan peninsula was concerned, even if the animosity between the French and the Spaniards was far from over and it would manifest itself several times in the following two centuries.

Spanish control over southern Italy was nothing new; after all the Aragonese had ruled Naples since 1443, but the form that this control took from 1503 was new. The Viceroy was appointed by the Spanish Council of State, choosing from the candidates suggested by the Real y Supremo Consejo de Italia, which was a government office in Madrid with the task to oversee the Spanish territories in Italy. Under the Viceroy was the Consiglio Collaterale, which was appointed by the Viceroy himself and consisted of three lawyers (later five) and was the most important office within the city government. They had the task of making laws and in particular circumstances administrating justice and could even act as regents if the Viceroy was dead or incapacitated. Alongside the Collaterale there was the Regia Camera della Sommaria, which was responsible for the kingdom's finances, and the Gran Corte della Vicaria which was the kingdom's tribunal.[1] The distinctions between the specific areas of competence between the ruling offices were not always clear, particularly during times of crisis, which were not uncommon during the period of the Spanish Viceroyalty, which lasted until 1705. In those two centuries the city of Naples saw a volcanic eruption, a plague and countless riots and attempted rebellions, one of which, the Masaniello revolt, achieved a degree of success. All of these events tested the strength of the Spanish rulers and deeply affected the way in which the government choose to communicate with its subjects, as we will see in the pages that follow.

---

1 For a more in-depth analysis of the bureaucratic organization of the Neapolitan Vicerealm see Raffaele Colapietra, *Vita pubblica e classi politiche del Viceregno napoletano: 1656–1734* (Rome: Edizioni di Storia e Letteratura, 1961); Giuseppe Coniglio, *Il regno di Napoli al tempo di Carlo V* (Naples: Edizioni scientifiche italiane, 1951); Piero Ventura, *La capitale dei privilegi. Governo spagnolo, burocrazia e cittadinanza a Napoli nel Cinquecento* (Naples: Federico II University Press, 2018).

This book presents an exploration of the printing industry of Naples during the Spanish Viceroyalty. In particular, the focus will be on popular print and its role in building a relationship between the people of Naples and the Spanish authorities and how this particular type of publication was used to shape the public opinion of the citizens of Naples. I have always been somewhat sceptical of the view of the dynamic between Neapolitan people and Spanish rulers as one rooted exclusively in conflict. It did not seem possible, were that to be the case, for the Spanish Viceroyalty to have lasted as long as it did, despite the numerous obstacles. Therefore, I decided to take a closer look at the communications between the Spanish rulers and their subjects as a way of gaining insight into what I suspected to be a more complex and multifaceted dynamic. Before diving into this subject, however, I would like to provide a brief discussion of the historiography available on the subject, highlighting why this particular topic has been, up to this point, almost completely ignored by Italian and foreign scholars alike, as well as point the attention to the few notable studies on the subject that do exist.

Alfonso v of Aragon (1396–1458) was the embodiment of the Renaissance *mecenate*. He held books and letters in the highest regard, so much so that his first act upon entering the city in 1445 was to establish the first library of the city, as well as a number of scholarships to educate a new generation of young scholars. The interest in letters, books and the cultural enrichment of the realm was something that was shared by the Aragonese sovereigns and increased further when the new invention of movable type printing reached the city of Naples in 1470. The first book printed in Naples for which we have an exact date is *Lamentatio Nigro Pontis*, printed in 1470 by Sixtus Riessenger (*c.*1440–ca. 1505), a German printer and typographer who is credited with bringing the new printing technology to Naples.[2] Between the marked interest of the crown and the favourable condition within the city, it should not come as a surprise that the printing industry in Naples prospered. It was a port city, there was a university, several government offices, a tradition of men of letters and a great number of churches and rich monasteries, all ideal customers for the book trade. After Subiaco (the first book printed in Italy was printed in the Benedictine Abbey there in 1465) and Venice (the first book printed there was Cicerone, *Epistulae ad familiares*, printed by Johann of Speyer in 1469)

---

2 [Anon.], *Lamenatio Nigropontis* (Naples: [Sixtus Riessenger], 1470), USTC 765133. There is only one surviving copy of this work (an in folio constituted of four leaves), preserved among the collections of the National Library of Prague. For further information on this copy see Kamil Boldan, '*Lamentatio Nigropontis*: an unknown print of Sixtus Riessenger, a prototypographer of Naples', *Acta Musei Nationalis Pragae – Historia Litterarum*, 67, 1–2 (2022), pp. 5–12.

INTRODUCTION

Naples appears to be among the first cities in Italy in which the new technology immediately thrived.[3] During the fifteenth century there were over 180 booksellers that worked in Naples and its provinces, while in the same period in Rome there were 150.[4] In the beginning, these booksellers sold manuscripts and printed books alike, given that the technology was fairly new and expensive, but gradually the manuscripts began to fade from booksellers' catalogues as printed books gained popularity. The only obstacle that printers faced was the Church's opposition, but it was something that they quickly found a way around. There was a surprising number of books printed in Pozzuoli, a small city in the province of Naples, because apparently the diocese of Pozzuoli was more lenient when it came to granting permission to print books.[5] Despite the fact that, for reasons that we will discuss shortly, the printing industry in Naples has been mostly ignored by scholars, it was a thriving and prosperous trade and the city and its governors proved to be eager exponents of this new technology.

My interest on the topic of cheap print has been something that accompanied me throughout my studies, therefore when I decided to start a PhD directing my interest to this subject was a natural choice, and I soon decided that Naples was the perfect city for this investigation. The reasons why I choose this city from the beginning, and why I decided to focus particularly on the period of the Spanish Viceroyalty as the geographical and chronological object of my research, are various. One of them is that the historiography on the subject, especially in English, is meagre. But the same could be said for the entire history of Naples, particularly if we look into the history of popular print and its readers. What makes the Spanish Viceroyalty stands out is that during the two centuries of Spanish domination a succession of unusual events and catastrophes offer a unique opportunity to examine popular print in different circumstances. Given the importance of these political events, and considerable historical interest in natural disasters, it is surprising that these events have not received more attention. To identify why this should be the case we need to turn to the historiographical context. What we find is a general scarcity of studies on cheap print and popular print in Italy, particularly by Italian scholars, a scarcity all the more evident when it comes to Naples and Southern Italy.

---

3 In 1470 we have news of a book printed in Foligno, thus Naples and Foligno are both candidates for the title of third Italian city to have a printing press.

4 Gianni Macchiavelli, *Dizionario dei librai di Napoli nel Rinascimento* (Naples: M. D'auria Editore, 2012); Angela Nuovo, *Il commercio librario nell'Italia del Rinascimento* (Milan: Franco Angeli, 2003), p. 68.

5 Pietro Manzi, *Annali di Giovanni Sulzbach* (Florence: Olschki, 1970), p. 21.

1 Cheap Print and the Problem of Readership

In the field of book history, increasing attention has been given in recent years to the study of cheap print and ephemeral publications. This was a kind of literature that was cheap to produce, usually made out of a single sheet of paper, and quick to distribute and consume. Because of its volatile nature and the fact that it was a kind of literature intended to be consumed, it rarely survives and, as a result, has often been overlooked while studying print culture. This lacuna has to some extent been addressed in recent decades, with a number of studies focusing specifically on printed ephemera in various European countries.[6] Book historians have come to the realisation that it was indeed this kind of literature that constituted the backbone of the printing economy and therefore any study of history of printing would be incomplete without including the ephemeral product of the printing presses.[7] When we look closer at what exactly constituted this ephemeral world of printed words we find a great variety of materials: from broadsheet of public ordinances to religious and political pamphlets, from newspapers to ballads. All these materials circulated in the streets of European cities, posted on walls, given away for free at street corners or sold in bookshops, bookstalls or from the satchel of itinerant pedlars. In the early modern period, the streets of Italy, as well as those of the rest of Europe, were flooded with printed products of many different kinds. From news sheets to broadsheets, from *avvisi* (printed or manuscript sheets that were used to communicate military and political news) to pamphlets, a great deal of literature was intended for wide public dissemination. It is now acknowledged that this kind of cheap print was indeed read and valued by people of all social classes, and we can expect that as such it had a great influence on popular opinion. However, what exactly was this influence, how it worked, who were the readers and how were they influenced by what they read is still a subject less studied. Since the people were those to whom the State communication was directed and where the addressee of this particular communication strategy, it is natural to assume that they were influenced by it, because it was designated to do so. Many examples of this are offered in Chapter 3, as a further demonstration that an intentional communication strategy was implemented by the Spanish authorities, particularly in a time of crisis.

---

6 For example, the series that is being published by the Oxford University Press *Oxford History of Popular Print Culture* As we write the following volumes have been already released: 1 (Britain) and 5–6 (United States).

7 Flavia Bruni and Andrew Pettegree (eds), *Lost Books: Reconstructing the Print World in Pre-Industrial Europe* (Leiden: Brill, 2016), p. 25.

INTRODUCTION

One of the reasons why this particular aspect, concerning the readers of cheap print, is investigated far less is because of the belief that the majority of common people were not able to read and therefore incapable of accessing this kind of content. However, the link between oral and written culture in Early Modern Europe in general and in Italy in this specific case, is particularly strong, to the point that the question of literacy becomes almost irrelevant.[8] The spoken word had a very important role and place in the cultural environment of the illiterate, and it was through that that the people received necessary information concerning their everyday lives. Broadsheets were recited out loud in city squares and street corners and sometimes, if the subject was particularly relevant, even from the pulpits of every church in town. This was the case for example of the broadsheet that communicated the end of the plague in the city of Naples and the subsequent lift of the travel ban to and from the city.[9] Furthermore, street performers and preachers contributed to spreading important news and dramatized versions of the same things that were narrated in pamphlets, contributing to a rich and vibrant oral environment that was an echo and reflection of the written one. Therefore, it seems that there were numerous ways for the mass of people to access the information that circulated in written form, in a more or less filtered way, and their readership level was only one.

If we focus our attention on Italy and in particular on Naples and southern Italy, we find very little scholarly work on this material. Although comprehensive studies on cheap print are a relatively new thing, there have been several noticeable studies of information culture, such as the works of Brendan Dooley on the news and newspapers.[10] As far as Italy is concerned, there are relevant works by Mario Infelise and Filippo de Vivo on news and communication in Venice.[11]

---

8   See *The Italianist* 34, 3 (2014), particularly Brian Richardson, 'Oral Culture in Early Modern Italy. Performance, Language, Religion' (pp. 313–317).

9   This is mentioned in a letter that the Neapolitan publisher and writer Antonio Bulifon sent to Antonio Magliabechi; see BNCF, *Magliabechiano*, VIII, 632, 51bis (23 February 1692).

10 Brendan Dooley (ed), *The dissemination of News and the Emergence of Contemporaneity in Early Modern Europe* (Farnham: Ashgate, 2010); Brendan Dooley, Sabrina, A. Baron (eds), *The politics of information in Early Modern Europe* (London: Routledge, 2011).

11 Mario Infelise, *Prima dei giornali: alle origini della pubblica informazione secoli XVI e XVII* (Bari: Laterza, 2002); Filippo De Vivo, *Patrizi, informatori, barbieri. Politica e comunicazione a Venezia nella prima età moderna* (Milan: Feltrinelli, 2012); Luigi Braida, Mario Infelise, *Libri per tutti. I generi editoriali di larga circolazione tra antico regime ed età contemporanea* (Turin: UTET, 2010).

6 INTRODUCTION

The work undertaken by Ottavia Niccoli on communication in the Papal State are also noteworthy.[12] While in all of these works the focus is often on just one aspect of the ephemeral world of cheap print, they do touch, although marginally, on a number of different sources and different questions that are of the utmost relevance when studying these particular materials. Who were the producers and the recipients of cheap print? What kind of information circulated through such media and what was the reaction of the authorities to these printed products? De Vivo, in particular, focused on how the State authorities used cheap print to spread political information throughout the entire Venetian state; the authorities were involved not only in censoring this kind of publication but also in producing and distributing it. This is particularly pertinent since we will see in this book that the same thing happened in Naples, thus establishing a parallel between two cities that have always been regarded as completely opposite. The most complete work on cheap print, as far as Italy is concerned, is *Ephemeral City* by Rosa Salzberg.[13] In her book, she attempts to reconstruct the printed ephemera of Renaissance Venice in its entirety, rather than focus on a specific media. She explored many kinds of cheap print and, using a geographical approach, she was able to construct a map of Venice built on the places in which these printed products were produced, sold or read.

These authors also share a common perception that, after the Council of Trent, censorship mechanisms put in place by both civic and religious authorities all but put an end to the circulation of information through unofficial media, mostly constituted by cheap print. This would seem to be especially true for southern Italy, crushed under strict Spanish rule. The view of cheap print as something illegal, clandestine, and, in a more general sense, as something deeply connected with a time of crisis is a fascinating one, albeit one that does not find confirmation in reality. In fact, it was the authorities who were the first producers and distributers of cheap print, for print was recognised from the incunabula era as the easiest and quickest way to communicate with their subjects, a fact that is now being recognised for other European countries as well. De Vivo is aware of this connection, as well as Rosa Salzberg, but there still seems to exist a huge disjunction between cheap print, often viewed as something made for the people by the people, and therefore illegal and subversive, and state communication. Even though the media used by the State are the same ones that make up the broad category of cheap print, it is difficult to

---

12   Ottavia Niccoli, *Prophecy and People in Renaissance Italy* (Princeton: Princeton University Press, 1990); Id., *Rinascimento anticlericale* (Bari: Laterza, 2005).

13   Rosa Salzberg, *Ephemeral City. Cheap Print and Urban Culture in Renaissance Venice* (Manchester: Manchester University Press, 2015).

INTRODUCTION

find a study that deals with both faces of the cheap print industry, especially when it comes to Italy. Ottavia Niccoli, despite being one of the more prolific and committed authors in the field of the history of popular culture, failed to recognise state communication as a source of popular culture.

2   A Note on Sources and Terminology

The majority of sources used in this book are printed materials, specifically what we call "popular print." Under this broad umbrella definition, we can find a varied array of products, that go from broadsheets proclaiming the law to pamphlets discussing comet's sightings. But what do these things have in common? In the introduction of the first volume of the *Oxford History of Popular Print*, Joad Raymond, the editor-in-chief, addresses some of the methodological questions and definitions that each of the terms chosen for the title poses, starting with *popular*. In the Early Modern period, printing was expensive and was produced by a group of professionals; moreover, a large part of the population was illiterate so surely popular could not mean 'produced by the people' nor 'widely read by them'. Nevertheless, Raymond argues against the use of the term 'cheap print' instead of popular culture because those two categories are not interchangeable: the first focuses on the nature of the materials while the latter on their purposes. They are both necessary to describe the object of our investigation.

Since the beginning of the Protestant Reformation, Protestants first and then, later and with less success, Catholics began to use cheap print as a tool for guiding and influencing public opinion. In this regard, Raymond too uses the term *popular* 'to describe a usage and a mode of reading', along with the interaction that existed between writers and readers for political, religious and propagandistic purposes.[14] It is popular in the sense that, given its political aim, cheap print and street literature were used as a means to shape public opinion and thus, to a certain extent, it ends up being a representation of what the public, the people were thinking. In this context, *political* refers to anything related to the government. Communicating the new law on the type of carriages that are allowed in the city, for example, is a kind of "political print." A pamphlet narrating the Vesuvius eruption and emphasizing the great example provided by the Viceroy in such a tiring circumstance is not political, but rather propagandistic. Meaning that its purpose, or rather one of its purposes, is to spread a positive image of the government.

---

14   Raymond (ed), *Cheap Print*, pp. 11–15.

The existence of cheap print and street literature is proof that complex levels of interaction and interdependence between different social strata indeed existed, thus overcoming the strictly dualistic and antagonistic nature of the predominant view of popular culture within the Italian academy. Moreover, it offers us written primary sources that did not originate through a dynamic of conflict between upper and lower classes, thus moving us beyond the model of a popular culture that was transmitted exclusively orally. If instead, we look at the small number of contributions on this subject produced by Italian scholars, the definitions we encounter are vastly different. Still very much attached to an idea that popular written culture was almost non-existent, the term 'popular print' appears to be almost an oxymoron and it is usually reserved and used as a synonym for clandestine print. The kind of publications that we are going to analyse in this book collectively referred to as 'cheap print' was usually distinguished by its small format and brevity (not more than twelve pages). These publications were cheap to produce, printed on low-quality papers and often with low-grade ink that deteriorated with time. This is true even for most of the official print. They were often published without indications of the place and year in which they were printed. Once again, the correlation to clandestine print is strong, especially if we consider that scholars such as Francesco Novati and Ottavia Niccoli, whom we can regard as the more modern Italian cultural historians, sometimes use the term popular print as an indication of the large dissemination through the uncultured lower social classes. The Italian definition, therefore, appears to be more focused on the material aspect of these kinds of printed products and secondarily on its recipients, while the Anglophone definition seems to be primarily focused on the readers and the purpose of such publications rather than on the material aspect. Without focusing too much on the geographical differences, it appears to me that cheap print could be considered the correct term from a book historian's perspective, since it highlights the economic aspect of the production of the material, while popular print appears to be the preferred choice for those who study social history, focusing on the purpose of a particular publication and on its readers. Since the main focus of this book will be on the political use of popular print in Naples and how it affected its readers, the preferred term that I will use is indeed popular print, but I will also sometimes use cheap print, now that we have clarified the meaning of both these categories.

We have seen that we can make a distinction between an "official" cheap print and a more "mundane", "commercial" one. The first question that one needs to ask oneself is by whom were these documents produced? Why? And who were the intended recipients? If we are talking about "official" cheap print, the answers to these questions are actually rather simple. Considering that the

INTRODUCTION 9

majority of what we can consider official cheap print were law proclamations, the purpose was to ensure the correct and smooth functioning of the city. Whether to make sure that the citizen had access to the necessary information regarding the law or to ensure that all the parts of the complex bureaucratic and administrative system in the realm were functioning smoothly, cheap print was an invaluable tool for the government and the intended recipient was the entirety of the population.

If we move our attention to the more "commercial" type of cheap print, and here I am referring mainly to pamphlets, providing answers to these questions becomes a bit more complex. Such pamphlets were produced by writers, academics, literates and sometimes even by the printers and publishers themselves with a dual purpose. To communicate something and to make money. Where things get trickier is when it comes to the question of who was the intended public. If we read pamphlets regarding the Vesuvius eruption of 1631, for example, they appear to be rather complex whether in the style in which they are written or in the explanation that they offer for the phenomenon.[15] At a first glance these do not appear to be destined to the general public but rather something written for a fairly educated audience. Why then did I choose to include such publications in my source material? In my opinion, while it is true that the intended audience was made up by educated readers and nobleman, the authors were aware of the fact that the content of their work often went beyond the mere distribution and circulation of the work itself. Given the fact that it was a fascinating and "trending" topic, and this is true for the majority of pamphlets, it was something that was almost certainly discussed on the streets. Moreover, street performers, charlatans, theatrical companies, all contributed to the diffusion of such works because they would take those and spread them in a way that would go beyond the media in which they were originally produced and thus give access to those contents to a broader audience.[16]

Besides printed material I used archival sources as well, but more as a secondary source used primarily to build the context and framework, given that these could not be consider "popular". I am talking about contracts, bank receipts, trial records and other such documents. When we are dealing with archival material the question of who and for whom they were produced is fairly straightforward. The producers and recipients were often one and the same, meaning that these were produced by clerks and government officials for their colleagues, with the purpose of keeping track and ensuring the proper functioning of the State. The public in this kind of material is not a factor, these

---

15   These will be discussed in Chapter 3.

16   Ottavia Niccoli, *Profeti e popolo nell'Italia del Rinascimento* (Bari: Laterza, 2007).

were not things intended for a broader consumption. The only way in which regular people could interact with such materials was if they had a specific need. For example, if they were the subject of a trial or if they were entering a contract or borrowing money.[17] When dealing with these sources there is also the matter of the intentionality in the survival rate and conservation of such documents, but we will discuss this particular question later on.

3 Popular Culture in Italian Historiography

With this many contributions and groundbreaking studies on the use of cheap print by the authorities, the question as to why this field of research is still very much marginalized in Italian historiography remains. Why does it feel like the predominant idea is still of a strong dichotomy between what was produced by civic and religious authorities, and a cheap print, which was often illegal and clandestine and was indeed aimed at the masses when in reality the boundaries between these two are not so clear?

One can argue that this dichotomy is a direct consequence of a historiographical trend, particularly prevalent in Italy, that considers written culture as something that moves vertically along the societal axis. The higher strata of society are those who produced printed products for the lower classes, and those who wrote cheap print were not those who read it. A big difference existed between producer and audience for such media and therefore a difference between official and popular cheap print.[18] This idea stems from two works in particular: Burke's synthesis of popular culture and Ginzburg's work on popular religion and superstitions in northern Italy. Ginzburg's work is still regarded as the most famous example of a study of popular culture, despite the fact that he did not use any real popular sources.[19] Meanwhile, the interest in various ritualistic aspects of popular culture was infiltrating the field of cultural anthropology, particularly thanks to the works of Ernesto di Martino

---

17   On the importance of civic writing and the way in which the public interacted with archives see Alexandra Walsham (ed), *The Social History of the Archive: Record-Keeping in Early Modern Europe*, particularly Jennifer Bishop, 'The Clerk's Tale: Civic Writing in Sixteenth-Century London', *Past and Present*, 230, supplement 11 (2016), pp. 112–130.

18   On the different approach to official and popular cheap print see De Vivo, *Patrizi, informatori, barbieri*, chapters 3 and 4.

19   Peter Burke, *Popular Culture in Early Modern Europe* (London: Temple Smith, 1978); Carlo Ginzburg, *I Benandanti: stregoneria e culti agrari tra Cinquecento e Seicento* (Turin: Einaudi, 1966); Id., *Il formaggio e i vermi: il cosmo di un mugnaio del '500* (Turin: Einaudi, 1976); Francesco Benigno, *Parole nel tempo. Un lessico per pensare la storia* (Rome: Viella, 2013).

INTRODUCTION

on popular religion and magical rituals in southern Italy.[20] The popularity of these works within the Italian academy incubated a marked interest in the field and, in the 1970s and 1980s, several studies that focused on popular culture, particularly on popular religion and popular belief, were published.[21] All used the same premises of popular culture as something primitive, often rooted in pagan superstitions that found their most vivid expression through rituals and festivities. This is a view of popular culture that relies on evidence from a very particular type of source material, especially inquisition and civic trial records. We have to ask whether any written testimony spun from the often-antagonistic encounter between upper and lower classes could be relied upon to offer an accurate portrayal of popular culture. Furthermore, with such a strong focus on the oral dimension these studies completely failed to acknowledge the reality of the intermingling between orality and written culture.

This is an obsolete and far too simplistic view, one that was later renounced even by Burke himself.[22] However, a new definition of popular culture with which the majority of the Italian academy can concur failed to take its place and that is why, in the Italian historiographical world, popular culture is a field that is often neglected. In recent years, there have been some attempts to rectify this oversight, but these works failed to achieve the same resonance, both within the academia and to the public, that Ginzburg and Burke had in their time and to some extent still have to this day.[23]

---

20   Ernesto de Martino produced many important works on this subject, here I will cite just two of them which are the most comprehensive: Ernesto De Martino, *Il mondo magico: prolegomeni a una storia del magismo* (Turin: Einaudi, 1948) (most recent edition: edited by Marcello Massenzio. Turin: Einaudi, 2022⁴); Id., *Sud e magia* (Milan: Feltrinelli, 1959) (most recent edition: edited by Fabio Dei and Antonio Fanelli. Rome: Donzelli, 2015⁴).

21   Alberto Mario Cirese, *Cultura egemonica e culture subalterne: rassegna degli studi sul mondo popolare tradizionale* (Palermo: Palumbo, 1973); Piero Camporesi, *Il libro dei vagabondi. Lo Speculum cerretanorum di Teseo Pini, Il vagabondo di Rafaele Frianoro e altri testi di furfanteria* (Turin: Einaudi, 1973) (most recent edition Milan: Garzanti, 2003²); Id., *Rustici e buffoni: cultura popolare e cultura d'élite fra Medioevo ed età moderna* (Turin: Einaudi, 1991); Id., 'Cultura popolare e cultura d'élite fra Medioevo ed età moderna', In Ruggiero Romano and Corrado Vivanti (eds), *Storia d'Italia: Annali. 4: Intellettuali e potere* (Turin: Einaudi, 1981), pp. 81–157; Annamaria Rivera, *Il mago, il santo, la morte, la festa: forme religiose nella cultura popolare* (Bari: Dedalo, 1988).

22   Peter Burke, 'Cuarenta años después: Bajtín y la cultura popular del Renacimiento', in Tomàs Antonio Montecon Movillan (ed), *Bajtín y la historia de la cultura popular. Cuarenta años de debate* (Santander: Universidad de la Cantabria, 2008), p. 17.

23   Besides the already mentioned works done by Francesco Benigno and Ottavia Niccoli, see Furio Bianco, *Storie raccontate, storie disegnate. Cerimonie di giustizia capitale e cronaca nera nelle stampe popolari e nelle memorie cittadine tra '500 e '800* (Udine: E. & C., 2001) which is one of the very few works focused on popular print.

Research from the Anglophone academy proves that things are not quite so definite: the social classes were indeed more mixed than what we might have originally thought, with constant interaction between upper and lower classes and it was indeed in these exchanges that the 'street literature' came into being.[24] Although this is a widely recognised truth in the Anglophone world, few Italian historians have grasped the concept and that is why the study of cheap print is sadly lacking in the Italian academy.[25]

The Spanish Black legend, the idea that Spanish rulers were absolutely inflexible, repressive, and brutal, and that therefore all of the Spanish Empire during the Early Modern period was subject to a fierce religious and political repression and intellectual and artistic stasis, deeply affected the historiography of the Spanish Viceroyalty of Naples.[26] Naples was, after all, part of the Spanish domain and as such suffered the same fate. The politics and conflicts of the Spanish Viceroyalty have been studied at length for the better part of the last century. More recent is the interest in the administrative organisation of Naples. Despite its reputation, the Spanish Viceroyalty, particularly in the seventeenth century was one of the most vibrant and prolific for Neapolitan culture. Don Pedro de Toledo, Viceroy from 1532 to 1553, was a patron of the arts, as were many of his successors. With their aid, architecture, music, and theatre enjoyed great success, in a period known as the 'Barocco Napoletano'. I find it interesting that, while historians of art, as well as music and theatre, have always recognised the value and importance of the contributions that Spanish patronage brought to the city, for Italian traditional historians the narrative that prevails is still that promoted by Galasso, who characterised the Spanish centuries as a period of repression and cultural desolation, a new 'Dark Middle Ages' for Southern Italy.[27] One of the goals of this book is to prove that, contrary to popular belief, Naples was indeed a city with a vibrant printing industry and that the Spanish authorities were the first to use this industry to shape and mould public opinion in their favour. Although the idea that

---

24 See Joad Raymond, 'The Origins of Popular Print Culture', in Id. (ed), *Cheap Print in Britain and Ireland to 1660* (Oxford-New York: Oxford University Press, 2011).

25 Ottavia Niccoli, 'Italy', in Raymond (ed), *Cheap Print*, pp. 295–307; Id., 'Cultura popolare: un relitto abbandonato?', *Studi storici*, 56, 4 (2015), pp. 997–1010.

26 On the Spanish Black Legend see Benjamin Keen, 'The Black Legend Revisited: Assumptions and Realities', *Hispanic American Historical Review* 49, 4 (1969), pp. 703–719; Jocelyn Nigel Hillgarth, 'Spanish Historiography and Iberian Reality', *History and Theory* 24, 1 (1985), pp. 23–43; Friedrich Edelmayer, 'The 'Leyenda Negra' and the Circulation of Anti-Catholic and Anti-Spanish Prejudices', *European History Online* (2011).http://ieg-ego.eu /en/threads/models-and-stereotypes/the-spanish-century/friedrich-edelmayer-the-ley enda-negra-and-the-circulation-of-anti-catholic-and-anti-spanish-prejudices.

27 Giuseppe Galasso, *L'altra Europa. Per un'antologia storica del Mezzogiorno d'Italia* (Milan: Mondadori, 1982).

INTRODUCTION

a communication strategy aimed specifically at the lower classes existed and was carried on by both religious and civic authorities, particularly in event of a great crisis, is definitely not a new one, there are after all several studies highlighting this relationship, it certainly appears to be a novelty for Neapolitan historiography.[28]

Having established the focus of our investigations on what the people of Naples were reading and how it shaped public opinion, the problem of readership appears to be of the utmost importance. A book, or, in our case, a pamphlet or any other kind of cheap print product, is an object unlike any other. You can study it as an object, focusing on how it was made, looking at the paper, the typographical character used, the binding or the lack of it; you can, in short, look at it from a strictly material point of view, studying the object that it is the book. You can look at its content: what is written in it, both by the author and by the occasional scholar who would jot down his notes on the book itself. Looking at the content you can study the relationship between various books, how the particular object you are looking at communicates with other books, and whether they follow the same narrative as all the others or if they say something different. The first approach is the one that is often followed by book historians, although, the lines between these various approaches are often blurred. Looking at the object you cannot ignore the odd note on the marginalia, as well as the traces that censors sometimes left on the book. These particular alterations to the object book are traces left by someone who read the book, who took that object and made it into something else, something more. A book is not only a passive object but an active carrier of information and therefore has the power to affect those who came in contact with it. This line of thinking is what opens the door to a third approach, a 'book history from below' in which the focus is on the act of reading and the readers instead of the object book.[29]

Already in 1989, Robert Darnton pointed out how, with their studies, book historians could easily identify who read what, when and where; what is more difficult to determine is how and why.[30] To this list I would also add another consideration, in fact, the main question that lies underneath my entire

---

28   Niccoli, *Prophecy and People*; De Vivo, *Patrizi, informatori, barbieri*; Salzberg, *Ephemeral City*; Domenico Cecere et alia (eds), *Disaster Narratives in Early Modern Naples. Politics, Communication and Culture* (Rome: Viella, 2018), Vincenzo Caputo, Lorenza Gianfrancesco, Pasquale Palmieri (eds.), *Tales of two cities, News, Stories and Media Events in Early Modern Florence and Naples* (Rome: Viella, 2023).

29   David Finkelstein, Alistair McCleary, *An Introduction to Book History* (London-New York: Routledge, 2013), p. 24.

30   Robert Darnton, 'First Steps Toward a History of Reading', *Australian Journal of French Studies* 23, 1 (1986), pp. 5–30: 8.

research: how what people read changed the way in which they acted, and how those changes, in turn, affected what was given to the people to read. It is generally assumed that Italy in general and southern Italy, in particular, was one of the parts of Europe with the lowest literacy rates in the Early Modern period.[31] In some of the legal proceedings against printers and sellers of prohibited books, that can now be studied in the Archivio Storico Diocesano in Naples, we find professional figures of the book industry claiming to be illiterate.[32] While this could certainly be a ruse to avoid a conviction (one that apparently worked because it was the norm to pardon those involved in these kinds of proceedings if they could not read or write) it nevertheless shows that illiteracy was widespread in the realm of Naples. However, we cannot assume that, because the level of literacy was low, the public had no access to the content of cheap print. We need to make a distinction between being able to read and being able to write. It was not always the case that people possessed both these skills; indeed, the number of people that could read was definitely higher than the number of people that could write or do both. Moreover, every single proclamation and official communication that was issued by the authorities was read aloud in every major square in the city, besides being posted on the walls, as proved by the conventional phrase printed at the bottom of every broadsheet:

> On 27 July 1691, I, Luigi Moccia, town-crier of the royal edicts, hereby declare that I read the aforementioned edict with the royal trumpeters in all the usual and regular places of this most loyal city of Naples, and in its villages, districts, provinces and in every municipality.[33]

Additionally, we need to take into account those professional figures, like doctors, parish priests and artisans, that definitely had the ability to both read and write and therefore contributed greatly to the spread of information through

---

31 Robert Houston, 'Literacy', *Europäische Geschichte Online* (2011), pp. 1–23. http://ieg-ego .eu/en/threads/backgrounds/literacy.

32 Archivio Storico Diocesano, Naples (ASDN), *Sant'Ufficio*, 608 A (1645–1652), also mentioned in Maria Consiglia Napoli, 'Lettura e circolazione del libro tra le classi popolari a Napoli tra '500 e '600', in Maria Rosaria Pellizzari (ed), *Sulle vie della scrittura. Alfabetizzazione, cultura scritta e istituzioni in età moderna* (Naples: Edizioni Scienfiche Italiane, 1989), pp. 375–390.

33 "A dì 27 Luglio 1691. Io Luigi Moccia Lettore delli Regii Bandi, dico di havere pubblicato il sopraddetto Bando con li Regii trombetti nelli luoghi soliti, e consueti di questa fedelissima città di Napoli, e ne' suoi borghi, Ristretti, e Casati ed in ciascun Rastello."[Deputati della Conservazione della Salute], *Appartenendosi a noi ...* (Naples: per Carlo Porsile, 1691); Archivio Storico Municipale Napoli (ASMNa), *II serie, Diversi Bandi ed Editti*, 12, n.n.; USTC 1752418.

INTRODUCTION

cheap print, both as authors and as intermediaries, passing content on to those who could not read it for themselves.[34] There is no direct correlation between the number of people who could read and the number of people who, in one way or another, were aware of what was written in the cheap publications that littered the street of Naples. Regardless of the literacy level of the people in the city, we can assume that both official communication and seditious publication managed to find their way to the ears of Neapolitan citizens, thus rendering the question of literacy less pertinent.

We have seen how and why the historiography concerning Neapolitan cultural history is lacking, but things are not much better if we look at the field of book history. We do not know very much about the print industry in Naples during this period. The greatest contributions to the history of print in Naples can be found in the Atti dell'Accademia Pontaniana. This is an Accademia founded in the sixteenth century and then re-founded in 1807 in the tradition of modern humanism of Benedetto Croce (1866–1952). The majority of its members are not historians, but archivists and bibliographers: nevertheless they produced the bulk of works on Neapolitan printing. Many of their works are bibliographical repertoires or bibliographical dictionaries of famous printers but there are some more historical contributions in their conference proceedings, although limited to the more material aspects of the history of print, such as a particular bookbinding technique or typographical character.[35]

4 Into the Archives

We have seen how, due to both the particular approach of the Italian Academic community towards cultural history and the deeply rooted prejudices and misconceptions about the Spanish rulers, the historiography of the Spanish Viceroyalty of Naples remained mostly conventional and unadventurous without much concern for the newest trend of global historiography. There is one further obstacle that historians have to take into consideration when studying Neapolitan history, and that is the nature of Neapolitan archives themselves. Before talking about the specificity of the Neapolitan situation, however, it is important to address the question of what was preserved and especially why.

---

34   Napoli, *Lettura e circolazione*, p. 377.

35   Giuseppina Zappella, *Tipografia campana del Cinquecento: centri e stampatori. Dizionario storico-bibliografico* (Naples: Accademia Pontaniana, 1984); Silvia Sbordone, *Editori e tipografi a Napoli nel '600* (Naples: Accademia Pontaniana, 1990); Antonio Garzya (ed), *Per la storia della tipografia napoletana nei Secoli XV–XVIII. Atti del Convegno Internazionale – Napoli 16–17 dicembre 2005* (Naples: Accademia Pontaniana, 2006).

As it was argued in recent studies toward a social history of the archives, there was almost always an intentionality in what was kept and what was disregarded.[36] The trials of time notwithstanding, we can learn as much from what is there as from what is no longer preserved. As we will see in Chapter 3 and 4, for example, the number of pamphlets on the Vesuvius eruption of 1631 is an indication of the marked and deep interest in the event. An interest that manifested itself not only in the number of pamphlets that were printed but also in how many of those survived to this day, thanks to a precise will to preserve narration surrounding this extraordinary event.

As will become evident in the course of this book, the portrait that I offer of the relationship between Spanish authorities and their Neapolitan subject is mostly harmonious. This does not mean that I choose to ignore the tense moments or dissenting voices. However, given that I chose to focus mainly on cheap print as my source material, the voices of dissent are necessarily more silent because almost nothing survived. And this is further proof in favour of my argument but also of the importance of looking at the void, at what is missing, as historiographic evidence in itself. My argument in fact is not that there was no dissent against the Spanish rulers but rather that the communication strategy that the authorities employed was so effective that between a capable use of censorship – both before and after publication – and a thorough campaign of "counter-information" any dissenting voice was dealt with in a timely and effective manner. So much so that it is rare to be able to find proof of their existence at all. I will elaborate further on this later on. What I wanted to point out here is that there is a known tradition when it comes to the deliberateness with which the Spanish authorities approached the matter of creating their archives and especially using it. This is evident if we look at the creation and running of the central archive in Simancas. Built in the second half of the 16th century as a place designed to collect all the papers from all corners of the Spanish Empire, it showed from the very beginning the political nature of such a project, designed to be a place to preserve paper but at the same time lock them away. Whether the documents were destined to be preserved, destroyed or forgotten depended very much on their nature and on the political climate.[37]

---

36   Alexandra Walsham (ed), *The social history of the archive: Record keeping in Early Modern Europe* (Oxford: Oxford University press, 2016).

37   For more information on the use of Simancas see Arndt Brendecke, 'Knowledge, oblivion, and Concealment in Early Modern Spain: The Ambiguous Agenda of the Archive of Simancas', in Liesbeth Corens, Kate Peters, Alexandra Walsham (eds) *Archives and Information in the Early Modern World* (Oxford: Oxford University Press, 2018).

INTRODUCTION

The archival heritage of Naples is scattered among many different archives and libraries with a clear distinction between religious and civic archives. For religious sources, the most important archive is the Archivio Storico Diocenso; located inside the main cathedral, this is the biggest religious archive, holding anything that has to do with the Church in Naples from *c.*1110 to 1943, including the proceedings of the Holy Inquisition. However, this is not the only archive; almost every major church in Naples was connected to a convent and, if the church and the religious order behind it still exist, they retain their own library and archive. These institutions include but are not limited to the Monastero di Santa Chiara, Chiesa di San Francesco, Chiesa di San Domenico, and the Jesuit archive. Unfortunately, none of these archives has been thoroughly catalogued and not all of their collections are available to scholars, due to poor conservation and a lack of archivists. There are partial catalogues of certain archival collections of the Archivio Storico Diocesano, while for the archive of the single churches, the best you can hope for is a manuscript non-descriptive catalogued compiled by a friar in the nineteenth century; these are not always reliable.

Things are far worse for the civic archives. The two major resources are the Archivio Storico Municipale and the Archivio di Stato. The collections of both archives are severely compromised, especially the documents from the Spanish period. About 50% of the documents from the Spanish period held in the Archivio di Stato were destroyed during World War II while, after the war, a fire did similar damage to the collection of the Archivio Municipale. For what is left there are no descriptive inventories and, more often than not, the inventories that do exist are not updated with the losses that occurred during the war.[38]

Due to all of these obstacles, scholars that wish to do research are forced to proceed in the dark, relying on old, non-descriptive catalogues and on the expertise of the archivists to aid them in their research. Still, despite all the losses, which were undoubtedly severe, both archives still hold sources of incredible value that have been gravely neglected by historians. I believe that the well-known disorganisation of Neapolitan archives and the lack of catalogues contributed greatly to keeping foreign scholars away from Neapolitan

---

38   For the Archivio Storico Municipale the only catalogue is Bartolomeo Capasso, *Catalogo ragionato dei libri registri e scritture esistenti nella sezione antica, o prima serie dell'Archivio municipale di Napoli (1387–1806)* (Naples: stab. Tip. F. Giannini, 1899), while for the Archivio di Stato the closest thing to a catalogue that can account for what was lost during World War II is Jole Mazzoleni, *Le fonti documentarie e bibliografiche dal sec. X al XX conservate presso l'Archivio di Stato di Napoli* (Naples: Arte Tipografica, 1974).

archives while the known losses in the Spanish archival collections encouraged local historians to focus on other periods.

Besides these two major archives, there are a number of smaller resources, such as the Archivio del Banco di Napoli (a financial archive), the Archivio del Monte di Pietà (an archive of one of the oldest charitable enterprises in Naples, that carried out works of mercy). Several private archives, the most important of which is the archive of the D'Avalos, a Spanish family that was in charge of appointing the city customs officers for the entire period of the Viceroyalty, are also important. Most of these private archives are not even known to the Soprintendenza dei Beni Artisitici, Archivistici e Librari, the Italian government authority that deals with the preservation of cultural heritage, and therefore is really complex to know what they possess, let alone gain access to them.[39]

Various libraries complete the mosaic of Neapolitan archival heritage. The National Library, the Biblioteca della Società Napoletana di Storia Patria, the library of the Istituto Italiano di Studi Storici Benedetto Croce as well as the Biblioteca Provinciale Giulio e Scipione Capone in Avellino all hold important materials, in the form of both printed and manuscript sources, from the Spanish Viceroyalty. Collectively, these resources demonstrate once and for all that there are indeed plenty of primary sources for a history of the Spanish Viceroyalty in Naples. Of course, we cannot pretend that the destructions of World War II never occurred; all the diplomatic correspondence between the Spanish court and the Viceroy held in Naples was lost, however, copies still survive in Spain and that is why the Archivo General de Simancas is an important destination for historians of the Spanish Viceroyalty. The fragmented and dispersive nature of the Neapolitan archives is without a doubt an obstacle for researchers and, while definitely not the main reason, is probably one of the reasons for the lack of more work on the Spanish Viceroyalty.

Given the dispersed nature of the archival heritage in Naples and the lack of online catalogues and inventories my research needed to be very 'hands on', a feat that was made more difficult by the COVID pandemic. The pandemic is the reason why I was able to take only one short trip to the Archivo General in Simancas or to the Archivio della Congregazione per la Dottrina della Fede in Rome, and also the reason why I was not able to access any of the other archives in Rome that could be useful for my research.[40] Moreover, even

---

39 A survey of Neapolitan private archives can be found in Archivio di Stato di Napoli, *Archivi privati: inventario sommario* (Naples: Arte tipografica, 1967, 2 vols).

40 Particularly the Archivio Apostolico Vaticano (AAV) which has an entire section called *Nunziature di Napoli* that supposedly should hold all the correspondence between the

INTRODUCTION   19

after the lockdown eased, none of the archives and libraries in Naples went
back to work at full capacity, but maintained severely limited opening times
and even more limited available seats; this rendered any archival research
slower and more complex.[41] Despite this, I decided nonetheless to keep my
research focused on Neapolitan archives, for two main reasons. The majority
of works that have been done on Neapolitan history by non-local historians
relied almost exclusively on ambassadors' correspondence, particularly from
the archives in Venice, Milan, Simancas and Florence, disregarding the local
sources. Also, already during my short trip to Naples before the pandemic hit, I
got the impression that there was, indeed, an incredible and unexplored richness of materials that could be found there, if only one had the patience to
search, look and talk with the most unlikely people. So that is what I did, and I
believe my efforts paid off. During the course of my research, I went to fifteen
different archives and libraries where I analysed more than 500 archival documents and 3,500 printed materials, adding more than thirty new records to
the USTC.

One thing that is worth keeping in mind while researching in Naples is that
a coffee can open many doors and lead to many interesting conversations and
insights. It was during my very first trip to the Archivio di Stato when, over a
coffee, I started talking with the retired head archivist whom, besides pointing
me in the right direction within the Archivio di Stato itself, arranged for me to
visit the Archivio Storico Municipale. This archive was closed to the public at
the time and this act of kindness enabled me to go through the very few surviving documents from the Comitato di Salute Pubblica and the Portolano. The
printed documents that I found pertaining to the Comitato, in particular, were
extremely interesting and a lucky find, given that they had just been recently
rediscovered during inventory works in the archive, having been wrongly filed
in the Second Series of this archive, that hold documents from the nineteenth
century. In the Archivio di Stato, my research was initially focused mainly on
the documents from the Delegazione della Real Giurisdizione, a section in
which I was able to find over fifteen legal cases involving printers and booksellers and the city government, a particularly important source to shed light

---

Neapolitan Church and the Holy See and the Archivum Generale Ordinis Praedicatorum
(AGOP) which is the general archive of the Dominicans. These are all archives that I still
plan to visit in the future, to expand and enrich my research.

41 As an example, the BNN was opened only two mornings per week, and the manuscript
section allowed only two scholars per day; the SNSP was open to four scholars two days
a week, the AFBN was only opened for two hours on Friday mornings, same as the ASDN,
and the ASNA was opened Monday through Friday but only to 8 scholars per day and with
a waiting list over two months long.

on the power dynamic that existed within the printing industry. In this same archive, through trial and error given the lack of inventories, I was nonetheless able to find many interesting documents that, even when not related directly to the printing industry or the time span of my research, were nonetheless invaluable for gaining insights on the general context. For example, I learned that, in order to apply for a licence, a copy of the book or pamphlet needed to be submitted to the authorities. These copies, from 1703 onward were stored in a library that no longer exists, the Biblioteca di Sant'Angelo a Nilo, but its catalogues are still held at the National Library. Another gem was the incredibly rare and, fundamental for my research, contract between Camillo Cavallo, printer, and the city government in regard to the *jus prohibendi* on the *Gazzette*.

It is almost pointless to try and talk about something that was produced and sold without taking into consideration the economic aspect of the trade, and that is why I spent a long time, or as long as I was able to given the COVID restrictions, in the Archivio Fondazione Banco di Napoli. This is an archive that holds ledgers from all the civic offices, as well as six charitable offices founded in the seventeenth century. Moreover, if any private enterprise had an account at the Banco di Napoli, there should be traces of their economic activities in their ledgers. This is the archive in which, through various credit slips, I was able to gain insight into the cost of living in Naples during the Spanish Viceroyalty and the costs of the print industry, both from the perspective of the printers themselves and that of the buyers.

The hardest part of my archival research was, without a doubt, the religious archives. The Archivio Storico Diocesano is the main religious archive within the city, and in theory should hold all the documents produced by religious authorities within the dioceses of Naples, as well as archives from various churches and monasteries throughout the city. This, however, is only in theory. A surprising number of churches, even relatively small ones, still hold on to their archives. Such is the case, for example, of the Chiesa dei SS. Filippo e Giacomo, a church that can be found on S. Biagio street and that was funded by the guild of silk and wool in Naples, in which the archive of the Chiesa of San Gennarello is now held. This was the first church in which the booksellers and printers that worked on that street used to congregate, and its archive still held, although in a dismal state of conservation, the wedding registry, as well as the ones recording births and deaths.

Things do not become easier when searching in larger churches or convents. The documents pertaining to S. Domenico Maggiore, for example, are divided between the Archivio di Stato, the Archivio Storico Diocesano and the library within the Church of S. Domenico itself. This is something that I discovered after a lengthy and insightful conversation with Padre Gerardo Imbriani, the head librarian in S. Domenico, who helped me locate the convent's ledgers, the

INTRODUCTION   21

books that were printed in this church and the convent journals, all sources
that are scattered between these three archives without any clear logic. In the
Archivio Storico Diocesano my main focus was on the documents from the
Holy Office, which held some valuable proceedings against famous printers
and booksellers. Navigating this particular collection was not an easy feat, partially due to the poor conservation of the majority of the documents and partially due to the outdated catalogues available there, and once again I have a
coffee to thank for the help of Professor Giovanni Romeo. Thanks to his help, I
was also able to search among the correspondence of Annibale di Capua, the
Archbishop responsible for bringing the Tridentine Decrees in Naples.

Speaking of religious archives, my only and undoubtedly too short visit in
Rome, at the Archivio della Congregazione della Fede, was nevertheless useful. Besides various examples of letters written from Naples to Rome in search
of advice on how to censor or promote particular pieces of print, the series
known as *Tituli Librorum* offered interesting suggestions for further research.
It is a series that features letters from local inquisitors of various Italian cities
to the central office in Rome containing the requests made by printers who
applied for a license, as well as asking what to do in cases of suspicious publication. Unfortunately, the letters from Naples are no longer in this archive (it
is possible that copies are held in the Archivio Apostolico Vaticano in Rome)
but I found something interesting among the letters from the Inquisitor from
Bologna. He wrote in 1657 to the Inquisitor in Rome because he was concerned
about two pamphlets that were circulating in Bologna, one printed first in
Palermo and then in Bologna and the other previously printed in Rome. Both
of them, however, were about Naples and it is clear from the subject and the
writing style that they were first produced in Naples; I would argue that they
were printed, as it seems unlikely that they circulated in manuscript form. They
concerned the Neapolitan plague and the role of Saint Rosalia and S. Gaetano
in saving the city. Both of them were condemned by the Roman Inquisition,
which replied to the Bologna Inquisitor *supprimat utramque impressionem*.
What is particularly interesting about these, besides the content of the pamphlets themselves (both were attached to the letter) is the fact that there is
no trace in the collective Italian catalogue (Sistema Bibliotecario Nazionale –
SBN) nor the Karlsruhe Virtual Catalog (KVK) of a Neapolitan edition. I believe
that there could be two possible explanations for this: there is no printed
Neapolitan edition or it was so successful that it sold out completely and
there are no surviving copies.[42] Both hypotheses are plausible but, given that

---

42   [Anon.], *Copia del decreto pubblicato in Napoli dall'illustrissima deputazione di questa
      Fedelissima Città, in riconoscenza del singolar beneficio ricevuto nella liberazione dal
      Contagio da suoi Santi Patroni e Nostra Gloriosa Cittadina Santa Rosalia* (In Palermo e in

there are no records of either the Roman or Sicilian edition in any Neapolitan library or archive, and it is highly unlikely that such pamphlets never reached Naples, I think it is safe to assume that either way these were popular pamphlets in Naples.

Research that focuses on popular print, however, could not be conducted only within the archives. Though the archival resources available exceeded my expectations and proved to be invaluable to gain information about life, struggles and undertakings of the printers and booksellers, my research needed to be moved to libraries in order to look at what these businessmen printed and what the people of Naples read. Once again, the richness of materials that I was able to find surprised me. The Biblioteca della Società Napoletana di Storia Patria is an obligatory visit for all of those who are interested in ephemeral print in Naples. Only about 60% of its collection has been catalogued online, but there are manuscript catalogues and inventories from the nineteenth century that are available in the library. Sadly, the archive of this library was destroyed during World War II, so it is impossible to trace the history of how and why certain books and pamphlets came to be there, but there they are nonetheless. The *Sismica* collection in particular, which held over 400 pamphlets written about and around the eruption of Vesuvius in 1631 was one of the main sources for my research, as it was the impressive collection of Neapolitan *Gazzette*. Several manuscript chronicles about the plague and Masaniello's rebellion can also be found in the collections of this library, as well as a surprising number of broadsheets and official proclamations from the entire time span of the Viceroyalty.

All these sources, plus several other pamphlets on various subjects, provided me with a clear understanding of the variety and richness of popular print in Naples. The amount of materials that I found within this library would have probably been more than enough (as it is, I was obviously not able to include everything that I found in this book) but I could not declare my research to be completed without looking at the Biblioteca Nazionale di Napoli. Here, I focused my attention on two specific collections within the Manuscript section. The collection known as Biblioteca di San Martino is a collection of manuscripts and miscellaneous printed volumes that were previously held within the charterhouse of San Martino. This is a collection of over 10,000 books and pamphlets focused exclusively on Neapolitan religious and political history.

Bologna: Gio. Battista Ferroni, 1657), USTC 1752419; [Anon.], *Supplica della città di Napoli alla Santità di N.S. Alessandro VII. Con attestazioni pubbliche della liberatione della medesima dal contagio, per l'intercessione del S. Gaetano Tiene, fondatore dei Clerici regolari. Per ottenerlo Protettore* (In Roma e in Bologna: per gli HH del Dozza, 1657), USTC 1731477. More about this in Chapter 5.

INTRODUCTION

Of particular interest is a collection of over 150 broadsheets from the time of Masaniello's rebellion, which provided a detailed understanding of the communication strategies employed by the government in a time of unprecedented crisis. The other collection on which I focused my interest is the Brancacciana. The first public library in Naples, the Brancacciana was opened in 1691 according to the will and testament of Cardinal Francesco Maria Brancaccio. It was closed in 1848 and, after several attempts to find a new home, the 90,000 volumes of this library were brought to the Biblioteca Nazionale in 1937. Within this particular collection, the most important resources for my research were the manuscript chronicles of the Spanish Viceroyalty, which provided insights into the daily life, events and ceremonies of the time, often referencing printed products of which we have no other traces.

Although it is evident from this brief overview that I focused the majority of my attention and efforts on Neapolitan sources that could be found in Naples, I nevertheless briefly ventured outside the city to gain some external perspective to enrich my research. This is why I made brief trips to Venice, Florence, Milan and Simancas.

5   Aim and Structure of the Book

The goal of my book is to examine what was published in Naples, what Neapolitan people read or were exposed to and how this literary production contributed to the shaping of public opinion and the construction of a politically-informed population. I used archival sources and manuscripts to shed light on all the activities related to printers, printing business and readers, such as proceedings for buying and selling prohibited books, but also concessions for printing certain works, who were the appointed printers for civic offices, and which books were imported. I believe it is crucial not only to know how the printing industry worked and what was printed in a general sense but also what was written in those books and pamphlets. For this purpose, I examined the printing products themselves. The result is this book, set out in five chapters, each focusing on a particular aspect of the printing industry in Naples.

Chapter 1 will represent a brief overview of the state of the printing industry in Naples. It will focus on the laws regulating printing within the realm, the rules and regulations according to which the printers operated as well as providing biographical details for some of the most renowned printers of the Spanish Viceroyalty. Having provided the legislative background within which printers operated and an overview of the general state of the industry, the following chapters will be focused on popular print produced by different agents in various circumstances. Chapter 2 will focus on the political use of the printing press. We will discuss the role of the royal printer and the use of printed broadsheets to communicate matters of public interest implemented by the State. We will also discuss the propagandistic value of public print with a focus on the *Gazzette* and the political and military pamphlets.

With our survey view of the printing industry in Naples as well as the political and propagandistic value of popular print, we will then delve into the impact of specific events. Chapters 3 and 4 will both deal with catastrophic events that shook the city and somehow affected and changed, however temporarily, popular print in Naples. Chapter 3 will deal with probably the most famous event in Spanish Naples: Masaniello's rebellion. We will see the different communication strategies put in place by the Spanish authorities, the rebels and the French during this time of political and social upheaval. In Chapter 4, the focus will be on science and natural disasters. We will discuss pamphlets, *avvisi*, news, and broadsheets on scientific knowledge and popular beliefs, like sightings of comets, popular medicine and charlatanism. After this brief excursion, the focus will be on natural disasters, namely the eruption of Vesuvius in 1631 and the plague in 1656. We will discuss popular print during these calamities and its role in shaping public opinion. Lastly, chapter 5 will deal with the relationship between the Church and the printing industry, discussing the censorship strategies implemented by the Neapolitan Church but also the popular printing of religious subjects and the relationship between the Church and popular devotion as it is told through print.

CHAPTER 1

Printing in Naples

Having encountered a copy of the letter written to the most illustrious Lord Abbott Peretti from his secretary in regards to the prodigious accidents of Mount Vesuvius, I wanted to print it with the name of Your Most Excellent Lordship, because for the regard that you hold for the author I am sure you will see this gladly and thus this will serve me as a shield against the complaint he could make against me for the liberties I took in printing it. May the gift please Your Most Excellent Lordship, a symbol of the devotion I have for you, while I pray the Lord will grant you to reach the greatness you deserve.

In Naples, 12 January 1632.[1]

∴

This letter was written by Egidio Longo, who at the time was the royal printer, as a preface to the pamphlet *La strage di Vesuvio*, and it offers a perfect example of some of the distinctive features of the Neapolitan printing industry. This was a business regulated by many laws and practices put in place by both civic and religious authorities, that relied heavily on the relationship between clients and patrons and on the personal abilities of printers and booksellers to find a path amidst all the bureaucracy to be able to print what they wanted to print.

For a very long time, historians believed Spanish Naples to be a cultural wasteland, a city in which the strict control exercised by the Spanish

---

1 "Essendomi capitata una copia della presente lettera scritta all'Illustrissimo Signor Abbate Peretti dal suo Secretario in relazione de' prodigiosi accidenti del Vesuvio, ho voluto ch'esca dalle mie stampe col nome di V.S: Reverendissima, che per l'affetto, che ella professa all'Autore me assicuro che la vedrà volentieri, e mi servirà di scudo contra le querele, ch'egli potrebbe far meco della licenza che io mi son presa in pubblicarla: gradisca V.S: Reverendissima il dono, in corrispondeza della divotione, con ch'io l'accompagno, mentre per fine proego il Signore l'esalti ad ogni meritata grandezza. Di Napoli li 12 Gennaro 1632." [Domenico Benigno] *La strage di Vesuvio* (Naples: per Egidio Longo, MDCXXXII) SNSP, SISMICA 06.B.15.3, USTC 4011559. Every translation is my own unless otherwise stated.

© KONINKLIJKE BRILL BV, LEIDEN, 2025 | DOI:10.1163/9789004549401_003

26   CHAPTER 1

authorities combined with the iron fist of the Counter-Reformation Church made it almost impossible to publish anything without having to go through a very lengthy, frustrating and almost always unsuccessful bureaucratic procedure. While this may be true to some extent (the process to obtain a printing license was indeed quite lengthy), it fails to acknowledge the determination of printers and booksellers to exercise their profession and their willingness to begin a dialogue with the authorities in order to obtain what they wanted. This old-fashioned view of the Spanish government also completely dismisses the important role that many of the Viceroys had in shaping the Neapolitan baroque. Don Pedro de Toledo himself was a great patron of the arts.[2] While it is true that regulating the printing business generated a large number of rules, laws, and proceedings, it was precisely this that often left room for constructive interpretation of the laws.

In recent years, some studies on the subject of print in Naples nuanced the view of the Spanish Viceroyalty as a time of cultural impoverishment. In 2010, Giampiero Di Marco published a list of all printers, booksellers, and typographers who were active in Naples during the seventeenth century; this list contains 557 individuals, demonstrating without any doubt that the printing industry in Naples was far from a dying business.[3] In this chapter, I will provide a brief survey of printing in Naples, the laws that regulated this commerce, as well as introduce some of the most notable printers of the time.

1   An Organization for Booksellers and Printers

If you walk the street of Naples from the old city centre, in which you will find San Biagio de Librai, as well as the Chiesa del Carmine and Piazza della Carità, key places for the Masaniello's rebellion, and Piazza San Lorenzo, one of the most important squares for markets in the city, to the Royal Palace in Piazza del Plebiscito you will find yourself on Via Toledo. As the name suggests, this street was built by the Viceroy Pedro de Toledo, and he also built the Spanish Quarters (Quartieri Spagnoli), a network of streets adjacent to Via Toledo that from there reaches up to the top of the hill on which sits Castel Sant'Elmo. This entire part of the city was built in the sixteenth century and it became a city

---

2   Carlos Josè Hernando Sánchez, 'La vida material y el gusto artístico en la corte de Nápoles durante el Renacimiento. El inventario de bienes del virrey Pedro de Toledo', in *Archivo Español de Arte*, LXVI (1993), 261, pp. 35–55; Id., *Castilla y Nápoles en el siglo XVI. El virrey Pedto de Toledo (1532–1553) Linaje, estado y cultura* (Salamanca: Junta de Castiglia Y Leon, 1994).

3   Di Marco, Giampiero, 'Librai, editori e tipografi a Napoli nel XVII secolo', *La Bibliofilia* 112 (2010), pp. 21–60, 141–184.

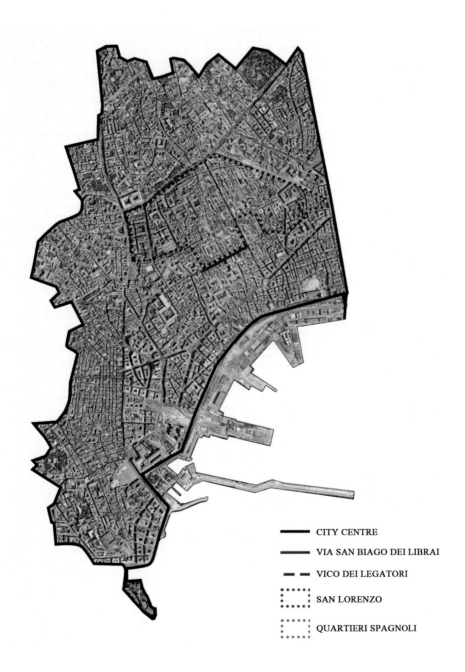

MAP 1.1   Map of Naples city centre as it appears today
SATELLITE VIEW COURTESY OF GOOGLE MAPS

within a city: its architectural layout closed it off to the rest of the town. When it was built, this was the place where Spaniards lived; soldiers and commoners in the modest accommodation of the Spanish Quarters, noblemen in the rich palaces that surrounded the area.[4] Along with the expansion of the city limits and the consequent construction of new city walls, the Viceroyalty of Toledo saw an increase in the number of inhabitants of the city, which grew from the 110,000 registered at the end of the Aragonese period to the 210,000 that were registered during the census of 1547. The population continued to steadily grow until the plague of 1656 when the number of people in Naples declined from over 360,000 to 160,000.[5]

On the opposite side of Via Toledo and the Spanish sector is the old city. Part of the original settlement from Roman times, it remained for centuries the heart and soul of Naples. There are more than 200 churches in this part of the city alone, the majority of them built or re-built during the sixteenth century. Even when the city began its expansion towards the sea and the seat of political power was moved to the Maschio Angioino, this remained the living heart of the city. It was here that most of the city population lived and had their businesses.[6] The names of the streets remind us, to this day, of the ancient stores and businesses that took place here. The neighbourhood of St Lorenzo, with Via San Biagio de' Librai (booksellers), Vicolo de' legatori (bookbinders) immediately behind the church of San Biagio, Vico alla carta (paper alley), Vico Nuovo alli Librari, was the centre of the printing industry in the city.

Although in Naples there was no guild nor corporation for booksellers and printers, such as those we can find in Venice and many other European cities, this does not mean that there was not some sort of association among these professional figures. The first traces of an organized structure can be found, unsurprisingly, in the archives of the old church that stood in the heart of the neighbourhood of St Lorenzo. This part of the city, full of narrow streets, churches, and old buildings, today is one of the most frequented and loved by tourists and locals alike. Here, on the corner between via San Biagio and Via

---

4 The toponymic of the city and its monuments still bears traces of the Spanish presence. Besides the obvious and ever famous Spanish Quarters, we can find churches such as the Chiesa di San Giacomo agli Spagnoli or the Chiesa della Santissima Trinità agli Spagnoli, as well as palaces such as the Palazzo Spagnolo. On the Spanish city within Naples see Pierre Civil, Antonio Gargnano, Matteo Palumbo, Encarnación García Sánchez, *Fra Italia e Spagna: Napoli crocevia di culture durante il vicereame* (Naples: Liguori, 2011).

5 The census data are from Bartolomeo Capasso, *Sulla circoscrizione civile ed ecclesiastica e sulla popolazione della città di Napoli dalla fine del sec. XIII fino al 1809* (Naples: Tipografia della Regia Università, 1892).

6 For more information on the layout of the city of Naples see Emilio Ricciardi, *Appunti per una storia dell'urbanistica napoletana* (Viterbo: Betagamma, 2002).

San Gregorio Armeno, one of the most famous streets in the city, there is a small church: San Gennarello all'Olmo, the church where printers, booksellers, and typographers first came together. Most of them had their shops and homes in the surrounding streets, and it is in the registry of this church that we can find weddings, baptisms, deaths, and traces of the lives that these people lived. The wedding registry in particular is of the utmost importance. Without the means to navigate the enormous series of notarial deeds held in the Archivio di Stato, is through this small parish registry that we can trace the evolution of the community of printers and booksellers. The death of someone in the business family was usually followed by someone else's marriage, and often with the precise goal of keeping the business alive. This can be demonstrated through the recurring of names within the wedding registry, the same family names that we can find in documents and sources about the professionals of the book industry.[7]

Although they started there, the church that is usually associated with the printing world in Naples is a different one. Adjacent to San Gennarello is the church of San Biagio, which gives the name to the street as well as the section of the neighbourhood, *San Biase alli librai*, San Biagio de' Librai, as it is known today; San Biagio of the booksellers.

FIGURE 1.1
Street sign
PHOTO BY THE AUTHOR

---

7   Unfortunately, at the time in which I am writing this the documents from San Gennarello are not accessible. The wedding registry in particular is no longer held in that church but should be in the church of ss. Filippo e Giacomo however the archive of that particular church is currently close therefore there is no way to confirm this information. The last person that was able to see it was Giovanni Lombardi. See Giovanni Lombardi, *Tra le pagine di San Biagio. L'economia della stampa a Napoli in età moderna* (Naples: Edizioni Scientifiche Italiane, 2000).

Although Neapolitan printers and booksellers were never forced into a guild by the local authorities, this does not mean that they did not act like one. During the seventeenth century they even had their own printer's device: the Virgin Mary, standing between San Biagio and San Gennaro, was the symbol of the Società de' librai napoletani, who made up the unofficial San Biagio guild.[8] The first recorded mention of some sort of organisation within the Church of San Biagio is on 21 June 1543 when the parishioners came together to fund the *monte elemosiniere in S. Biagio Maggiore*, a common fund to which every male of the congregation had to contribute, and that was destined to help widows and families of booksellers, bookbinders, and printers who were struggling. It is clear that the organisation in S. Biagio had a strong religious and charitable imprint, but although it was not specifically a guild it is still an organisation that is relevant for our topic: with this document printers and booksellers became a group, a collective that had a common legal identity and that was identifiable with a particular location within the city.

> *In primis*, the most magnificent Masters and Governors of the said Church and hospice of the Nunziata, to which Church and Hospital the said Church of Saint Blasio along with the Church of Saint Gennarello belongs, that they hereby grant in *perpetuum quo ad usum* the said Chapel of Saint Blasio, along with the terrain before it. Henceforth in this Chapel, they will hold a guild with this name and be able to appoint masters, establish a fund and collect charitable offers from other guild members and here they will do as they please and at the end of the year they will keep a true and legal registry of their work to be passed on to the following master that they will appoint in said church without any restriction.[9]

Some of the parish registers for baptisms, weddings, and funerals are now held in the private archive of the church of s.s. Filippo e Giacomo; some papers of more ecclesiastical nature are in the Archivio Storico Diocesano, a couple of financial reports are in the Archivio di Stato. Unfortunately, apart from these papers hidden amidst the complexity of the Neapolitan archival network, the majority of the documents from the churches of S. Gennarello and S. Biagio are lost. Despite this, in a legal statement from 1628, the importance placed

---

8 Giampiero Di Marco, 'Librai, Editori e Tipografi a Napoli Nel XVII Secolo', *La Bibliofilia* 112 (2010), pp. 21–60, 141–184.

9 ASN, Cart. Culto 2, Reale Stabilimento dell'Annunziata di Napoli, fasc. 8 bis *Patronato della S. Casa sulla Chiesa di S. Biagio Maggiore*. The transcription can be found in Costanza Silletti, 'Alle radici dell'editoria nel Regno di Napoli. I capitoli statutari della Confraternita di S. Biagio dei librai a Napoli', *Bollettino Storico della Basilicata*, 18 (2002), pp. 255–263.

PRINTING IN NAPLES

on the charitable aspect of this association is most evident, as it is the strong geographical orientation.

11. In regards to the charitable enterprises exercised by the said Governors, they are obliged to follow the following rules. 1 ° in regards to the concession of dowry, this cannot and should not be done without the participation of all governors, and a private contract (*albarano*) should be drawn up and signed by all of them and then be registered in the appropriate book, and said book would be in itself a private contract signed by all of the governors so that every requirement can be met. 2. That the women chosen for this charity would only be the poorest and most honourable from the street of S. Gennarello, those for whom the loss of their virtue would be most grievous. 3. That those that have reached their majority should be preferred, both for the assignation of a dowry and the writing of a private contract; and in the case of a private contract, in any case, the woman should not be less than fifteen years and she should be Neapolitan or a citizen of the Neapolitan Kingdom and should have lived in this street for no less than five years and even if she could be the recipient of a private contract, she should not obtain a dowry unless she will get married in the parish of S. Gennarello, adjacent to the said church of S. Biaso and if any of the poor women in the said street should wish to become a nun then she should be granted a dowry, on the condition that upon her death it will be reimbursed [to us], minus the expenses and 8%. 4 ° that [the women that are chosen for this charity] are born from legal matrimony. 5 ° that those who are orphaned of both Father and Mother should always be preferred 6 ° that the utmost care is taken in choosing those [women] who are at most risk in their virtue. This the governors should do with the utmost care.[10]

---

10 "11.Che a rispetto delle opera di carità solite esercitate dalli detti Governatori debbano osservare le seguenti regole, 1 ° a rispetto dei maritaggi non possano ne debbano fare se non con intervento di tutti i governi facendosene albarano quale dovrà sotto scriverse da tutti essi et dopo registrarse nel libro a tale effetto destinato, et nel medesimo libro debbiano sottoscriventi registrato sarà detto albarano acciò si possano osservare tutte le condizioni in quelle opposte. 2 ° che si eligono le più povere della strada di santo Gennarello tanto honorate, et le più pericolose di perdere l'honore. 3 ° che siano preferite quelle di maggiore età, non solo nel darseli in maritaggio ma anco nell'eligersi per albarano, et quando se li farà l'albarano non sia minore di anni quindici e che o sia napolitano o sia del regno che abbia per il meno abitato in questa strada per anni cinque, et che ancorchè abbia albarano non se ne dia il maritaggio se non si farà il matrimonio nella parrocchia di San Gennarello contigua a detta chiesa di santo biaso e quando alcuna povera di detta strada vorrà monacarse allora se dia il maritaggio con pleggeria di restituirsi dopo

The rules of residency not only applied to those women eligible for a dowry but also to men who wished to be appointed governors; there was not, however, any rule concerning the profession that men should have. The identification of the street and church of San Biagio as a space pertaining to those who made their living printing, buying, and selling books has more to do with the nature of the shops in the street than with a strict rule that dictates it to be this way. From what we can gather from the surviving papers, more often than not the Governors of San Biagio were indeed printers and booksellers.[11] The organisation that had its home in the church, however, was not a professional guild; its purpose was more in the field of providing assistance to those who needed it and regulating the life of the neighbourhood. It is worth mentioning that, although neither printers nor booksellers had a guild, many of the professions in Naples did, including the *Arte della seta e della Lana* (Guild of Silk and wool), with which printers had a close relationship, and some more singular associations such as the guild of the *tarallai*, bakers of a particular kind of savoury bread famous in Naples.[12] We should thus not assume that the lack of guilds related to the book industry was a sign that it was not a profitable enterprise or that the government was not interested in such an industry.

2 A Thriving Industry

When Gonzalo de Cordoba vanquished the French army in Garigliano, securing the entire Kingdom of Naples for the Spanish crown, he became the first Viceroy of the realm. He entered the city and assumed his powers on 16 May 1503, and one of his first official orders was to re-open again many of the businesses that had previously shut down, with an explicit mention of the

---

la morte di quella, o vero se li corrisponda delle spese alla ragione dell'otto per cento 4° che siano nate da legittimo matrimonio 5° che siano sempre preferite quelle figliole che siano prive di padre e madre 6° s'abbia mira a preferire quelle che saranno con maggior pericolo dell'onore a che li governatori faranno ogni diligenza." ASN, CM, Statuti e Corporazioni, fs. 1205/115, *S. Biagio Maggiore, Governo*, 1628. For further papers on the structure and organization of the parishioners of San Biagio see ASN, ms 176/2 *Librari St. Biasij*.

11 In 1649, for example, the Governors of the guild of S. Biagio were Vincenzo Bove (editor and bookseller), Francesco Balsamo (editor), Domenico Montanaro (editor, bookseller and printer) and Agostino Bertaldo (bookseller). Cfr ASDN, *Sante visite di A. Filomarino*, v. IV, f. 95v.

12 For an excursus about the guilds in Naples during the Spanish Viceroyalty see Antonio Follieri de' Torrenteros, *Quattrocento anni di vita operaia napoletana. 1882–1884* (SNSP, MS XXXIV A 42).

PRINTING IN NAPLES

printing press as one of the businesses that needed to be reopened in the city post haste.[13]

It was common practice for printers in Naples to leave the city during times of crisis, and the war between the French and Spaniards, along with the famine and plague that accompanied the conflict, had led many businessmen to flee the city. It warrants notice that already in the very early days of the Spanish Viceroyalty the government showed an interest in the printing press and from that point onward the interest of the crown in taking an active role in the diffusion and control of print never wavered. This is demonstrated by the number of laws on the matter that were issued, particularly from the reign of Don Pedro de Toledo onward, when the government took up its role of regulator of all things print. Between *Prammatiche*, decrees and proclamations, a new order regarding print (or the repetition of an old one) was issued almost yearly.

The interest of the government in the printing business and the desire to make it thrive was indeed of long-standing in the kingdom of Naples. In 1536 Charles v issued a law exempting from tax imported paper, books, typographic fonts, wooden matrices, and everything else that could possibly be of use to printed books.[14] This exemption remained active, with some exceptions, throughout the seventeenth century, thus providing a favourable economic environment for printers and booksellers. This is evident from the occasional document addressed to customs officers that can be found in the Neapolitan State archive.

> Pro Horatio Salviani bookseller.
>
> Alfonsus d'Avolos, etc. To all and every *dohanieri, arrendatori, credenzieri, gabelloti, passaggieri, piazziari, dazieri, pontieri, guardian di qualsivoglia passo et ponte, exultori et percettori di tutti et qualsivoglia vectigale*

---

13 Gianni Machiavelli, *Dizionario dei librai di Napoli nel Rinascimento* (Naples: M. D'Aura Editore, 2012).

14 Giovanni Lombardi, *Tra le pagine di San Biagio. L'economia della stampa a Napoli in età moderna* (Naples: Edizioni Scientifiche Italiane, 200) p. 163.

    The law would have been recorded in the paper of the Sommaria, but unfortunately most of the documents from that particular office were lost during a fire at the beginning of the Nineteenth century. Even if we do not have the decree, we can find references to this law in various papers from the Regia Dogana. "We undersigned Royals Custum Officers ... attest that we never have nor will exact a fees nor a fine for printed books that are brought within this city both from outside and inside the Kingdom both by printers, booksellers and any other person and for printed books that from this city are taken elsewhere. This by the privilege granted with the everlasting memory of the Emperor Charles v. This we witnessed and we still carry in this Royal Custom Office. Datum ex aedam Regia Dohana Neap. 18th January 1622." ASM, Miscellanea Storica, cartella 60.

et diritti [i.e. these are all different kind of government officers in charge of collecting the kingdom's taxes and duties in different places and for different goods, such as customs officers, tax collectors, fees collectors etc.] who are working in this Kingdom now or will work in the future, and to all their subordinates and replacement, both working for the King or the noble families and to all and every who will receive this. Since Horatio Salviani bookseller wants to bring and send to different cities, places and territories of this kingdom printed books, both bound and unbound, to sell them and because for said printed books there is no need to pay any *deritto nè vectigale alcuno di dogana, gabella, passo, datio, scafa, ponte, piacza, pedagio, cortisia nè altro deritto* [i.e. these are all different kind of taxes and fees that were in place on the import and export of goods in the Kingdom of Naples.] with this we remind each and every one of you above mentioned and in the name of the King whose authority we represent we command you to let said Horatio Salviani and those who carry the aforementioned printed books pass through the places and borders of your jurisdiction without any issue or payment of any *dohana, cabella, datio, passo, piacza, ponte, pedagio, cortesia nè qualsivoglia vettigale et deritto* and we warn you to not do otherwise if you want to obey His Majesty's orders under penalty of one thousand ducats. This, *singulis vicibus*, has been seen, read and returned to the proprietor. Naples, 27 June 1577.

Franciscus Antonius de David pro Magno Camerario.[15]

---

15   "Alfonso D'Avalos, ecc. A tutti et singuli dohanieri, arrendatori, credenzieri, gabellotti, passageri, piazzari, dazieri, pontieri, guardiani di qualsivoglia passo et ponte, exactori et perceptori di tutti et qualsivoglia vectigale et deritti in tutto lo presente regno constituti et constituendi presenti et futuri o vero a lloro a chi la presente pervenerà et sarà in qualsivoglia modo presentata insolidum salutem. Perché lo nobile Horatio Salviani libraro intende per diverse città terre et lochi et castelle del detto regno portare o mandare per causa in quelli vendere libri de stampa legati et non legati, et perché per decti libri di stampa non se deve pagare pagamento deritto né vectigale alcuno di dogana, gabella, passo, datio, scafa, ponte, piacza, pedagio, cortisia, né altro deritto, per tanto a voi sopradetti et a ciascuono di voi per tenor de la presente ve deciamo et officii regia autorithate qua fungimur ordiniamo et comandamo che a detto Oratio Salviani libraro, o vero li delitari e portatori de li supradetti libri de stampa debbiati lassare passare per li lochi et passi de le vostre jurisdictioni liberamente et senza impedimento né pagamento alcuno di dohana, cabella, datio, passo, piacza, ponte, pedagio, cortesia né altro qualsivoglia vettigale et deritto atteso non è tenuto, et non fate né ciascun di voi faccia lo contrario, per quanto teneti cara la gratia de la Regia Maestà et pena di ducati mille, etc. La presente, singulisi vicibus, per voi vista et letta restituereti al presentante. Datum Neapoli, etc., Die 27 mensis Junii 1577. Franciscus Antonius de David pro Magno Camerario." ASNA, *Sommaria, Partium*, vol. 785, f. 78v.

PRINTING IN NAPLES

The practice of instituting laws to favour a particular type of business, thus attracting to the city commerce and money was a common one all throughout Europe and it proved to be particularly effective when it came to the printing business in Naples, as it is evident by the great number of foreigner printers active in the city. Just to make a few examples, Giacomo Raillard, Antonio Bulifon and Stefano Monliver were French. The first printed book in Naples was printed by a German. Secondino Roncagliolo was from Milan, Domenico Ferrante Maccaramo from Rome and the Beltramo family came from Genoa.[16]

Given the favourable conditions for the printing business, what kind of books were printed or sold in Naples? According to surviving booklists, a great variety of books spanned all of the main genres of publication. Religious and juridical texts were among the most popular genres in Naples but by no means the only thing that was printed in the city. Chronicles, histories of the city, medicinal text and even cookbooks were printed there. Being a port city and part of the Spanish empire the number of goods that circulated in the city was impressive, and books were a part of this import trade. Unfortunately, due to the poor survival rate of such documents, it is difficult to ascertain precisely what kind of books were sold in the city that were printed elsewhere, while it is an easier task to ascertain what was printed in Naples, thanks to the USTC and other bibliographies. Pietro Manzi, did an incredible work in the redaction of the *Annali* for many of the major printers active in Naples during the sixteenth and seventeenth centuries; these are bibliographies of some of the most relevant printers of the sixteenth century, compiled using several libraries' catalogues. For the seventeenth century, the authority has been Giustiniani, according to whom in Naples more than 4,000 books were printed, almost four times the amount of books printed in the previous century.[17] Writing in 1793, Giustiniani obviously could not have access to exact data. The USTC registers 1,414 books published in sixteenth-century Naples, and 2,749 for the first half of the seventeenth century. For the second half of the century, 3,256 books were printed in Naples.[18] Adding to these the few surviving inventories from booksellers provide us with a glimpse of what kind of books circulated in Naples.[19]

---

16   All of these are important names in the printing business in Naples. For more information on their activity and role see Appendix.

17   Lucio Giustiniani, *Saggio sulla tipografia storica napoletana* (Naples: Orsini, 1793).

18   For this datum I have to thank my colleague and friend Giovanni Petrocelli.

19   Pietro Manzi was a Neapolitan bibliographer who compiled a list, based on library catalogues, of the book printed by some of the more active printers in Naples during the sixteenth and seventeenth centuries. The majority of booksellers' catalogues can be found in the Archivio Storico Diocesano, either in the Holy Office section or in the Censorship

36   CHAPTER 1

Here I transcribe the catalogue of the booksellers Giovan Giacomo de Rosano, compiled on 21 May 1579 by the ecclesiastical censor. Where possible, I will indicate the precise edition to which the record refers.

Dated 21 May 1579
Books that belong to Jo. Iacovo de Rosano
1 Tre parte del campo primi studii di Gabriele Simion.
Gabriele Simeoni, *Le III parti del campo de primi studii* (Venice: per Comino da Trino di Monferrato, 1546), USTC 856447.

2 Le epistole ad Atti(co). Cicero stampa ade altimatur.
Cicero, *Le pistole di Cicerone a Attico* (Venice: in casa de figliuoli di Aldo, 1555), USTC 822368.

3 Rudimenta grammatices Nicolai Pirotti.
Niccolò Perotto, *Rudimenta grammatices* (Naples: per Matias Moravus, 1480 or Naples: [M. Moravus?], 1483), USTC 992303 or USTC 992291.

4 Capricci Medicinali di messer Fioravante.
Leonardo Fioravanti, *De capricci medicinali* (Venice: appresso Lodovico Avanzo, 4 editions between 1564–1573), USTC 829656; USTC 829659; USTC 829663; USTC 829669.

5 Lettere di D. Antonio di Juvara.
Antonio De Guevara, *Letters.* 4 vols; published throughout several years. Probably one of the two complete editions available at the time. Venice, appresso Vincenzo Valgrisi, 1565, or 1575.
USTC 835305; USTC 835335

6 Della religione di cavalieri hierosolimitani.
[not identified]

7 Roma ristorata et Italia illustrata del Biondo di Forlì.
Flavio Biondo, *De Roma instaurata and De Italia illustrata.* Unknown edition printed between 1503 and 1527, presumably in Venice. Could be one of these USTC 814547 or USTC 814546.

---

one. This means that we only get to look at what those printers who at some point or another had trouble with the law sold.

PRINTING IN NAPLES   37

8 Appiano Alessandrino.
Unknown edition of Appian of Alexandria's Roman History.

9 Grammatica Urbano Greco.
[not identified]

10 Operetta verità di fra Battista da Crema ordinis predicatorum.
Giovanni Battista Carioni, *Via de aperta verità* (Venice: per Gregorio de'
Gregoriis 1523), USTC 812854.

11 Secreti di D. Alexio Piemontese.
Unknown edition of Girolamo Ruscelli's Secrets.

12 Paragoni della lingua toscana e castigliana di messer Io. Maria Alexandri.
Giovanni Mario Alessandri, *Il paragone della lingua toscana et Castigliana*
(Naples: appresso Mattia Cancer, 1560), USTC 808598.

13 Opera toschana di Luigi Alemanno.
Plausibly one of the four editions of Luigi Alamanni, *Opere Toscane* Printed
between 1532 and 1542.
USTC 808163; USTC 808164; USTC 808165; USTC 808166.

14 Rime di diversi signori napoletani.
One or more volumes from a series only partially preserved entitled *Rime di
diversi illustri signori napoletani, e d'altri nobilissimi ingegni* Volume III and V
were printed in Venice by Gabriele Giolito de Ferrari between 1552 and 1555.
USTC 803574; USTC 803573; USTC 803735.

15 Cons. tr.
[not identified]

16 Avvisi del India deli Padri Gesuiti.
Nuovi Avisi dell'India de Reverendi Padri della Compagnia di Giesù (Rome: per
gli heredi di Antonio Blado [1570]), USTC 804746.

17 Expositione sopra Orlando Furioso.
[Lodovico Dolce], *Espositione di Historie, favole, allegorie, et di vocaboli diffi-
cili, che nell'Orlando Furioso si contengono* (Venice: per Gio. Andrea Valvassori
detto Guadagnino, 1553), USTC 810776.

18 Isitutione di tutta la vita del homo di Alexandro Piccolhomino.
One of the six editions of Alessandro Piccolomini, *De la institutione di tutta la vita de l'huomo nato nobile, e in città libera* (Venice, 1542–1559), USTC 848289; USTC 848290; USTC 848291; USTC 848293; USTC 848304; USTC 848321.

19 La confessione et conversion di Santa Maria Magdalena del Reverendo P. fra Pietro Giaves.
Pedro de Chaves, *La conversione, confessione, et penitentia di Santa Maria Maddalena* (Naples: appresso Gio. Maria Scotto, 1561), USTC 821843.

20 La repubblica di Venezia di Messer Donato Gionnotti.
Donato Giannotti, *La republica di Vinegia* (Lyon: per Antonio Gryphio, 1569, 1570, 1572 or 1577) USTC 832715; USTC 832716; USTC 130041; USTC 832717; USTC 832747.

21 Compendio del regnio di Napoli di messer Pandolfo.
Pandolfo Collenuccio, *Compendio delle historie del Regno di Napoli composto da Messer Pandolfo Collenuccio* (Venice: M. Tramezzino, 1541), USTC 823403.

†22 Terentio dela stampa di Aldo Manuzio.
Terentius, *Comedies* (Venice: in aedibus Aldi et Andreae Asulani Soceri, 1517 or 1521), USTC 858679; USTC 858691.

23 Beato stampato per Agostino Guidone, et Cornelio Acchillo Tacito.
[not identified]

†24 Il dialogo Cicerone.
Cicero, *Il dialogo dell'oratore di Cicerone tradotto da Lodovico il Dolce* (Venice: appresso Gabriel Giolito de Ferrari. Between 1547 and 1556), USTC 822365.

25 Elegantie di Aldo Manuzio.
Unknown edition of Aldo Manuzio the Younger, *Eleganze, insieme con la copia della lingua toscana, e latina*; Printed between 1556 and 1576. USTC 822289; USTC 822354; USTC 822365; USTC 822156.

26 Li discorsi del Reverendo monsignor Francesco Patricii.
Francesco Patrizi, *De discorsi ... sopra alle cose appartenenti ad una città libera, e famiglia nobile* (Venice: in casa de' figliuoli di Aldo, 1545), USTC 762223.

PRINTING IN NAPLES

27 Le nove fiamme di messer Lodovico Paterno.
Lodovico Paternò, *Le nuove fiamme* (Venice: per Gio. Andrea Valvassori, detto Guadagnino, 1561) or (Lyon: appresso Guglielmo Rovillio, 1568), USTC 847020; USTC 154683.

28 Jeronimo a docto halicarnasso.
[not identified]

29 Le Istorie del Perù di Pietro Cieza.
Unknown edition of Pedro de Cieza de Leon, *La prima parte dell'historie del Perù* Printed between 1555 and 1576. USTC 822620; USTC 822621; USTC 822622; USTC 822625.

†30 Comentaria di Io. Cesarea.
i.e. John Chrysostom et al., *Commentaria in sacrosancta quatuor Christi Evangelia ex Chrysostomi aliorumque veterum scriptis magna ex parte collecta* ... (Leuven: ex officina Rutgeri Rescii, 1543), USTC 400711.

31 Familiare clericorum.
Familiaris clericorum liber Unknown edition printed in Venice between 1530 and 1570.

32 Rime di Messer Ludovico Dolce.
Lodovico Dolce ed, *Rime di diversi, et eccellenti autori* (Venice: appresso Gabriel Giolito de Ferrari. 1556 or 1563, 2 voll), USTC 803814.

33 Assolani et rime di messer Pietro Bembo.
Unknown edition of Pietro Bembo, *Gli Asolani* printed between 1505 and 1575.

34 Opera di messer Lodovico Martelli.
Lodovico Martelli, *Opere* (Florence: appresso Bernarno di Giunta, 1548), USTC 841134.

35 Privilegii di frati minori di fra Gaspar Passarelli.
Gaspare Passarello ed, *Privilegia per complures summos pontifices ordinis fratrum minimorum concessa, & communicata* ... (Naples: in officina viri Oratij Salviani, 1573), USTC 1752417.

40   CHAPTER 1

36 Trattato del governo di Aristotele.
Aristotle, *Trattato dei governi* ... (Florence: appresso Lorenzo Torrentino, 1549
or 1559), USTC 810925; USTC 810951 or (Venice: per Bartholomeo detto l'Imper-
ador, et Francesco suo genero, 1551), USTC 810933.

37 Petro Bella Pertica, sopra la Istituta.
Pierre de Belleperche, *Super librum institutionum* ... [Pavia: Giovanni Giolito de
Ferrari the Elder, b. 1520] USTC 848498.

38 Bartolo [da Sassoferrato] sopra la Istituta.
Bartolus de Saxoferrato, *Super Authenticis, & Insitut.* ... (Venice: apud Lucam
Antonium Iuntam, 1567 or 1570), USTC 812537 or USTC 812538.

39 Lo organo de Aristotile.
Unknown Latin edition of Aristotle's *Organon* Printed between 1536 and 1571.

40 Nicolai Belloni sopra la Isituta.
Niccolò Belloni, *Super utraque parte institutionum lucubrationes* (Venice: apud
Cominum de Tridino Montisferrati, 1563), USTC 813317 or (Venice: ex officina
Ioan. Bapt. Somaschi, 1573), USTC 813319.

†41 Tito Livio Paduano.
Unknown edition of Livy's *Ab urbe condita*

†42 Le epistole di Seneca.
Unknown edition of Seneca the Younger's *Epistulae Morales ad Lucilium*

†43 Francesco Petrarcha.
Unknown edition of Francesco Petrarca's works.

44 Antonio Andrea super Artem veterem.
Antonio Andrés, *Super Artem Veterem* (Venice: [Ottavianus Scotus the Elder,
1508] USTC 817275 or (Venice: per Simonem de Luere, 1509), USTC 809281 or
(Venice: per dominum Lucantonium de Giunta Florentinum, 1517), USTC
809285.

45 Consuetudine di Napoli.
Consuetudines Neapolitanae (Naples: per magistrum Antonium de Frizzis
Corinaldensem, 1518), USTC 844151 or (Naples: apud Joannem Paulum
Suganappum, in platea Armeriorum, 1546) USTC 844168 or (Naples: apud
Joannem de Boy, 1567), USTC 844185.

PRINTING IN NAPLES

46 Vita di Carlo v del Signor Alfonso Villanova.
Alfonso de Ulloa, *Vita dell'invittissimo, e sacratissimo imperator Carlo v* (Venice: appresso Vincenzo Valgrisi 1566 or 1573 or 1574), USTC 861578; USTC 861585; USTC 861586 or (Venice: dalla bottega d'Aldo, 1575), USTC 861587.

47 Le Istorie di Venezia di messer Pietro Bembo.
Pietro Bembo, *Della historia vinitiana* (Venice: [Gualtero Scotto], 1552), USTC 813419 or (Venice: per Giordano Ziletti, e compagni, 1570), USTC 813453.

48 Stato di religiosi di Fra Paulo Morgia.
Paolo Morigia, *Stato religioso, et via spirituale* (Venice: appresso Domenico Farri, 1567), USTC 843583.

49 Rimi di diversi eccellenti bressani.
Girolamo Ruscelli ed., *Rime di diversi eccellenti autori bresciani* (Venice: per Plinio Pietrasanta, 1553 or 1554), USTC 853878 or USTC 853882.

50 Horii Augusto messer Cornelio Tacito.
Tacitus, *Le historie auguste di Cornelio Tacito, novellamente fatte italiane* (Venice: appresso Vincenzo Vaugris al segno d'Erasmo, 1544), USTC 857891.

51 Avisi di fauriti.
Antonio De Guevara, *Aviso de favoriti e dottrina de cortegiani, con la commendatione della villa* Unknown edition printed in Venice between 1544 and 1562.

52 Andriano Cardinale.
Adriano Castellesi, *Ad Ascanium cardinalem Venatio* (Venice: apud Aldum, 1505), USTC 819393.

53 Nicolai Renardi.
[not identified]

54 Io. Baptista Arcutio.
Giovanni Battista Arcucci, *Naupactiaca victoria* (Naples: apud Franciscum Falconem, et Joannem Antonium Sportellum, 1572), USTC 810285.

55 Le Istorie di Monsignore Argentone.
Philippe de Comines, *La historia famosa di monsignor di Argenton delle guerre & costumi di Ludovico Undecimo Re di Francia* (Venice: [s.n.], 1543), USTC 823594 or (Venice: per Michel Tramezino, 1544), USTC 823597.

42　　　　　　　　　　　　　　　　　　　　　　　　　　　　　　　　　　　　CHAPTER 1

56 Filosophia naturale Alexandro Piccolomino.
Alessandro Piccolomini, *Della filosofia naturale* (Venice: presso Giorgio de'
Cavalli, 1565), USTC 848341 or (Venice: appresso Daniel Zaneti, et compagni,
1576), USTC 845389.

57 Pietro Bembi.
[not identifiable]

58 Desione di Mattheo de Afflitto.
unknown edition of Matteo D'Afflitto ed., *Decisiones sacri concilii neapolitani*
Printed in Venice between 1552 and 1575.

59 Vocabularium Juris.
plausibly *Vocabolarium Juris* (Venice: impressum Georgii de Rusconibus, 1517),
USTC 800492.

60 Io. Battista Montini medico.
unknown work by Giovanni Battista da Monte. Presumably printed between
1554 and 1565.

61 Le istitute.
plausibly an unknown edition of Justinian

†62 Il cortigian di messer Baldassar Castiglione.
unknown edition of Baldassare Castiglione's *Il Cortegiano*.

63 Cinafonte spagnuolo.
Xenophon, *Las Obras* (Salamanca: por Juan De Junta, 1552), USTC 339255.

64 Le confession di Santo Agostino.
unknown edition of Saint Agustin's Confessions.
Signavi signo crucis non vendantur absque licentia.
Franciscus Joele actuaries.[20]

Besides proving the argument that books of various genres were sold in Naples,
this bookseller catalogue offers us another interesting information. The

---

20　　ASDNA, *Carte Diverse sulla censura dei libri*. The catalogue was compiled by the censor
　　　and the † mark the books that he indicated should not be sold without an ecclesiastical
　　　licence. Cfr. Pasquale Lopez, *Inquisizione, stampa e censura nel Regno di Napoli tra '500 e
　　　'600* (Naples: Edizioni del Delfino, 1972).

PRINTING IN NAPLES

majority of books here listed are printed in Venice, some in other Italian cities and there are even some printed in France, Spain, Belgium and Switzerland. This proves the international nature of the book trade in Naples.

The commercial relationship with Venice were particularly strong when it came to the book trade, with agents for both the Giunta and the Manuzio family being particularly active in Naples, as it is proven by numerous bank statements.

> To Luise di Leo ducats 600 and from him we pay [those] to Luca Antonio Giunta, from Venice, as a partial payment for the expenses that he will have in printing a corpus of books in five volumes and bring those to Naples in a year time.[21]

Furthermore, out of the 64 books here listed, only six were printed in Naples, and one cannot help but wonder at this curious fact. Although we do not have nearly enough information on the book trade in Naples during the sixteenth century, what little we do have led me to believe that some of the characteristics of this trade that are present in the seventeenth century can be found in the previous century as well. Namely, the fact that the vast majority of printers had their own bookshop from which they would sell their own books. Indeed, it was quite unusual for a professional figure involved in the book trade to be just a printer, only 16.94%. It was more often the case of printers being also publishers, booksellers, editors and sometimes even authors, as it is the case for Domenico Antonio Parrino and Antonio Bullion.[22]

Unfortunately, given the poor survival rates of documents from the sixteenth century within the Neapolitan archives, I was able to find only a couple of booksellers' catalogues, but although it is a limited resource and it would be wrong to generalise based on such small evidence, these two catalogues combined with the *Annali* provide an interesting example of what one could find in a bookshop in Naples.[23] It stands to reason that the books that were printed and were part of booksellers' inventories were those that sold best. We can see that in the sixteenth century, Naples was still very much a Renaissance

---

21   The transcription can be found in Lombardi, *Tra le pagine* ... (2000) p. 26.

22   In the Appendix, you will find a graphic representation of the book-trade in Naples during the seventeenth century. This list was compiled combining data from De Marco's article, libraries catalogue, archival documents and the USTC. It features 490 names, only 83 of which were just printers (16.94%).

23   On the importance of catalogues as a tool for book historians see Arthur der Weduwen, Andrew Pettegree, Graeme Kemp (eds), *Book Trade Catalogues in Early Modern Europe* (Leiden: Brill, 2021). Particularly Chapter 1.

city, with a Renaissance culture. This is evident from the number of classical texts printed and sold, along with books of jurisprudence, a smaller number of religious texts, some history books (both local and from other corners of the Spanish Empire), and even the odd item of more popular genres. The selling of used books, particularly those that came from the personal libraries of the clergy, was a lucrative business, particularly toward the end of the sixteenth century and in the seventeenth.

Of course, along with these more serious, expensive publications, we cannot fail to mention a more commercial type of print. Small pamphlets, cheaply and quickly made, actually constituted the bulk of the printing business, particularly those of a legal nature. These cannot always be found in booksellers' inventories because they were often distributed for free or sold within government offices. Unfortunately, we do not have surviving account records for printers but we do know that several of them owed a substantial portion of their income to contracts with various government offices and banks, printing documents for their internal use and copies of proclamations and lawyers' discourses both to be used in court and to be sold on the streets. Evidence of these kinds of contracts can be found in the papers of the archive of the Fondazione Banco di Napoli.[24]

> To said [governors] eleven ducats, four tari and 10 grana and from them [this sum] is paid to Secondino Roncagliolo as the price for four and a half *resme* [reams] of printed pamphlets that [he] delivered because of his contract to the royal warehouses and houses of their Office along with the list of the pamphlets he delivered and they are pleased with the results. And for him, 11.4.10 ducats [are given] to Pietro Andrea Grassi. To said [governors] thirty-eight ducats and from them, there are given to

---

24 Between 1500 and 1600 eight different public banks opened in Naples, to accommodate the increased volume of commercial exchange within the city, due to the growth of the population as well as the relevance of the city within the Spanish Empire: 1. Banco della Pietà (1539–1808); 2. Banco dei Poveri (1563–1808); 3. Banco dell'Annunziata (1587–1702); 4. Banco di Santa Maria del Popolo (1589–1808); 5. Banco dello Spirito Santo (1590–1808); 6. Banco di S.Eligio (1592–1808); 7. Banco di S.Giacomo e Vittoria (1597–1809); 8. Banco del Salvatore (1640–1808). The archive of the Fondazione Banco di Napoli preserves the account registers for all these different banks and it is one of the most well preserved archival resources in Naples, with many papers related to the affairs of printers. With a source such as this, it came as no surprise that the majority of studies done up until now on the subject of print in Naples went for an economic approach.

PRINTING IN NAPLES

Gio Antonio Venderosa for books, papers, ink, quills and the rest that was delivered to be used in their office.[25]

This particular business was so lucrative that, when the government tried to regulate it, the majority of printers rallied together against this decision, as we will see.

Books were printed in many languages, particularly Spanish and Latin, along with of course Italian. The circulation of books in Spanish, both printed in Naples and imported from Spain, was particularly relevant and made up a good portion of the book market in Naples, as is to be expected given the high numbers of Spanish people who resided in the city. According to the USTC, between 1503 and 1650 275 books were printed in Spanish in the city. The community of booksellers in S. Biagio was of varied geographical provenance, with many foreign printers and booksellers who chose to make their home and business in the busy streets of the San Lorenzo neighbourhood. One of the most important Neapolitan printers of the eighteenth century, Antonio Bulifon, was French, born in Chaponay and he arrived in Naples in 1670, when he immediately opened a bookstore in San Biagio street and, two years later, began also to work a printer. Of course, he was not the only foreigner; French, Spaniards, Germans, as well as professionals from outside the Kingdom of Naples, operated in Naples, including a branch of the renowned printing family of the Giunta.

3   Laws and Regulations

Before introducing some of the most renowned printers and booksellers from the period of the Viceroyalty, it is worth mentioning something about the laws that regulated their business. What was the position of the government with regard to print? Which laws existed in Naples for printers and booksellers? What was the procedure to obtain a printing licence? In order to be able to print anything legally, from books to news sheets and everything in between,

---

25   "Alli detti d. undici tarì quattro grana 10 e per essi a Secondino Roncagliolo se li pagano per il prezzo de resime quattro e mezza bollettini stampati che ha consignato per servitio delli regij fundaci e subfundaci del loro arrendamento justa la lista li bollettini consignati e resta soddisfatto del passato e per esso a Pietro Andrea Grasso per altrittanti d.11.4.10; Alli detti d. trentotto e per essi ad Gio Antonio Verderosa se li pagano per tanti libri carta inchiostro penna et altro consignati per servitio del loro arrendamento" This is a contract from the Banco di San Giacomo for the office that held the contract to collect the payment of taxes on salt. AFBN, BsG, gb. 1646–47, d.38, 3 Luglio 1647.

printers needed to apply to the Real Cancelleria, while, at least at the beginning, seeking permission from the Archbishop was necessary only for books on religious subjects.

A printer who wished to publish something needed to send a manuscript or printed copy of the work to the Real Cancelleria; his petition would then be forwarded to the Consiglio Collaterale, which had the task of deliberate whether the license for said print should be granted or not. Once a license was granted, the book or pamphlet could be printed, and on the front page or the last page *Con Licenza de' Superiori* would attest to the legitimacy of the print and that the proper process had indeed been followed. This is just in regard to the civil authority. As we have seen with the bookseller's catalogue, the ecclesiastical authorities often wished to have their says in the matter of what was printed and sold, and for religious texts as well as some of the classics of philosophy an ecclesiastical licence was also needed. Given the quite lengthy process that went into the obtaining of a license and the risk that this license could be refused, it is unsurprising that clandestine and illicit print flourished in Naples.

The authorities were very much aware of this particular problem. Between 1544 and 1611 no fewer than eight laws were promulgated reiterating the need to apply for a license in order to publish any work, and this is not counting the numerous edicts addressed directly to printers and booksellers detailing the consequences for those who were caught printing or selling unlicensed books: 'Hereby we order printers and bookseller to print neither theology books nor the Holy Scriptures without permission of the Archbishopric.' (1544) 'Hereby we order printers and booksellers to print no books, nor letters, pamphlets or any kind of print without a license.' (1550).[26] The number of laws, as well as the numerous mentions of clandestine printing in legal proceedings and in reports between the various offices of the Neapolitan bureaucratic machine, show us that clandestine printing was indeed an issue and that preventive censorship was not working as planned.[27]

While the civic authorities struggled to control what was printed and sold in the Viceroyalty of Naples, the Church inserted itself in the debate. At first content to police only religious texts and ensure the rigorous application of the Tridentine Index, faced with what appeared to be an incapability to control the printed market on the part of the civic authorities, the Archbishop of Naples

---

26   Lorenzo Giustiniani, ed. *Nuova collezione delle prammatiche del Regno di Napoli* 15 vols. (Naples: Stamperia Simoniana, 1803–08).

27   This was a common problem throughout Europe. See Nina Lamal, Jamie Cumby, and Helmer J. Helmers (eds), *Print and power in Early Modern Europe (1500–1800)* (Leiden: Brill, 2021). Particularly Chpater 7 (The Netherlands), chapter 11 (England), and chapter 15.

PRINTING IN NAPLES

and the local inquisitor took the task upon themselves. In 1617, the Archbishop decided to reissue a Papal decree of some years standing that stated that everything that was printed needed to be submitted for the approval of the local inquisitor. This implied that the jurisdiction of religious and civic powers overlapped. Now the printers needed to apply to both Church and State before being able to print anything. Or at least, this is what it was supposed to happen: a system of control carried on by two different offices should have ensured a reduction of clandestine print.

What actually happened was that Neapolitan printers and booksellers took advantage of these overlapping jurisdictions to appeal to a third office, the Real Giurisdizione, therefore managing to immerse licensing in a lengthy and complex bureaucratic and legal process that dragged on for more than 30 years, creating a lot of grey areas in which they could operate in relative safety. Although the Archbishop's decree referred to everything that could be printed or sold in Naples, it was followed by a more detailed regulation, that explicitly mentioned religious and legal texts as to the kind of work that deserved more close scrutiny. And it was precisely this distinction that offered printers and booksellers the opportunity to appeal. They send their complaints to the Real Giurisdizione, the Neapolitan office that had the task of deliberating on matters for which it was unclear if they were the competence of a spiritual or lay tribunal, using the obligation to the public for them to be aware of legal matters as an excuse to appeal against the Archbishop and his threat of excommunication.

> The printers of this most faithful city of Naples hereby inform Your Excellency that for the longest time, such that there is no one alive who can recall otherwise, they printed judicial sentences, lawyer's discourses and accounts of the cases that are being discussed in this royal courthouse and while they kept on printing those, an order suddenly came from the Archbishop that under the threat of being excommunicated they could not print such works anymore without a licence from the Archbishop's Court. Once the licence was obtained a new one was to be requested every time for every work. This is causing much damage not only to those who are now appealing to Your Excellency and that earn their living by printing but also to the public, because having such legal papers printed instead of only available as manuscripts is cheaper and more expedient. The Archbishop's licence is needed for printed books, which we have observed in the past and are still doing because they can include something that goes against the sacred word, but not for such legal pamphlets, who are printed to be used only by lawyers who have

to defend the cases and judges who have to deliberate upon them .... Because of this, we are now appealing to Your Excellency to please resolve this, in a way that nothing new will change and we can continue to print such legal papers as we are doing now, without a further licence from the Archbishop's court.[28]

The authorities of the Real Giurisdizione appeared willing to talk with printers and booksellers and work with them to find proper solutions. The chancellor himself, Giovanni Giordano, inquired with the vicar of the city as to this edict, demonstrating that the complaints made by printers and booksellers had merit. The response of the Vicar was one of deflection: he was not the one who had issued the law (given that it was a papal decree) and that the person to question about it should have been the Cardinal, who exceeded his with further proclamations on the matter. Significantly, this document is dated 1630, some years after the decree which they were discussing, showing that the matter was taken seriously by all the parties involved and that until a clear answer could be found it would not be put to rest. It also shows that in the meantime the Cardinal of Naples kept making demands on Neapolitan printers and booksellers, who were taking advantage of the legal quarrel to ignore his demands. Upon receiving a positive response to their plight, printers and booksellers became bolder.

They maintained communication with the authorities, both as a group and as individuals, and whether it was to reiterate their appeal against the

---

28   "Li Stampatori di questa fidelissima Città esponeno a v.e. come da tempo immemorabile che tale che non vi è memoria d'homo in contrario hanno stampato, et stampano l'allegatione in iure, et note di fatto, che fanno l'avvocati, et causidici per le liti che sono in questi regij tribunali, et mentre sequitavano fare dette stampe li è venuto ordine di monsignore arcivescovo di Napoli, che non possino stamparle sotto pena di scomunica latae sententiae senza licenza della sua Corte Arcivescovale né dopo stampate ancorche con detta licenza pubblicarle dopo senza nova licenza dell'istessa corte, con il qual'ordine stanno impediti di stampare dette allegationi, et note di fatti in molto danno non solo d'essi supplicanti li quali vivono con detta lor'arte di stampare, ma anco del pubblico, si per il minor dispendio, che corre in dette stampe che nelli scritti a mano, si anco per maggior comodità dell'istessi avvocati et giudici che hanno da decidere, et terminare dette liti, et la licenza di detta corte che si ricerca nelle stampe deve esser à rispetto delli libri, conforme anticamente s'è osservato, et si osseva, nelli quali vi potria essere qualche cosa contro li sacri canoni, ma non a rispetto delle allegazioni le quali si stampano solamente per li giudici che hanno da votare nelle cause, et per li avvocati che le hanno da deffendere ... Perciò ricorreno da v.e. et la supplicano darli quel rimedio che conviene, acciocche non s'innovi cosa alcuna circa detto antico solito in stampare dette allegationi com'in ogn'altra cosa solita, et possino continuare dette stampe senza altra licenza della Corte Arcivescovile." ASNA, Delegazione della Real Giuridisizione, processi, vol. 182/1, f.7.

PRINTING IN NAPLES

Archbishop, plead their loyalties to the Real Giurisdizione or support their cause, they began signing with their own names and by their own hand all further communications. Even the Viceroy deemed it appropriate to intervene in this particular debate, issuing his own orders. Speaking on the authority of the King of Spain he reinforced the necessity to maintain firm control over book circulation in the Neapolitan Viceroyalty. Besides addressing the need to have approval before printing anything he also brought into focus the need to exercise control over books printed abroad and imported into the Neapolitan territory. Despite being addressed to the officials of the Regia Dogana, under the Spanish order there is a note in Italian, reinforcing the need to obey this particular regulation to maintain order in the city, that is signed once again by the chancellor of the Real Giurisdizione highlighting how with the continuing uncertainty as to who should be in control of printing the task fell once again upon the very office with which the printers and booksellers were in dialogue. Twenty-five years after the Archbishop's decree the Real Giurisdizione reached a conclusion, issuing its own decree and promising dire consequences to those who would print anything without asking for the proper authorization.

> Under penalty of the payment of 100 ducats the first time, 200 the second, 300 the third and other corporal penalties established by His Excellency, it is ordered that from today onwards they must neither print nor publish any sort of books or works of any matter, science and profession if these are not first seen and authorized by us.[29]

Authorisation needed to be requested from the Real Consiglio and reinforced by the Real Giurisdizione. The final ruling was against the Archbishop and apparently in favour of printers and booksellers, despite what the severity of the penalties established here may indicate. It is also worth mentioning that appealing to the Real Giurisdizione was not the only way around the Archbishop's regulation and control of the Church. The diocese of Pozzuoli, for example, was notably less strict than Naples and therefore printers frequently sent their work there for approval after a rejection from the Neapolitan diocese.[30] This was not the only instance in which printers and booksellers came together, presenting a united front against the authorities. As we have

---

29 "Sotto pena di pagamento di ducati 100 per la prima volta, 200 per la seconda, 300 per la terza e altre pene corporali così come stabilite da S.E. si ordina che da questo momento in avanti essi non possano né stampare né pubblicare qualsivoglia sorta di libro o opera su nessun argomento, materia e professione senza che questo sia prima visto e autorizzato da Noi." ASNA, Delegazione della Real Giurisdizione, *Processi*, vol. 449/4, f. 263.

30 Giampiero di Marco, *Librai* (2010), p. 146.

50 CHAPTER 1

seen at the beginning of the chapter, these professionals of the printed word were not organised in a guild, but they did have an organisation of some sort and the collective and charitable dimension of the organisation allowed them to work together, supporting each other for the sake of greater profit to be had by all.

This is all the more evident in the cases that appeared before the Real Giurisdizione on the matter of printing licences and patents. We have mentioned that in order to be able to print anything legally within the Kingdom it was necessary to obtain a printing licence; some of these were exclusive, granting to a single printer the right to publish a book, or to a single seller the right to sell it. Of course, the breach of an exclusive licence was a serious offence, but this did not stop printers and booksellers from trying to find their way around it, particularly when there was an economic advantage to be had. The connection established between various printers, be it by marriage, apprenticeship or business arrangement became particularly relevant in appeals against exclusive printing privilege and the archival documents provide an opportunity to bring some of these connections to light. An example of this is the case that several booksellers of San Biagio, led by Antonio Bulifon, presented to the Real Giurisdizione against the exclusive licence held by Giuseppe Abbate for the *Ordinario Romano*. In 1679 Abbate obtained an exclusive licence for printing and selling this particular book for the duration of ten years. Immediately, other booksellers appealed to the Real Giurisdizione on the basis that the privilege should not have been granted in the first place, because

> [the *Ordinario Romano*] can be printed anywhere in the world where the Church has jurisdiction and the Mass is performed. Particularly within this Kingdom, it is printed every year in all the various dioceses and it is printed differently because of the celebration for the Patron saints that change every year. Moreover, an exclusive licence is granted when the printing of a book is either a great expense or long labour which is not the case for this book, that is made up of very few pages and it is copied from the one in Rome. Lastly, if such a commonly used book is sold by only one the poor priests would be gravely mistreated with the price.[31]

---

31 "Mentre può il medesimo stamparsi per ogni parte del mondo et dovunque si stende la giurisdizione, e rito della Santa Chiesa, e per quel che tocca in particolare à questo Regno, è solito stamparsi ogni anno, per varie diocesi e per quella di questa fidelissima città, si stampa con distintione in riguardo de santi protettori ò feste, che si celebrano, in essa solamente che può ricevere mutatione in ogni anno; oltre che quando, un solo tiene prohibitione che altre non possa stampare, un libro necessario che sia ò per una spesa grandiosa, ò per una grande diligenza o faticha, il che non si considera, in questo

PRINTING IN NAPLES

Bulifon's plea was favourably received and Abbate lost his privilege. Of course, he tried to fight back, appealing to the Collaterale that he had invested 300 ducats for the print run of the Ordinario Romano and that he was sure that the only one who was actually against his privilege was Antonio Bulifon 'because he wanted me to give him 150 copies of the Ordinario for free'.[32] Bulifon replied with a renewal of his plea against the exclusive licence, this time signed by ten other printers and booksellers, all connected to each other by economic and business alliances. Once again a crucial role was played by the knowledge and understanding of the intricacy of the Neapolitan bureaucracy; the case was moved from the Collaterale, the office that had granted the privilege in the first place, to the Real Giurisdizione but Abbate still appealed to the Collaterale. Bulifon was quick to inform the Delegate of the Real Giurisdizione of this misstep and thus the ruling ended up being in favour of Bulifon and his associates.

Not all the instances in which printers came together ended on such a victorious note. In 1661, in fact, every single printer within the city of Naples was arrested, including the royal printer Egidio Longo. Amidst tensions between the Church of Rome and the Spanish authorities on the matter of whom was entitled to collect fees paid by the Church, the publication of a pamphlet on the Inquisition attributed to Giuseppe Campanile proved to be the last straw. In this pamphlet, the author declared himself against the institution of the Inquisition as a whole, but more specifically against the Spanish Inquisition, arguing that its introduction into the Kingdom of Naples was illegitimate.[33]

---

    libro, che consoste in pochissimi fogli, e si copia, da quello di Roma che può aversi da ogni uno, e per l'ultimo, quando questo libretto, così usuale, si venda, da un solo li poveri sacerdoti sarebbero angariati, nel prezzo, mentre hoggi si vendono a prezzi dolci et con la prohibitione si venderiano a prezzi alterati." ASNA, Delegazione della Real Giurisdizione, Processi, vol. 337/177, f.1.

32   ASNA, Delegazione della Real Giurisdizione, Processi, vol. 337/177, f.4.

33   I believe the pamphlet in question to be *Raggioni per la fedelissima città di Napoli negli affari della Santa Inquisizione* (Pesaro: Gio. Battista Giotti, 1661), USTC 1752420 The imprimatur is almost certainly a false one, given that there are no records of anything else ever being printed by Gio. Battista Giotti nor any kind of information about him can be found. The attribution of the pamphlet to Giuseppe Campanile is done by Fuidoro and then repeated by Galasso, *Napoli spagnola dopo Masaniello* (Florence: Sansoni, 1982) p. 185 but I believe this to be a pseudonym. In my opinion, the author of the pamphlet here in exam is actually Pietro Di Fusco, as he is the author of a manuscript with the same subject and title. The content of the manuscript is the same as the pamphlet and it appears to be directed to the Spanish crown and presents arguments for keeping the Holy Office out of Naples. Di Fusco is also the author of a second work on this same subject, addressed to the Duke of Alba, being a defence of Naples' historic right to keep the Holy Office under the control of the Viceroy, quoting legal precedents from the Neapolitan archives, mostly from the second half of the sixteenth century.

The Viceroy's reaction was swift and immediate; given that the pamphlet was anonymous and without imprimatur he ordered that every printer within the realm was to be arrested. Not even holding a royal office was enough to be spared this punishment, as even Egidio Longo was brought before justice. According to the account of this event provided by Innocenzo Fuidoro (1618–1692), the incarceration was brief and the following day the printers were once again free.[34] It is not clear whether this was the end of this particular incident, suggesting that the arrest was motivated in the first place more by the desire to send a signal to printers that the crown was watching and policing their activity rather than a real desire to discover and bring to justice those who were guilty of a crime.

Throughout this brief exploration of legal proceedings concerning printers and booksellers, we have witnessed how the balance of power and the leverage that these professional figures could exert varied depending on the political climate. Another clear example of this is the controversy between Antonio Bulifon and Domenico Antonio Parrino when it came to be the first to be able to publish a history of the Neapolitan Vicerealm that went up to their days. In 1692 Parrino published the first volume of his own *Teatro Eroico, e Politico de'Governni de'Sig. Viceré di questo Regno*, a work in three volumes – the other two would be published over the next two years – containing the history of Naples from the beginning of the Spanish Viceralm until Parrino's days. In this book, there is a copy of the verdict issued on 19 August in favour of Parrino and against Bulifon, forbidding the latter to publish his history of Naples and ruling that Bulifon can publish his work but only up until the beginning of the reign of Ferdinand the Catholic, when Parrino's book starts. Already at the beginning of 1688, on 26 January Parrino petitioned the Viceroy himself, Francisco de Benavides, to obtain a privilege for his upcoming work which was granted for 10 years. A ten-year privilege issued for a work that was not yet published was a rarity. In the meantime, Bulifon 1690 published the first volume of his history of Naples, known today as Cronicamerone, which was titled *"Giornale Historico delle cose memorabili del Regno di Napoli."*. On 13 March of that same

---

34   Innocenzo Fuidoro, *I giornali di Napoli* (4 vols., Naples: Società napoletana di Storia patria, 1934), I, pp. 96–97. The real name of the author was Vincenzo D'Onofrio, born in Naples in 1618. In his *Giornali* he details day by day the major political and social events of the city. This work covers the period between the beginning of February 1660 and the end of 1680. In his narration D'Onofrio is often extremely critical and satirical toward the rich and powerful elite of the city and also toward the Church, and probably this kind of attitude is the reason why he chose to hide himself behind a pseudonym. It is Antonio Bulifon in the *Cronicamerone* (Naples: G. Rosselli, a spese dell'autore, 1690), the ideal follow up to the work of Fuidoro, who reveals the real identity behind the name.

year, Parrino appealed to the Consiglio Collaterale. Using the privilege that he obtained on January 1688 as his legal justification, he asked for the narration in the *Cronicamerone* to stop before the kingdom of King Ferdinand the Catholic (he became king of Naples in 1504), when the *Teatro eroico* started. His request was granted with a ruling issued on 22 September, effectively putting an end to Bulifon's editorial enterprise. This was made possible solely thanks to the political allies and connections that Parrino had managed to establish and cultivate during his career, particularly thanks to his role as the official printer and publisher for the *Gazzette*.

One thing should have been made abundantly clear by now. Far from being a dying business, strangled by irrational laws and caught between the rigidity of ecclesiastical censorship and a political government unaware of the potentiality of print, printing was a thriving business in the Spanish Viceroyalty. Naples was a port city, a bridge between different parts of the Spanish empire, with a rich intellectual community and an ancient university, all aspects that made Naples a city rich with books.

The allegation that print in Naples was mostly cheap, with limited print runs and poor quality has been proved wrong in recent years. One needs only to look at the already mentioned Manzi's work and the catalogues of the most important libraries in Naples to realize that a number of richly illustrated editions, expensive works of the greatest quality, were printed in Naples during the sixteenth and seventeenth centuries; according to the USTC 222 of the 1,414 works known from the sixteenth century were in folio. Here we will mention just some of the most relevant examples.[35] Histories of the city and its rulers, along with guidebooks of Naples, were among the most popular genres in the seventeenth century. Works such as *Notizie del bello e del Curioso* by Celano and *Historia della città e Regno di Napoli* by Summonte were particularly popular at the time and because of their popularity, these are still some of the preferred sources for historians.[36] And of course, we cannot forget the entire scientific

---

35 Besides Manzi and the catalogues of the National Library of Naples, the Girolamini Library and the National Library of Florence, some of the most unusual suggestions come from Leo S. Olschki, *Choix de livres anciens, rares et curieux* (13 vols., Florence: Olschki, 1907–1966), particularly vols. 4, 5 and 6.

36 Carlo Celano, *Notizie del bello, dell'antico e del curioso della città di Napoli* (10 vols., Naples: G. Raillard, 1692); Giovanni Antonio Summonte, *Historia della città e del Regno di Napoli* (Naples: Giacinto Passaro a spese di Antonio Bulifon, 1675). On the financing of Summonte's work "To Antonio Bulifon ten ducats and for him to mister Luca Antonio de Fusco. Four of those as the remains of fifteen ducats, the entire price for some wooden matrices figures for Summonte's book that he sold [us]; the other six [ducats] are a deposit for the continuation of the printing of [not legible in the original text]. Signed Luca Antonio de Fusco, d.10." AFBN, BP, g. 1674, m.684, d.10, 28 sett.

54   CHAPTER 1

and philosophical production of Giovan Battista Della Porta; all his works were
printed in Naples between 1563 and 1614, in both luxurious, richly illustrated
editions, and in cheap ones; they were sold and reprinted across Europe.

4   Biographical Notes on Notable Printers

Before moving on to a different sort of publication, a more popular one, and a
discussion on the political use of such media, as we will see in the next chapter, I would like to provide some information on certain printers and booksellers, who by now we have already encountered several times, and who will
be relevant in the following chapters both because of their professional and
political roles.

Egidio Longo was one of the most important printers in Naples. Longo's
printing press was established in 1598 by Tarquino Longo, who was active until
1620. Between 1620 and 1622 the imprimatur became 'Apud heredes Tarquinii
Longi' but already in 1621, we can find some titles printed under the name Egidio
Longo. He remained active until 1679 when he died without heirs, leaving his
business to the convent of S. Maria della Pace: the last works printed by him are
some legal pamphlets sold for 'due grana l'uno' (two granas for each pamphlet)
and printed in July. He was the royal printer from 1630 to 1637 and then again
from 1641 until his death, but that was not all; he was also chief of the Ottina di
San Biagio during the plague of 1656 and held a similar role during Masaniello's
rebellion.[37] His double role as administrator and printer became particularly

---

37   Charles VIII granted the people's right to gather at their own seat with a royal decree
      on 15 May 1495. The location for the *Sedile del Popolo* was in the cloister of the convent
      of St. Agostino alla Zecca. Unlike the nobles' seats, the popular one was organized in 29
      ottine – places in which the Neapolitan families gathered, one for each of the 29 ancient
      streets of Naples – and the *Eletto del Popolo* ruled with 29 captains, one from every *ottina*.
      At the beginning, the *ottina* was made by eight families – later they became 10 – and for
      each of them a leader was elected. The Capitano was chosen between six candidates, who
      were nominated through a secret vote, by two *procuratori*. During the Spanish Viceroyalty
      the task to nominate the *Eletto del Popolo* became a prerogative of the Viceroy, who also
      choose candidates for the role of *capitano dell'ottina*. The first to describe this complex
      organization was Carlo Celano.
          "Afterwards the people of the twenty-nine streets or ancient alley of Naples began to
      meet in the cloister of S. Agostino, to deliberate upon their businesses. These streets or
      alleys were called since old times *Ottine*, unlike the Noble's ones that were called *Tocchi*,
      and each of them made up, as we said, a *Seggio*, composed by eight or ten families and
      that was subject to the *Seggio maggiore*. A *Capitano* was the leader of the *ottina*; and when
      the general meetings of the municipal administration where held every person from their
      respective *ottine* would come togheter. And because their number and participation was

PRINTING IN NAPLES

relevant during times of crisis. Especially during the plague, he was charged to print the government guidelines and make sure they were observed, as we will see in greater detail in Chapter 3.

At the opposite end of the spectrum, we can find Secondino Roncagliolo. He too held a government printing commission, as we have seen from the bank statement for the *arrendamento del sale* but during Masaniello rebellion, he decided to side with the rebels. He was active from 1608 to 1667, heir to a printing business established in Naples since 1577. He was also the head of the printing press associated with the convent of S. Domenico Maggiore (1618) and one of the first to print a gazette in Naples in 1642, the *Gli Avvisi di Roma e di altre parti del mondo*. After Masaniello's rebellion, he began to sign his works as *stampatore di questo fidelissimo popolo* and *stampatore della Serenissima Republica di Napoli*. When the French took control of the city in 1647 he was not able to maintain his role as state printer, as it is testified by the broadsheets issued under the command of Henry of Lorraine, Duke of Guise and printed by Lorenzo Graffaro *stampatore di S.A. Serenissima*. He was nevertheless able to carry on his business as a printer and even leave it to his heirs, who were active until 1676.

Bulifon's political journey was of a different sort. Printer, author and editor, he began his career in Naples as a bookseller working for Raillard but immediately began tightening his connection to Naples with a local marriage. In 1673, he married Maddalena Criscuolo to evade the edict decreeing the expulsion of the French, thus acquiring Neapolitan citizenship. He soon began to build a relationship with Spaniards close to the ruling classes, so much so that around 1680 he was officially known as *libraro di Sua Maestà*. From that point forward, his business continued only to grow. He did not open his own printing press but used the one of his colleague Giuseppe Rosselli. He had many contacts within the intellectual elites of Naples and soon became the go-to person for purchasing foreign editions, particularly French, in Naples. This, along with his work in publishing fundamental books such as Della Porta's "*Magia naturale*", several legal and juridical texts, alongside more commercial and popular works made him a very rich man. He is probably one of the most important editors of the second half of the century, not to mention the incredible historical value of his *Giornali* and *Cronicamerone*, as we will see in later chapters. His printing press was shut down in 1707, but at that point, his son Nicola had

---

so great, among the best of these people eight would be chosen, and these eight togheter would choose the *capitano dell'ottina* and it is because of this election of eight people that the streets were called *ottine*. This name is known since the time of King Manfredi, and more precisely King Robert in the year 1315." Celano, *Notizie del bello*, p. 300.

mostly taken over the work and Antonio had sought refuge in Madrid, where he died in 1714.[38]

The other prominent publisher active in Naples in that same time is Domenico Antonio Parrino. He came from a family of booksellers and theatre people. He started working in his father's bookshop but soon decided to join a theatre company in order to make more money and this venture brought him to Modena, where he became part of the troupe of the Grand Duke. He went back to Naples in 1680 where he bought out from the shop of his father (which in the meantime was passed down to extended family) and opened his own print house and bookshop. He never had the same monetary disposition of his rival, Bulifon, but his business was quite successful, particularly given his focus on works about Naples and from Neapolitan authors, and of course the contract that he had for printing the *Gazzette*, that we will see in the next chapter.

Now that we have sketched the general background, in the next chapters, we will move on to study how these general rules changed and shifted to accommodate different circumstances, and how printers and readers reacted to those changes.

---

38   Antonio Bulifon, Nino Cortese, *I giornali di Napoli dal 1547 al 1706* (Naples: Società Napoletana di Storia Patria, 1932); Bulifon, *Cronicamerone*.

CHAPTER 2

Print and Politics

With this provision, we order and command that there will be no one, no matter their status or birth or condition, who will dare to buy wheat and barley in all of the Terra di Lavoro to keep them in warehouses or to sell them for profit, but only what it is necessary for their life.[1]

• • •

And because the natural magnanimity of His Excellency made him wish to be a part of the general and universal happiness in such a unique occasion, this is why His Excellency on Friday morning took himself to the prison at the Vicaria and there, sitting upon his throne, granted their freedom to more than one hundred prisoners as well as changing the sentence from harsh to mild to a similar number of convicts. And the command that the prison of the Great Admiral, known as Visitatore, and the one of the *Art of wool* (the guild of wool and silk) were to be opened, and all those poor souls let out. It is not possible to explain the immense kindness and compassion displayed by His Excellency on this occasion, as well as all the favours that he granted to all of those who asked him and because it is impossible to understand all from the brief public broadsheet I will not give any more details here, but I will write a separate *Relazione* in the upcoming week.[2]

∴

As we have briefly mentioned in the previous chapter, one of the most lucrative enterprises for printers was obtaining a government commission. Whether

---

1 [Pedro da Toledo], *Bando e comandamento da parte dell' Illustrissimo signor Don Pietro de Toledo* (Naples: 1551), SNSP, OP.1.SER.331(4), USTC 1752437.
2 [Domenico Antonio Parrino], *Gazzette di Napoli* (Naples: Per Domenico Antonio Parrino, 17 Settembre 1686). SNSP, S.G.B.1 vol. 2.

© KONINKLIJKE BRILL BV, LEIDEN, 2025 | DOI:10.1163/9789004549401_004

58   CHAPTER 2

this was as Royal Printer, who was in charge of printing every broadsheet and
law, or a supplier for one of the many offices that would require printed forms
and papers, such as a printed form for a stall at the market, it was one of the
most rewarding jobs in economic terms. This was less because of the compen-
sation per piece and more because of the great quantities that were requested
and the competitive prices for the materials.

A bank receipt issued to Secondino Roncagliolo in 1647, for example,
showed that he was paid 'for 5, 8 ½ and 4 ½ reams of printed bulletins 13 ducats, 22 ducats and 11.4.10 ducats.'[3] Considering that in 1629 a yearly rent for
two shops and three rooms was 65 ducats, this means that the monthly rent
was 5,41 ducats. Therefore for 5 reams of printed bulletin he was paid the
equivalent of two months' rent. It seems clear that Roncagliolo's work was
well paid.[4] It is not easy to determine with any certainty how much the paper
cost for printers, but thanks to the income and expenditure account from the
Convent of San Domenico we are able to determine that between 1615 and 1640
the price of paper remained pretty much consistently between 10–13 carlini
per ream.[5] If we assume that the price was the same for printers, we can calculate exactly how profitable these contracts with government offices were. From
the above invoice, we know that Roncagliolo received ca. 2.6 ducats (ca. 26
carlini) per printed ream, so if he paid ca. 11 carlini for the paper, he would
have a 100% profit. When we think of the large number of printed products
that he printed for his government commission, this was extremely lucrative.
A well-kept registry of the *Arrendamento del Sale*, the office responsible for
collecting salt taxes from the entire realm, shows several payments made to
both Secondino Roncagliolo and the royal printer Egidio Longo for great quantities of *bollettini*. This is a very generic term used to indicate anything from a
single sheet of paper to a pamphlet, but in this specific case, I think it referred
to a printed bank receipt that could be used as a promissory note. In six years
Egidio Longo printed 45,000 of them.[6] Despite the clear economic advantage
that was to be had in working for the authorities, not to mention the social
prestige that came with the job, the relationship between printers and power
was not always smooth. Moreover, the dynamic between power and print is
a complex one, that manifested itself in different ways. In this chapter, we
will analyse three different fields in which this dynamic would assert itself:

---

3 AFBN, BP, gc. 1647, 30 July. A ream is usually constituted of 500 sheets.
4 For a more detailed examination of the cost of life in Naples in relation to the cost of printed
   news see the last paragraph of this chapter.
5 The ledgers for San Domnico can be found in ASNA, Corporazioni religiose soppresse, 472
   (*Registro di cassa*).
6 ASFNA, BPop, gc. 1656, m.306, d.33.3.17, 27 Marzo.

PRINT AND POLITICS

communications and regulation for the smooth functioning of the city in its day-to-day life; censorship, and propaganda.

1   Broadsheets, Proclamations and the Communication of the Law

In terms of sheer quantities of printed materials, the largest portion of popular print dealt with everyday life. Almost every office required printed forms and documents for internal circulation and some of them had their own printing press or at least a designated official printer. This is helpfully confirmed by a rare discovery unearthed in the course of my research in the Archivio Storico Municipale. It is a handwritten receipt in which the civic office of the Portolano listed the expense for re-printing six leaves due to typographical mistakes, the binding of 100 booklets (*libretti*), some non-specified corrections and 50 pages of tariff variations printed on a broadsheet (*altre cinquanta tariffe, ristampate in foglio aperto*).[7] It is extremely difficult to give even a rough estimate of exactly how many broadsheets, placards, and fliers were printed, published and distributed every month in Naples. In the library of the Archiginnasio in Bologna there is an archival collection of more than 100 bound volumes containing every proclamation issued by the city from mid-1500 to mid-1800. This is an exceptional resource, though we can also find large quantities of printed ordinances for many other cities in Northern Italy. However, as is often the case, we are not so fortunate when it comes to Naples. The only collection of some substance is held at the National Library of Naples, but it refers exclusively to the time of Masaniello's rebellion and the Neapolitan republic.[8] Although it deals with a fairly short period of time, less than a year, it still contains around 400 items. It would be a mistake to try to extrapolate from this collection any estimate of the output in less turbulent times, but nonetheless, this combined with the numerous payment invoices issued to a variety of printers that explicitly reference this sort of works along with the quantities, makes me confident in my estimation that the everyday communication of the laws and regulations constituted the greater part of the political print in Naples. The various government offices were constantly releasing rules, regulations, provisions and laws

---

7   ASMNA, I, 410, fil. 289. This manuscript note is not dated, I think it is from the 1730s as the other documents in the same dossier, and it is not addressed to a specific printer.

8   It is also not a collection of broadsheets and placards exclusively, but rather five bound up volume of such materials are included in the collection of the Biblioteca di San Martino. The library of the Priory of San Martino became part of the collection of the Royal Library in 1799. It is a substantial collection, with more than 10,000 printed and almost 1,000 manuscripts, focused on the religious and civil history of Naples.

on all manner of things, from what clothes were appropriate to wear in the city, to communications on the mint, from the price of wine to the type of carriages that could be used inside the city walls. The citizens of Naples needed to be kept aware and informed of all of these communications, and what better way to do so than have them printed and pasted up all over the city? Not only that but every single broadsheet and official communication that was issued by the authorities was read aloud in every major square in the city, besides being posted on the walls. It is difficult to say precisely where these ordinances were affixed, given that they usually present the indication "it is to be posted in all the usual places", without further specification. We can, however, speculate that they were at the very least posted in Piazza Della Carità, given that it was the major market square in the city, near the Cathedral, near the Royal Palace, and near the courthouse. This means that of all the printed products that existed in Naples, this type of communication was the one that had the broadest audience.

Besides the singularity that was Masaniello's rebellion, which will be discussed in the next chapter, there is a distinct lack of propagandistic use and political intent behind this kind of publication. These were mainly administrative in nature rather than political, but I believe they still held persuasive power. This is naturally a source of wonder, given that we have established that it was the type of print with the broader audience. Moreover, as we will see in this and the following chapters, the Spanish authorities were not averse to the use of the printing press as a propagandistic tool, both to portray themselves in the best possible way and to impugn their political adversaries. Why then, did they not use their most popular medium to do the same? Once again, the inconsistent nature of the archival and library collections does not work in our favour and without a solid documentary base, it is very difficult to provide a definitive answer. All we can do is try to formulate a hypothesis as to why that is the case. I believe there are two different reasons for the absence of a propagandistic, or even a general political tone, within the everyday communication between the authorities and the citizen of Naples.

The control that the Spanish authorities had over the territories that they ruled in Italy was so strong that there was no need to try and re-affirm it in everyday communications. The goal of these communications was simply to keep their citizen informed and it was superfluous and unnecessary to muddy the waters and distract from the main objective by including propagandistic messages. Moreover, with the refusal to use their arguably most powerful tool in such a way, the Spanish authorities gave the impression, to both local and foreign readers, that their power and control were such that they had no need to reinforce it through print. The only exception is a proclamation announcing the beginning of the war between Spaniards and the Emperor and his Dutch and English allies (and later, the one that announced the end of the conflict) but even in these, the tone is far milder than the scathing remarks that can be found in the *gazzette* and the pamphlets. Once again, the aim appears to be to inform rather than to actively and forcefully sway the public's opinion.

> We received letters from your majesty on the 27th of July, whereby [we have been informed that] the [Holy Roman] Emperor, in alliance with the Dutch and English, has declared war on our lord the king (may God watch over him) and has since performed many acts of hostility in his majesty's dominions. He [in these letters] has ordered that war must be waged in this kingdom against the Emperor as well as against the English and the Dutch, in particular forbidding, from the day of the publication of this notice onwards, vessels and other ships under the authority of the Emperor, the English or the Dutch, to dock or land persons, goods and merchandises in any part of this kingdom under penalty of death and confiscation of goods, merchandises, vessels and ships. Likewise, the King has ordered that if they should happen to be in the ports, beaches, or other places of this kingdom by sea or land, the said persons shall be immediately imprisoned, and merchandise, goods, vessels, and ships seized.
>
> For the purpose of securing the execution of the orders contained in these royal letters, with the vote and advice of the Regio Collateral Consiglio assisting us, we have enacted this notice, whereby, in the name of the King our Lord (may God watch over him), we declare war on the above-mentioned Emperor, English, Dutch and their subjects. We have likewise informed and ordered all the subjects of the emperor, as well as the English and Dutch present in this city and kingdom, to depart, under penalty of death and confiscation of their property. Furthermore, we have ordered the people of Naples and the kingdom, as well as all those who dwell therein, under the same penalties of death and confiscation of property, not to be in any way in correspondence with vassals and subjects of the aforesaid. Moreover, if any of the inhabitants should have knowledge [of the presence in the kingdom] of any of them, they shall immediately notify us. Those who do so shall be rewarded with the sixth part of the goods confiscated. The same benefit shall be enjoyed by those who shall indicate to us where in this kingdom there are goods of the emperor's subjects, Englishmen, or Dutchmen, including goods and credits due to them. Likewise, we order that all those who sell or conceal these goods, or who in any way aid or abet the said persons and their goods,

shall suffer the penalty of death and confiscation of property. We likewise order that if the said persons, their merchandise, vessels or ships should be found in the ports, beaches or other places of this kingdom, the former shall be arrested and the latter seized immediately. The persons shall be taken to the prisons and the goods to the nearest places to the aforesaid ports, beaches or other places where they happen to be, and we shall be immediately informed of the same, so that we may take the appropriate decisions in the matter. We further declare that the aforesaid vassals of the Emperor, as well as the English, Dutch and other subjects of these principalities who at present reside in this most faithful city of Naples and its kingdom, must leave as already ordered, since the final term of six months (within which this order had to be carried out) established in the chapters of the peace of 30 October 1697 has elapsed. After the many acts of hostility perpetrated by the aforesaid principalities, we were obliged, by the Royal Pragmatic Act solemnly promulgated on 21 November 1701, to call to arms, on penalty of death, the vassals of His Majesty residing in their dominions. Desiring to show our clemency, we grant them [the emperor's vassals, as well as the English, Dutch, and other subjects of these potentates] fifteen days from the publication of the present notice [to leave the territories of the kingdom], after which they shall automatically be considered sentenced to the death penalty and confiscation of property as established in the present notice, extending the said term to twenty days from the publication of the same in this most faithful city for those residing in the [other] Provinces of the Kingdom. We charge the G.C. della Vicaria, the Regie Audienze Provinciali, as well as all officials and ministers, both royal and baronial, with the execution of the contents of this notice. Lastly, so that all may be informed of these provisions, we order that this notice be posted in the usual places in this most faithful city and the cities of residence of the aforementioned Regie Odienze. Promulgated in Naples, 25 August 1702.[9]

---

9   "Essendosi ricevuto ordine di S.M. con sue regali lettere de' 27 del passato mese di Luglio, con le quali havendo l'imperatore come principale, gl'Olandesi come ausiliari, e gl'Inglesi come confederati al medesimo dichiarato la guerra al Ré Nostro Signore (che Iddio guardi) & havendo finalmente fatti molti atti d'ostilità nel dominio di S.M. ha ordinato in esse che debbasi pubblicare in questo Regno la guerra così all'Imperatore, come agl'Inglesi & Olandesi, proibendo specialmente dal giorno della pubblicazione di questo avanti non possano li vascelli o altri navigli immediatamente sudditi dell'Imperatore Inglesi &Olandesi di qualunque d'essi venire con le loro persone, robbe e mercanzie in niuna parte del presente Regno sotto pena di morte naturale , e confiscazione di robbe, mercanzie, Vascelli e Navigli; ordinando similmente che quando capitano nelle porti, spiagge o altri luoghi di questo Regno così per mare come per terra respettivamente si debbano subito carcerare e sequestrare

PRINT AND POLITICS

Despite the promise of severe punishment for any English and Dutch that were to remain within the Kingdom of Naples, as well as for those Neapolitans found helping the enemies, along with the order to seize all properties of those said enemies, we are confronted with a fairly unemotional piece of communication. There is no emphasis on the duplicity of the enemies, nor on the magnificence and magnanimity of the Spaniards themselves. While the numerous *relationi* and news about the conflict are full of details and celebrations,

le dette persone, mercanzie, robbe, vascelli & navigli; che però per esequzione di d. Reali Lettere, col voto, e parere del Reg. Collat. Cons. appresso di noi assistente abbiamo fatto il presente Banno, col quale dichiariamo a nome del Re Nostro Signore (ch'Iddio guardi) la guerra alli suddetti Imperatore, Inglesi & Olandesi e loro sudditi; Dicemmo medesimamente, e comandammo a tutti e qualsivoglino sudditi immediati dell'Imperatore, Inglesi & Olandesi che se ritrovano in questa Città e Regno, che si debbiano partire e sotto le medesime pene di morte naturale, e confiscazione dei loro beni, ordinando ancora a tutte, e qualsivoglino persone di questa città di Napoli e Regno o habitanti in esso, che sotto le medesime pene di morte naturale , e confiscazione de loro beni, non debbiano in modo alcuno tener corrispondenza né comunicazione con vassalli e sudditi de' medesimi e se alcuno ne avrà notizia ce ne debbia subito dar avviso, che se li darà per premio la sesta parte delle robbe che si confiscaranno; dovendo similmente godere il beneficio di detta sesta parte chi metterà in chiaro ove siano in questo Regno robbe de sudditi dell'Imperatore, Inglesi & Olandesi o effetti e crediti che ai medesimi spettassero: e nell'istessa pena di morte naturale e confiscazione dei beni vogliamo che incorrano tutti quelli che li ricetteranno o occulteranno o in qualsivoglia modo daranno aggiuto e favore alle dette persone e loro robbe; Ordinando similmente che quando venessero le dette persone e le loro mercanzie, Vascelli o altri Navigli nelli porti, spiagge e altri luoghi di questo Regno, si debbano subito carcerare e sequestrare e portare le persone nelle carceri e le robbe nelli luoghi più vicini a d. porti & spiagge & altri luoghi di terra dove capiteranno, dandosene subito notizia a Noi, acciò possiamo ordinare quello, che si averà da fare; dichiarando però che detti vassalli dell'Imperatore, Inglesi & Olandesi o altri sudditi immediati di detti Potentati che al presente si trovarono ad abbitare in questa Fedelissima città di Napoli e suo Regno, i quali devono partirsi come di sopra s'è ordinato, benchè sia passato maggior termine delli sei mesi stabilito negl'ultimi Capitoli della pace delli 30 Ottobre dell'anno 1697, dopo li tanti atti d'ostilità usati da detti potentati, onde fummo obbligati in virtù della Regia Prammatica delli 21 Novembre del passato anno 1701, solennemente pubblicato, richiamare con pene capitali i Vassalli di Sua Maestà che ne' loro domini abitavano; con tutto ciò usando maggior benignità concediamo altro termine di 15 giorni decorrendi dal tempo della pubblicazione del presente, dopo del quale s'intendano incorsi nella sud. Pena della vita e confiscazione de beni contenuta nel presente Banno, dichiarando, che a rispetto di quelli che si trovarono ad habitare nelle Provincie del Regno s'intenda haversi possuto haver notizia di questo Banno 20 giorni dopo la pubblicazione di esso in questa Fedelissima Città; incaricando l'esecuzione di esso alla G.C. della Vicaria, Regie Audienze Provinciali & a tutti qualsisiano Officiali e Ministri così regi, come de' Baroni, & affinchè venga a notizia di tutti , volemo che il presente Banno si pubblichi nelli Luoghi soliti e consueti di questa Fedelissima Città, e nelle città di residenza di dette Regie Odienze, Datum Neapoli die 25 Augusti 1702." (Naples: 1702) SNSP, SALA A06 A 10.16 USTC 1752438.

official communications with the citizens are always very formal, in which the Spaniards appear to have absolute control over the situation.

Although we lack a comprehensive and cohesive collection of broadsheets, proclamations and flyers, there are several examples scattered in various archives and libraries in Naples. The oldest I was able to find are six civic law ordinances from 1551, held in the Biblioteca della Società di Storia Patria (half of them are not catalogued).[10] These ordinances are quite peculiar for several reasons: they are smaller in format than those published at later dates and in at least two of them, both offering rewards for the capture of wanted criminals, there is an explicit mention of the place in which they were sold.[11] I believe that, rather than to be exhibit on the streets, these particular ordinances were printed to be given to other public officials and from there passed on to other interested parties. In every other flier that I was able to see, there is always the indication that the particular broadsheet had been read aloud and posted in all the designated locations. This is a further proof in favour of the argument that there was a broad diffusion of such materials.

The topics covered in this kind of communication were extremely varied, and so were the formats and even the languages. Although the vast majority of the surviving copies within libraries and archives are in Italian, there are some notable examples in Spanish and, even more interesting, some printed both in Italian and in Spanish.[12] It is not easy, with an incomplete collection, to discern what was actually published in which language and why. We do have communications announcing the beginning of a war, something that one would expect to be of interest for everyone, both Spaniards and Neapolitans, only in Italian while others, apparently less significant communication, such as an ordinance in regards to extortions within the walls of the jail, are written in both languages. We could argue that the lack of documentary evidence does not necessarily mean that such documents never existed in Spanish, merely that they did not survive.

Communications on new taxes, new coins, and maximum prices for goods such as wheat and wine were fairly common and I have found several examples for each of those.[13] Of course, besides being of the utmost importance when it came to the running of the city, economic news could also be used as

---

10   These are all bound in the same volume, SNSP, OP.I.SER.331.

11   [Regno di Napoli], *Reformatione del banno contra i forasciti* (Naples: per Andrea Maffuccio, [1551]) SNSP, OP.I.SER.331(16), USTC 844159.

12   [Regno di Napoli], *Carolus Dei gratia rex* (Naples: per Carlo Porsile stampatore della Regia Corte, 1699) SNSP, Sala.A.10.A.10 USTC 1706589.

13   See for example BNN, San Martino LIX.7.1.22; BNN, San Martino LIX.7.1.6; BNN, San Martino LIX.7.1.8.

PRINT AND POLITICS

an effective means to portray the government in a good way without being too obvious that it was propaganda. Such is the case, for example, of an ordinance published on 29 April 1702 that announced the imminent arrival of the King in the city of Naples and subsequent reduction by half of the duty on wheat due to 'the incomparable love that His Excellency has for the city.'[14]

Financial matters were important not least because they were closely related to military developments. The outbreak of war and the subsequent victory or defeat of the Spanish empire often led to changes in the taxation on imported goods and even to the necessity of recalling every coin because new ones were forged, with less silver in them. The importance placed on these communications was such that we can find news of this kind not only in broadsheets and ordinances but also in the newspapers.[15] Mixed in with the occasional piece of gossip and news from 'every corner of the world', the newspapers were often the place in which the authorities could reiterate and reaffirm important pieces of communication that they had already issued through more formal media, such as ordinances. But before moving forward with our examination of the newspapers as a propagandistic tool, there is one other example of a close relation between official state communication and informal, propagandistic print: communications concerning public decorum.

A recurring subject in the public ordinances was public decency and the regulation of behaviour. In an ordinance from June 1620, detailing the kind of carriages that could be used within the city walls, it is explicitly mentioned that the reason behind this ordinance and the prohibitions that it contained, stemmed from the need to regulate and control where and how courtesans could move within the city 'so as not to mistake them for noble-women'.[16] This is not a public security concern, but rather a matter of decency. Naturally, on the occasion of important public events within the city, the need to regulate every aspect of the attendees' behaviour was of the utmost importance. Several ordinances were issued on occasions such as the death of the Queen Mother, or a visit from the King.[17] It is interesting to take note of the emphasis that the

---

14   SNSP, Sala A10 A6.4.

15   The first two numbers of 1689 are almost exclusively dedicated to the new coin: SNSP, S.G.B.1 vol. 3 n.28 and 30.

16   SNSP, SALA D.X.B.24.4.

17   A couple of examples are: [Regno di Napoli], *Carolus Dei cratia* [*!*] *rex, &c.* (Naples: per Carlo Porsile regio stampatore, 12 June 1696) SNSP SALA A11 A 06.1 USTC 1706591.

   This is a broadsheet containing indications on how to observe the mourning period for the death of the Queen Mother. It explicitly refers to an ordinance printed in Madrid in 1691, saying that since that ordinance was never published in Naples the government is now remedying that by printing the present broadsheet to let Neapolitans know how they

authorities put on such occasions, doing everything that they could to make sure that everyone in the city knew what was expected of them: interesting, but not surprising, given that these celebrations were a powerful political and propagandistic tool to show the might of the Spanish government and the harmony between the authorities and their subjects. Spanish authorities would demonstrate their control over the city by taking prominent roles in public celebrations that once again would involve people from all of Neapolitan society, even though the majority were mere spectators. The entire affaire would then be recounted and narrated in celebratory pamphlets that would reach far and wide not only within the confines of the Kingdom of Naples, to show everyone the extent of the power of the Spanish crown, hence why these celebrations needed to be held with decorum.

The importance of public processions as a tool for keeping the pulse of the city but also to show the Spanish power and the harmony that existed between them and their subject was something very familiar to the Spanish authorities. It was something that they did regularly in Spain and that they implemented in Naples from the very first time they entered the city. And that first procession with which Gonzalo De Cordoba claimed his title of Viceroy of Naples set the tone for this particular political tool. Public ceremonies with grand processions were held, of course, whenever a new Viceroy was appointed. But also on the occasion of royal marriages, births, and deaths. Besides these monumental occasions, public ceremonies were also held during important religious festivities, but also during times of tension for the Vicerealm, for example during the Vesuvius eruption in 1631, as we will see in the next chapter. If celebrating joyous occasions or military victories through public procession seems a pretty straightforward way to assert and demonstrate political power, doing the same during times of crisis requires a closer look. In every celebration held by the Spanish authorities the public, the people of Naples, had a fundamental role. They were at the same time spectators and participants, witnesses and living proof of the Spanish power.[18] Whenever something happened that could shake

---

would need to dress and what activities were deemed acceptable to partake in during this time of mourning.

[Regno di Napoli], *Philippis Dei Gratia Rex* (Naples: per Carlo Porsile regio stampatore, 29 April 1702) SNSP, SALA A10 A 06.5 USTC 1752439. This is an ordinance that was issued on the occasion of a royal visit. In order to reduce the expenses for the celebrations and procession that such occasion granted, the government decided to issue an order according to which every baron could be accompanied by no more than six servants during the celebrations.

18   On the use of public ceremonies as way to reinforce the Spanish public image and the way in which this practice was tied with the practice of the "buon governo" see Celine

PRINT AND POLITICS

the hold that the authorities had on their subject and the equilibrium of society as a whole, like with cataclysmic natural events, Spanish rulers were quick to put forward every tool in their arsenal to reaffirm their control. In this sense, public processions were extremely useful. They had the dual purpose of reassuring the people that they were not alone in dealing with what was happening, thus providing a sense of kinship, but at the same time, they showcased the fearlessness of the leader and their efforts in solving the problem. But this is something that we will see in a more in-depth manner in the next chapter.

2   Newspapers and Propaganda

The fact that the authorities chose not to use the everyday communication of the law to impart propagandistic messages does not mean that they were completely oblivious to the power of print as a political and propagandistic tool. In this respect, newspapers could play an important role. The first official news sheet printed in Naples was *Avvisi di Roma* by Geronimo Favella who was entrusted by Viceroy Monterrey with a privilege for this publication around 1636. It was modelled after the newspapers that already existed in various European cities, featuring a section of news from other cities and countries and a section dedicated to news from the city itself, and it was very much dependent on these, as Favella did not have a personal network of informants and contacts from which he could receive his news. The *Avvisi di Roma* was primarily a copy of the Roman newsletter, that the Viceroy received alongside newspapers from other Italian and European cities.[19] The privilege granted to Favella was not as ironclad as the ones that would be granted in later times as many others printed news, *avvisi*, and histories. For the first true Neapolitan newspaper, independent from other newspapers and protected with an exclusive privilege, we have to wait until 1674, when Ludovico Cavallo obtained this monopoly. Cavallo's *avvisi* were consistent in format, size and layout, and the steadfast loyalty that Cavallo had for the Spanish government saw his privilege renewed on three consecutive occasions (1674–1681); it ended only with his death. Beginning in October 1684, the privilege for the *avvisi* was granted to Camillo Cavallo, one of the sons of Ludovico, and Domenico Parrino. It was

---

Dauverd, *Church and State in Spanish Italy: Rituals and Legitimacy in the Kingdom of Naples* (Cambridge and New York: Cambridge University Press, 2020).

19   The term newsletter indicates a manuscript, while we use newspaper for the printed version.

68   CHAPTER 2

Camillo himself, in his contract to re-negotiate the privilege, who credited his
father for the invention of Neapolitan newspaper.

> Since I, the undersigned bidder, have come to know that from the side
> of this Royal Office there is the intention of moving forward with a new
> lease for the *Jus Prohibendi* for the *Avvisi*, *Relationi* and others, I deemed
> it important to remind Your Excellency that the late Ludovico Cavallo,
> my father, in the year 1674 invented and began to print the *avvisi* from
> every part of the world. And the most excellent Marquess of Astorga and
> the Viceroy Los Vèles granted to Ludovico 3 privileges *ad tempus* during
> which no other printer nor bookseller both in this city and in this realm
> could have printed the abovementioned *avvisi*, but only Ludovico who
> invented this business and carried it onward with great satisfaction from
> the public. And when Ludovico died we signed the aforementioned lease,
> and it was given to me and Domenico Antonio Parrino for a period of 9
> years and the price of 520 ducats per year.[20]

Cavallo was the one in charge of the actual printing while Parrino focused his
effort on the sales of the *gazzette* from his bookshop; besides the direct sales,
courtiers and more prosperous citizens held annual subscriptions that were
paid in advance, but free copies were to be delivered to the government. The
first privilege to Cavallo and Parrino was granted for nine years at the cost of
520 ducats per year, but when it came to renewing it in September 1693 the
price was raised to 810 ducats per year.

> I have here 810 ducats and with these, I am paying one year of the lease
> for the Jus *prohibendi dell'Avisi, e Relationi*, starting with 21 October 1693
> and until 20 October 1698. [This is] the fifth year of the aforementioned
> lease for the sum of 810 ducats per year upon the *accensione di Candela*

---

20   "Havendo io sottoscritto offerente inteso, che da questa reale camera si vogli procedere
      al nuovo Affitto del Jus Prohibendi del' Avisi Relationi et altro, ho stimato conveniente
      prima, che si venisse con atto alcuno rappresentare a S.E. che il quondam Ldovico Cavallo
      mio padre nell'anno 1674 inventò e introdusse a stampare gli avvisi, e relationi di tutte le
      parti del mondo che però li ecellentissimi signori marchesi d'Astorga e de los véles vicerè
      in quei tempi, concederono a detto Ludovico 3 privilegi ad tempus che nessun'altro stam-
      patore o libraro tanto in questa città che nel regno havesse stampato li suddetti avvisi e
      relationi a riguardo solo che detto ludovico fu l'inventore di detto negozio, e che con tanta
      pontualità, e soddisfatione del pubblico l'esercitava, et essendo passato a miglior vita
      detto Ludovico si fece l'affitto suddetto e si pigliò da me sottoscritto unito a Domenico
      Antonio Parrino per il spazio di anni 9 a raggione di docati 520 l'anno." ASNA, Notai del
      Seicento, fs. 531/32, f.398r.

FIGURE 2.1 First page of the contract for the newspapers. ASNA, Notai XVII, 531–532. Naples, Archivio di Stato

[drafting of a payment commitment] in the presence of the Master Notary Filippo Giacomo Pepe to be paid every semester in advance D. 810.[21]

In a show of good faith and in an effort to maintain a good relationship between the government and the two printers, the steep rise in price was accompanied by a more stringently and enforced monopoly on *avvisi* and *gazzette*. This renewed concession lasted until June 1702.[22] Within twenty-four hours from the arrival in the city of the newsletter, the newspaper was ready to be sold. The first *privativa* bundled together gazzette, calendars, almanacs, prediction

---

21 "Introito di d. ottocento, e dieci per tanti importa l'estaglio di un anno dell'affitto del jus prohibendi dell'avvisi e relazioni, cominciando dalli 21 Ottobre 1697 e per tutto li 20 Ottobre 1698, quinto anno dell'affitto suddetto alla raggione di docati ottocento, e dieci l'anno iusta l'accensione di candela appresso il magnifico attuario Filippo Giacomo Pepe da pagarnosi ogni semestre anticipatamente. D. 810." ASNA, Dipendenze della Regia Camera della sommaria, f.395/1 *Conto del magistro Camillo Cavallo affittuario del ius prohibendi delle stampe d'avisi, e relationi comiciando dalli 21 ottobre 169*[3] *e per tutto li 20 Ottobre 1698*.

22 For more information on the rights and obligations granted to Cavallo and Parrino see Lombardi, *Tra le pagine*, pp. 191–194.

70 CHAPTER 2

books etc. ... and as such was extremely difficult to actually enforce. With the renewed concession it was limited only to Gazzette and avvisi and therefore became actually more enforceable.

The Neapolitan newspaper, unlike its European cousins, looked fairly simple and it was not of particularly high quality. There was no clearly marked title section, just a simple heading with the city and the date. The ink often bled a little due to the not-so-great quality of the paper and there were often typos due to the haste with which the newspaper was usually put together.[23]

Printing newspapers in the Kingdom of Naples was a very profitable business for everyone involved. By issuing a privilege for such publications, the civic authorities granted themselves tight control over what kind of news circulated in Naples and how this news was reported. For their part, Parrino and Cavallo used the prestige that came with printing the newspapers for advancing their business, with the newspapers themselves as a marketing tool, advertising in subtle, and sometimes not-so-subtle ways, upcoming publications from their printing press.[24] It was not unusual to find, at the bottom of the newspaper sheet, advertisements for popular books and anticipated bestsellers such as, for example, the promotion of:

> La novissima Historia della Guerra d'Ungheria, from the author Lopez, that begins from its origin to the surrender of Montcatz and Alba Reale. It includes woodcut portraits of all the Roman and Turkish generals, and these are very true to life, and all the cities that were captured by His Roman Majesty. It will be sold bound, and split into two volumes, from Cavallo in the press at the Spirito Santo and from Muti in San Giuseppe Maggiore. Carlini 8.[25]

On other occasions, particularly in regard to political news, Parrino generated anticipation for forthcoming publications through several issues of the newspapers, before the actual pamphlets came out. Such is the case, for example,

---

23   On the Italian newspapers see: Nina Lamal, *Italian Communication on the Revolt in the Low Countries (1566–1648)* (Leiden: Brill, 2023).

24   For the development of advertisement in newspapers see: Arthur der Weduwen and Andrew Pettegree, *The Dutch Republic and the Birth of Modern Advertising* (Leiden: Brill, 2020); Jason McElligot, "Advertising and Selling in Cromwellian Newsbooks." In Shanti Graeli (ed), *Buying and Selling. The Business of Books in Early Modern Europe* (Leiden: Brill, 2019), pp. 467–488.

25   [Domenico Antonio Parrino], *Gazzette di Napoli.* (Naples: Per Domenico Antonio Parrino, 8 Giugno 1688). SNSP, S.G.B.1 vol. 2. The book being advertised is Miguel Lopez, *Historia delle passate e correnti guerre d'Ungheria.* (2 vols. Naples, a spese delli soci Camillo Cavallo e Michele Luigi Muti, 1688). A third volume was published in 1691, and was once more advertised by Parrino in the issue 24 of the *Gazzette* (12 Giugno 1691). SNSP, S.G.B.1 vol. 3.

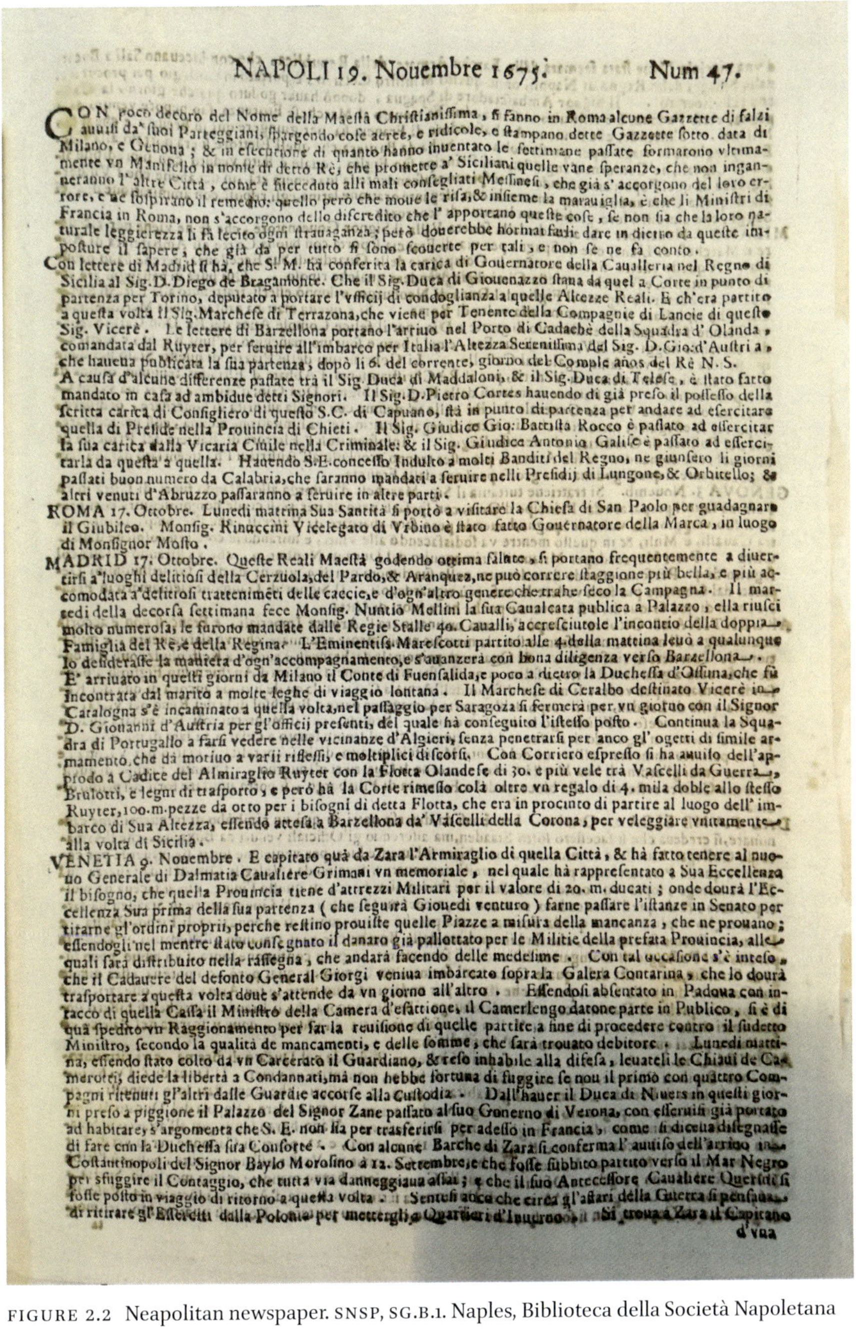

NAPOLI 19. Nouembre 1675. Num 47.

CON poco decoro del Nome della Maestà Christianissima, si fanno in Roma alcune Gazzette di falzi auuisi da' suoi Parteggiani, spargendo cose aeree, e ridicole, e stampano dette Gazzette sotto data di Milano, e Genoua; & in esecutione di quanto hanno inuentato le settimane passate formarono vltimamente vn Manifesto in nome di detto Rè, che promette a' Siciliani quelle vane speranze, che non inganneranno l'altre Città, come è successo alli mali consegliati Messinesi, che già s'accorgono del loro errore, e ne sospirano il remedio: quello però che moue le risa, & insieme la marauiglia, è che li Ministri di Francia in Roma, non s'accorgono dello discredito che l' apportano queste cose, se non sia che la loro naturale leggierezza li fà lecito ogni strauaganza; però douerebbe hormai farli dare in dietro da queste imposture il sapere, che già da per tutto si sono scouerte per tali, e non se ne fà conto.

Con lettere di Madrid si hà, che S. M. hà conferita la carica di Gouernatore della Caualleria nel Regno di Sicilia al Sig. D. Diego de Bragamonte. Che il Sig. Duca di Giouenazzo staua da quel a Corte in punto di partenza per Torino, deputato a portare l'vfficij di condoglianza a quelle Altezze Reali. E ch'era partito a questa volta il Sig. Marchese di Terrazona, che viene per Tenente della Compagnie di Lancie di questo Sig. Vicerè. Le lettere di Barzellona portano l'arriuo nel Porto di Cadachè della Squadra d' Olanda, comandata dal Ruyter, per seruire all'imbarco per Italia l'Altezza Serenissima del Sig. D. Gio: d'Austria, che haueua publicata la sua partenza, dopò li 6. del corrente, giorno del Comple años del Rè N. S.

A causa d'alcune differenze passate trà il Sig. Duca di Maddaloni, & il Sig. Duca di Telese, è stato fatto mandato in casa ad ambidue detti Signori. Il Sig. D. Pietro Cortes hauendo di già preso il possesso della scritta carica di Consigliero di questo S.C. di Capuano, stà in punto di partenza per andare ad esercitare quella di Preside nella Prouincia di Chieti. Il Sig. Giudice Gio: Battista Rocco è passato ad essercitar la sua carica dalla Vicaria Ciuile nella Criminale: & il Sig. Giudice Antonio Galise è passato ad essercitarla da questa a quella. Hauendo S.E. concesso Indulto a molti Banditi del Regno, ne giunsero li giorni passati buon numero da Calabria, che saranno mandati a seruire nelli Presidij di Lungone, & Orbitello; & altri venuti d'Abruzzo passaranno a seruire in altre parti.

ROMA 17. Ottobre. Lunedì mattina Sua Santità si portò a visitare la Chiesa di San Paolo per guadagnare il Giubileo. Monsig. Rinuccini Vicelegato di Vrbino è stato fatto Gouernatore della Marca, in luogo di Monsignor Mosto.

MADRID 17. Ottobre. Queste Reali Maestà godendo ottima salute, si portano frequentemente a diuertirsi a' luoghi delitiosi della Cerzuola, del Pardo, & Aranquez, ne può correre staggione più bella, e più accomodata a' delitiosi trattenimēti delle caccie, e d'ogn'altro genere che trahe seco la Campagna. Il marcedi della decorsa settimana fece Monsig. Nuntio Mellini la sua Caualcata publica a Palazzo, ella riusci molto numerosa, le furono mandate dalle Regie Stalle 40. Caualli, accresciutole l'incontro della doppia Famiglia del Rè, e della Regina. L'Eminentiss. Marescotti partito alle 4. della mattina leuò a qualunque lo desiderasse la maniera d'ogn'accompagnamento, e s'auanzerà con bona diligenza verso *Barzellona*. E' arriuato in questi giorni da Milano il Conte di Fuensalida, e poco a dietro la Duchessa d'Ossuna, che fù incontrata dal marito a molte leghe di viaggio lontana. Il Marchese di Ceralbo destinato Vicerè in Catalogna s'è incaminato a quella volta, nel passaggio per Saragoza si fermerà per vn giorno con il Signor D. Giouanni d'Austria per gl'officij presenti, del quale hà conseguito l'istesso posto. Continua la Squadra di Portugallo a farsi vedere nelle vicinanze d'Algieri, senza penetrarsi per anco gl' ogetti di simile armamento, che dà motiuo a varii riflessi, e moltiplici discorsi. Con Corriero espresso si ha auuiso dell'approdo a Cadice del Almiraglio Ruyter con la Flotta Olandese di 30. e più vele trà Vascelli da Guerra, Brulotti, e legni di trasporto, e però hà la Corte rimesso colà oltre vn regalo di 4. mila doble allo stesso Ruyter, 100. m. pezze da otto per i bisogni di detta Flotta, che era in procinto di partire al luogo dell' imbarco di Sua Altezza, essendo attesa a Barzellona da' Vascelli della Corona, per veleggiare vnitamente alla volta di Sicilia.

VENETIA 9. Nouembre. E capitato quà da Zara l'Armiraglio di quella Città, & hà fatto tenere al nuouo Generale di Dalmatia Caualiere Grimani vn memoriale, nel quale hà rappresentato a Sua Eccellenza il bisogno, che quella Prouincia tiene d'attrezzi Militari per il valore di 20. m. ducati; onde dourà l'Eccellenza Sua prima della sua partenza (che seguirà Giouedì venturo) farne passare l'istanze in Senato per titarne gl'ordini proprii, perche restino prouiste quelle Piazze a misura della mancanza, che ne prouano; essendogli nel mentre stato consegnato il danaro già pallottato per le Militie della prefata Prouincia, alle quali sarà distribuito nella rassegna, che andarà facendo delle medesime. Con tal occasione s'è inteso, che il Cadauere del defonto General Giorgi veniua imbarcato sopra la Galera Contarina, che lo dourà trasportare a questa volta doue s'attende da vn giorno all'altro. Essendosi absentato in Padoua con intacco di quella Cassa il Ministro della Camera d'esattione, il Camerlengo datone parte in Publico, si è di quà spedito vn Raggionamento per far la reuisione di quelle partite a fine di procedere contro il sudetto Ministro, secondo la qualità de mancamenti, e delle somme, che sarà trouato debitore. Lunedì mattina, essendo stato colto da vn Carcerato il Guardiano, & reso inhabile alla difesa, leuateli le Chiaui de Camerotti, diede la libertà a Condannati, mà non hebbe fortuna di fuggire se non il primo con quattro Compagni ritenuti gl'altri dalle Guardie accorse alla Custodia. Dall'hauer il Duca di Niuers in questi giorni preso a piggione il Palazzo del Signor Zane passato al suo Gouerno di Verona, con esseruisi già portato ad habitare, s'argomenta che S. E. non sia per trasferirsi per adesso in Francia, come si diceua disegnasse di fare con la Duchessa sua Consorte. Con alcune Barche di Zara si conferma l' auuiso dell'arriuo in Costantinopoli del Signor Baylo Morosino à 12. Settembre, e che fosse subbito partito verso il Mar Negro per sfuggire il Contaggio, che tutta via danneggiaua assai; e che il suo Antecessore Caualiere Querini si fosse posto in viaggio di ritorno a questa volta. Sentesi ancor che circa gl'affari della Guerra si pensaua di ritirare gl'Esserciti dalla Polonia per mettergli a Quartieri d'Inuerno. Si troua a Zara il Capitano

d'vna

FIGURE 2.2 Neapolitan newspaper. SNSP, SG.B.1. Naples, Biblioteca della Società Napoletana di Storia Patria

72   CHAPTER 2

of the publications emanating from the siege of Buda (1686). In issue 24, published on 29 October 1686, we can read:

> In the next week, we will publish the true journal of the siege of Buda, from the beginning to its capitulation, with a separate list of the deaths and the injured, both from the Christian army and the Turkish and it will also contain all the progress through undertaken done by our [soldiers] up until today. It will also feature the true and accurate map of Buda, which was under siege, and its position in the world, along with many other things that are worthy of notice.[26]

In the following number, Parrino reminds its readers once more that 'the promised diary of the siege of Buda will be published by the end of this week'.[27] Parrino also used the *Gazzette* to keep his customers updated on the location of his business, which changed at least 4 times during the years in which he held the privilege of printing the newspapers. In issue 14 of 1699, for example, he warned the readers:

> We now give notice that the *Avvisi* from 4 May onward will be sold in Toledo Street, near [the church of] Santa Maria delle Grazie where Parrino will be living. Furthermore, before Saturday we will publish as a pamphlet the peace treaty between the Holy League and the Turks.[28]

The veracity of the news printed in the *Gazzette* was of the utmost importance for writers and readers alike. Traditionally, the news was disseminated through verbal reports that circulated among the population, reaching even those who could not read via word of mouth. The invention of the printed news sheet did not put a stop to the circulation of manuscript *avvisi* and for a long time, the two media existed alongside one another, with the manuscript *avvisi* used mainly by the elites. With the competition provided by the older, and therefore

---

26 [Domenico Antonio Parrino], *Gazzette di Napoli* (Naples: Per Domenico Antonio Parrino, 29 Ottobre 1686). SNSP, S.G.B.1 vol. 2.

27 [Domenico Antonio Parrino], *Gazzette di Napoli* (Naples: Per Domenico Antonio Parrino, 5 Novembre 1686). SNSP, S.G.B.1 vol. 2. I am not sure if the publication advertised by Parrino was a pamphlet or a book, as he usually advertised both, but I believe it reasonable that the advertised book is [Anon.], *Distinto diario, ovvero relationi di quanto è accaduto nell'assedio di Buda* (Naples: per Camillo Cavallo e Michele Muti, si vende da Domenico Antonio Parrino, 1686).

28 [Domenico Antonio Parrino], *Gazzette di Napoli* (Naples: Per Domenico Antonio Parrino, 7 Aprile 1699). SNSP, S.G.B.1 vol. 5.

PRINT AND POLITICS   73

more trusted, medium, the newspapers, *avvisi*, *gazzette* and *relationi* alike had
to find alternative means to gain the public's trust.[29] The adjective True (*Vera* in
Italian) was often present in the titles of political news sheets and pamphlets,
alongside references to the source from which the author would gather information. All of this was intended to reassure the readers of the veracity of the
information provided. Gaining the readers' trust was useful to the newspaper
publishers since it meant more sales, and to the political authorities because
it granted them more control over the kind of information to which the public
had access. Moreover, particularly in the case of political and military news,
having access to a reliable, which in this instance is a synonym for controlla-
ble, source of information was paramount. Feeding false information to the
enemies could greatly affect the ongoing conflicts and tilt the scale on one side
or the other. Therefore, it should not come as a surprise to learn of a personal
interest in this matter from both Cavallo and Parrino, who often offered scathing remarks toward those who would spread false information, as well as those
that they deemed stupid enough to believe them.

> With little honour, the supporters of the King have published in Rome, in
> the name of His Christian Majesty [i.e. the French King] some Gazette of
> false news, full of ridiculous and made-up things and they printed them
> under the name of the city of Milan and Genoa. And continuing on from
> their made-up plan from last week they lately printed a broadsheet in the
> name of the King full of false promises to the Sicilian people, for which
> no other city could believe them. And the same has already happened
> to the unfortunate Messinesi, who discovered their mistake and are now
> hoping for a remedy. But what causes us to laugh and be incredulous is
> that the French emissaries in Rome fail to realize how this makes them
> untrustworthy, or maybe their natural frivolous disposition means that
> they do not care. But they should at least take back these falsehoods, as
> now everyone recognises them for what they are and they do not believe
> them.[30]

---

29 Mario Infelise, *Prima dei giornali. Alle origini della pubblica informazione* (Milan: Laterza,
    2002); Brendan Dooley, *The Social History of Skepticism* (Baltimore: Johns Hopkins
    University Press, 1999).

30 "Con poco decoro nel Nome della Maestà Christianissima, si fanno in Roma alcune gaz-
    zette di falsi avvisi da suoi Partegianni, spargendo cose aeree e ridicole, e stampano dette
    Gazzette sotto data di Milano e Genova; e in esecuzione di quanto hanno inventato le set-
    timane passate formarono ultimamente un manifesto in nome di detto Re che promette a
    Siciliani quelle vane speranze che non inganneranno l'altre Città, com'è successo alli mal
    consigliati Messinesi, che già s'accorgono del loro errore e ne sospirano il remedio: quello

This issue was more serious than it might appear.[31] Conflicting or outright false reports on the intentions and plans of the French could gravely harm Spanish subjects, and that is why the Viceroy did not let the matter rest. A follow-up on the event is provided in the following issue, dated 3 December 1675:

> The subjects that are discussed in the fake gazettes provided and printed by the French in Rome and neighbouring areas are already considered as such a mockery and joke that, to the great discredit of these Frenchmen, the people thought they were actually planning to put their ridiculous intentions into effect. It is a matter of some wonder that the ministers of France should be so foolish as to utter such jests, which receive less credit than they try to obtain by such childish and unworthy means. Once the captiousness and foolishness of these *avvisi* were discovered, they served to impress upon the memory of everyone, that the reports described in them are nothing but treasons, the account of which deserves little or no faith. Moreover, the peoples and nations of Europe well see that the French are only intent on sowing discord, inciting the subjects of other countries to rebellion, and being accomplices of those who rebel against God and princes, which is all the more disgraceful because it damages the Holy Church and Christendom. These French, having already set fire to all the northern countries, now seek to do the same thing in Italy, worse than they did in Messina, a city ruined by their charms and left exposed to a punishment that will affect them too ...
>
> Coming back to the invention and imposture of the gazettes, here the French promise new and adequate help to the Messina people, including the dispatch of new troops and even princes of the blood to enthrone that kingdom, even having the audacity to support all this with both a placard and a separately published broadsheet to warn and incite the Neapolitan nobility, using gazetteers and distributors in Rome as if they were the Royal Cabinet of Paris, circulating official missives and royal

---

però che move le risa & insieme la maraviglia, è che li Ministri di Francia in Roma, non s'acorgono dello discredito che l'apportano queste cose, se non sia che la loro naturale leggerezza li fa lecito ogni stravaganza; però dovrebbe hormai farsi dare indietro da queste imposture il sapere, che già da per tutto si sono scoperte come tali e non se ne fa di conto." [Ludovico Cavallo], *Gazzette di Napoli* (Naples: Per Ludovico Cavallo, 19 Novembre 1675). SNSP, S.G.B.1 vol. 1.

31 Newspaper 'battles' were fairly common. See Joad, Raymond, 'Exporting Impartiality', in Kathryn Murphy, Anita Traininger (eds) *The Emergence of Impartiality* (Leiden: Brill, 2014) pp. 141–167; Joad Raymond and Noah Moxam (eds) *News Networks in Early Modern Europe* (Leiden and Boston: Brill, 2016); Paul Arblaster, *From Ghent to Aix* (Leiden: Brill, 2014).

edits every week. They do not realise, however, that they are considered little better than storytellers, while the ministers who allow them to do this are regarded as fools who act without any restraint towards their own master. From the Neapolitan nobility, they received reproaches and easily predictable responses, as we shall shortly see. The nobles, moreover, have treated this placard not as a forgery but as a genuine document, and since they are accused of lacking that allegiance which is to them a most esteemed virtue, they will not allow this point to be questioned, either in jest or in earnest, without due resentment. Thus, this most faithful city, through its elected representatives, has presented this placard in the past few days to the Most Excellent Lord Viceroy, begging permission to respond to it and the *avvisi* of the French ... In fact, both the implacable hatred of the Neapolitans against that nation and the unparalleled love for its Catholic monarch continued to grow, to which is now added an uncommon disdain for the French, for such undignified encouragement and incitement.[32]

---

32   "La materia delle Gazzette false procurate e fatte imprimere da' Francesi in Roma , & in qualche altro luogo convicino alla medesima, era ridotta già in burla, e scherzo tale che con lor gran discredito si discorreva, che andassero in queste invenzioni ridicole trattando di avanzare i loro disegni, maravigliandosi ogn'uno che i Ministri di Francia havessero tanto poco cervello di dare in leggerezze simili, che apportano poco credito & meno opinione di quella che pretendono acquistare con mezzi così puerili e indegni, maggiormente che scoperta la macchina & rinfacciatili la loro sciocchezza, erano queli avvisi più tosto per ridurre alla memoria d'ognuno, che li loro progetti si riducono tutti a tradimenti, e che in fatti, &in parole, meritano poca o niuna fede; e che li popoli e Nationi d'Europa non vedono nelli Francesi altri negoziati che di poner zizzanie, seminar discordie , sollevar i vassalli altrui, farsi Parteggiani de Ribelli di Dio, e de' Principi; cosa tanto più indegna, quanto che resulta in detrimento di Santa chiesa e della Christianità; e che havendo attaccto il fuoco per tutti li paesi Settentrionali, hora procurarono a far il medesimo in Italia, più di quello che hanno fatto a Messina, la quale Città hanno rovinato con le loro seditioni & esponendola soggetta al castigo che non potrà mancarli ... E ritornando alle inventione & impostura delle Gazzette, nelle quali promettendo nuovi e validi soccorsi a' Messinesi, patrocinio di nuove armate & fino a mandarsi Principi del Sangue da promuovere al Trono di quel Regno, hanno attrevito a darne fuora Manifesto & poi in foglietto a parte avviso, & incitamento alla nobiltà Napoletana, disponendo li Gazzettari, e Menanti di Roma come dal Gabinetto di Parigi, ogni settimana brevetti e reami e non s'accorgano che sono trattati da Cantainbanco; e li ministri che lo permettono da huomini di poco senno, che oprano contro il decoro del loro Padrone, havendone riportato dalla Nobiltà Napolitana rimproveri, & potendone aspettare le risposte, quali di breve vederanno, mentre questa trattando il Manifesto come se non fosse d'inventione, ma verdatiero, e stimolata a mancar dal preggio stimatissimo della sua esperimentata fedeltà, non permette che questo punto se li tocchi né per burla, né da dovero, senza il dovuto risentimento, e così questa Fidelissima Città, per mezzo di tutti li Signori Eletti, si portò li giorni passati da questo Eccellentiss. Sig. Vicerè, supplicandolo a darli licenza di rispondere a tal

76   CHAPTER 2

This attitude toward the French is even more evident in the pamphlets. But before taking a closer look at those it is worth taking a moment to discuss the different kinds of political pamphlets and their use within the Kingdom of Naples.

Once again, the most common pamphlets were those containing military news. Ever since the Italian wars (1494–1559), the public showed itself eager for political and military news and both government and printers were quick to provide the desired content for this new market. Accounts of battles and sieges were written and printed as soon as the news reached the city, and it was not uncommon to find accounts by multiple authors of the same battle. Some were even advertised in the newspapers, printed and sold alongside with it, but the privilege granted to the *gazzettieri* did not extend in practice to such publications. Cavallo and Parrino paid the sum of 520 ducats per year to have the exclusive right to publish regular *avvisi* and *relazioni*, and even aspired to a monopoly of almanacks. This was going too far: despite their efforts, calendars and almanacks were not included, although they were apparently part of the original privilege granted to Ludovico. It seems though that when the privilege passed to Camillo, the authorities decided to bow to the pressure of other printers and booksellers and remove such publications from the privilege, as we can read in the contract between Cavallo and the Sommaria:

> As the contract was to be renewed, I offered to pay the above sum of 520 ducats per annum for a further nine years [for the printing] of *avvisi* and *relazioni*, leaving to the Royal Court the choice of the contractor [for the printing] of calendars, diaries, *chiaravalli* and astrological books, despite the fact that these were included in my previous contract. Furthermore, His Excellency, in view of the services rendered in the present procurement contract both by myself and by the aforementioned Ludovico, my father, who was the inventor of the said *avvisi* and *relazioni*, [stated] that I should be preferred to anyone else participating in the bidding process and that, regardless of the price established during the lighting of the candle, I should be offered [the contract] for the same sum. However, in spite of His Excellency's having made such statements in writing, the Royal House still decided not to accept my offer. Thus, I would like to

---

Manifesto, & avvisi de' Francesi ... crescendo tanto più l'odio implacabile de' Napolitani contro questa Natione, quanto l'amore impareggiabile al Cattolico Monarca suo Signore: & hora maggiormente con sdegno non hordinario a' Francesi, per così indegni stimoli, & incitamenti, li quali serviranno per altro a moverli, & indurli a nove, e continuate finezze di affettuosissime demostrationi d'ossequio verso la Maestà Sua." [Ludovico Cavallo], *Gazzette di Napoli* (Naples: Per Ludovico Cavallo, 3 Dicembre 1675). SNSP, S.G.B.1 vol. 1.

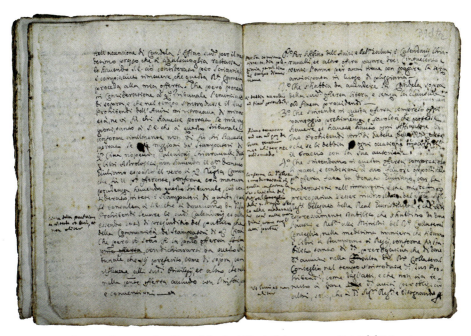

FIGURE 2.3 Contract between Cavallo and the Real Giurisdizione. ASNA, Notai del Seicento, fs. 531/32, f.398r. Naples, Archivio di Stato

bring to the attention of this court what has just been said, pointing out that at the time when the *Ius prohibendi* regarding the *avvisi* was introduced I was a minor, not to mention that at the time no one took my side either with Your Excellency or with this court, just as no one took the side of the printers of this city regarding [the management of the contract for the printing of] calendars, *chiaravalli*, diaries and astrological books. Furthermore, Donato Giuliano, in the presence of this Royal Chamber, did not declare the truth about who was the first bidder. Demonstrating wise caution, this Court has considered all this and after having listened to the city printers and consulted with His Excellency, [has deliberated] that the aforementioned *Ius prohibendi* should exclude said calendars and others, so as not to cause damage to the public or to the community of printers in this city. In accordance with this, I make the present offer, as mentioned above, requesting this Court to be favoured by virtue of the privileges that I enclose with this offer accompanied by the covenants and agreements set out below.

First. For the contract [to print] *avvisi* and *relazioni* (excluding calendars, *chiaravalli* etc) I offer 520 ducats a year for nine years, paying in advance the third part as a warranty.

Second. Let the candle be lit with regard to this offer, freely made and without the clause *ad finem providendi*.

Third. This offer includes all advantages, privileges and faculties granted to any contractor of *Ius prohibendi* having the role of tax collector of the Royal Court, which alone has the authority to impart them [i.e. advantages, privileges and faculties].

Fourth. This offer includes all the covenants and favourable conditions granted to Donato Giuliano as a result of his offer, with the exception of the images [i.e. etchings and engravings]. I further request that the esteemed Regent Delegate of the Royal Jurisdiction recognise me [i.e. grant me a personal title]. Furthermore, it is understood that copies of the notices and reports will be provided [free of charge] to the ministers of the Royal Collateral Council in the same way as it is customary to provide [them] with copies of the books that are printed in the kingdom and as was established at the time when the *Ius prohibendi* was introduced. In the same way, I shall not be obliged to supply copies of the said notices except to the Lord Regents. If then, for the purpose of arriving at a verdict in this matter, it should be necessary to furnish copies [of the *avvisi*] or do other services to the Royal Chamber, orders will be given to me accordingly.

Fifth. That it is prohibited to the copyists to write the aforementioned *avvisi* and *relazioni* to sell them for a profit, and if they were to be found in the act of doing so, may the same penalties be imposed on them as on those who print [clandestinely] to sell in accordance with this offer. However, should the said bidder wish to sell such copies, he must first submit them to the Delegate for his approval.

This offer is valid for fifteen days from today. Naples, 12 September 1693.

[I], Camillo Cavallo, offer [this] *ut supra*.[33]

---

33   "Dovendosi procedere al nuovo affitto offersi pagare la suddetta summa di docati 520 l'anno per altri anni nove dell'avisi, e Relationi con restare a' beneficio della Reale Corte l'affittare i Calendarij, Diarij, Chiaravalli, e libri Astrologici, non ostante, che stavano compresi nel primo Affitto, e che S[ua]. E[ccellenza]. a' riguardo delli servitij prestati tanto da me sottoscritto nell'Affitto suddetto quanto dall'esser detto Ludovico mio Padre l'inventore di detti avisi, e Relationi, d'esser poreferito [sic] ad ogn'uno altro, che concorresse in detto Affitto, e che li restasse nell'accensione di Candela l'Affitto suddetto per il medesimo prezzo, che a' qualsivoglia restasse; et havendo Sua Eccellenza ciò considerato per scritto no[n] si è compiaciuto rimettere, che questa Reale Camera proceda alla mia offerta. Che però ponendo in Consideratione a' questo Tribunale l'enunciato di sopra, e che nel tempo s'introdusse il Ius Prohibendi dell'Avisi mi ritrovava di minor età, né vi fu chi havesse portato le mie raggioni, tanto a' Sua Eccellenza che a' questo Tribunale, conforme similmente non vi fu chi havesse portato le raggioni de' stampatori di questa Città, rispetto

PRINT AND POLITICS

What emerges from this contract is that for Cavallo retaining the privilege was extremely important, we guess both for sentimental reasons, as he remarks how it was his father that invented the *gazzette*, therefore, staking some sort of inherited right, and for economic ones, as no sane businessman will hold this tight to a bad bargain. He was so determined to keep the *ius prohibendi* for himself that when Donato Giuliano tried to challenge this privilege with an offer of his own, Cavallo proved to be willing to relinquish his claim to calendars, almanacks and all other sorts of publications in order to keep the exclusive for the *gazzette* and *avvisi*.

A true monopoly over a kind of literature so ephemeral and varied would have been an impossible feat and therefore nearly everyone could print a

i Calendarij, Chiaravalli, Diarij e libri Astrologici, non havendo il quondam Donato Giuliano esposto il vero a questa Regia Camera che fu il primo offerente, conforme con matura prudenza, havendo questo Tribunale ciò considerato, intesi i Stampatori di questa Città sé consulta a' Sua Eccellenza che si dovevano da detto Ius Prohibendi levare li suddetti Calendarij, et altro essendo così di pregiuditio del publico, che della Communità de' Stampatori di questa Città. Che però io sottoscritto fo la presente offerta, con dichiararsi da questo Tribunale, che sij preferito, come di sopra, con riflettere alli suddetti Privilegij, et altro, che nella nella [sic] presente offerta accludo con l'infrascritti patti e conventioni.

Primo. Per l'Affitto dell'Avisi, e Relationi esclusi, i Calendarij, Chiaravalli, et altro, offero pagare docati Cinquecento e venti l'anno per anni nove con pagare la terza anticipata in luogo di pliggiaria [i.e. come garanzia].

Secondo. Che s'habbia da accendere la Candela sopra della suddetta offerta, libera, e senza la clausula ad finem providendi.

Terzo. Che s'intende in questa offerta ogni vantaggio, preminenza, e facoltà che potesse havere, et havesse havuto ogni Affittatore di Ius Prohibendi Arrendatori di Gabelle della Reale Corte e che se li debbia in ogni occasione impartirli il braccio con la sua autorità.

Quarto. Che s'intendano in questa offerta compresi tutti li patti, et condizioni a' suo favore opposti nella prima offerta fatta da Donato Giuliano, con le moderazioni nell'immagini. e che mi resta la prerogativa d'esser riconosciuto dal Spettabile Signor Reggente delegato della Real Giurisditione, e che resti espressamente stabilito, che s'habbino da dare l'avisi, e Relationi alli Ministri del Regio Collateral Conseglio, nella medesima maniera, che si danno i libri si stamano in Regij, conforme [come] fu stabilito, tanto di detta prerogativa, che di dare detti avvisi nella Consulta del Regio Collateral Conseglio, nel tempo [in cui] s'introdusse detto Ius Prohibendi, come dagl'altri, e che non sia tenuto a' dare detti avisi per obligo ad altri, solo, che a' detti Signori Reggenti e bisognando per questa Causa qualsivoglia aviso, e favore ricorrendo in essa Reale Camera, se li debbia con la sua autorità impartirli il braccio.

Quinto. Che è proibito per i copisti di scrivere le suddette relazioni e avvisi e venderli per profitto e che se verrano sorpresi a farlo siano nelle medesime pene, come a quelli li stampassero per venderli in conformità alla presente offerta, e volendo permettere a sottoscritto offerente, i detti copisti, acciò li vendessero, siano tenuti prima a farli rivedere dal spettabile sig. Delegato.

Vaglia la presente offerta per giorni quindeci da hoggi. Napoli, 12 settembre 1693.

Camillo Cavallo offero ut supra." ASNA, Notai del Seicento, fs. 531/32, f.398r–398ter.v.

80 CHAPTER 2

report about military operations, as long as the narrative was favourable to the Spanish crown, of course, and maybe without the word *relazione* in the title just to be safe. And of course, a fool-proof way to evade any kind of monopoly and unwanted consequences was to print in a clandestine way, anonymously, as is for example the case with a couple of printed anonymous letters. They are not in any catalogue, they do not have a title or an imprimatur and they recount the position of the French army during the Franco-Spanish wars in 1654. My hypothesis is that they could be a clandestine edition of the same manuscript letter sent to the Viceroy and made to be distributed in the city of Naples.[34]

It is worth mentioning that, in the bound volumes that made up the collection of Neapolitan newspapers held in the Biblioteca della Società di Storia Patria, alongside the *gazzette* there are several such pamphlets, alongside manuscripts letters and copies of political news. Unfortunately, as it happens too often when it comes to documents from the Spanish Viceroyalty, the archive of the library was destroyed during World War II, making it impossible to know when and how those bound-up volumes came to be. However, given the content of the pamphlets and manuscripts attached I feel that it is possible that they were bound together at an early date. Whoever collected the newspapers was most likely a member of the bureaucratic Neapolitan elite and therefore the recipient of political news through all three of the main media. Such an individual might well feel the need to keep together with the *gazzette* the pieces of news that were of the most interest to him. The fifty pamphlets bound there, demonstrate a marked interest in the war in Hungary, a strong dislike for the French and practical interest in all things military, as it is illustrated for example by the two different descriptions of the newest warship used by the British navy against the French in the battle of Dieppe.[35] Furthermore, it is

---

34 [Anon], [Anonymous letter about the french troops in the city] (s.l.n.d., dated 03.XII.1654). SNSP, CUOMO OP 02.SER 16 .6 USTC 1752427; [Anon], [Anonymous letter about the French troops in the city] (s.l.n.d., dated 27.XI.1654). SNSP, CUOMO OP 02.SER 16 .7 USTC 1752428.

35 Some of the pamphlets included are: *Relatione dello spaventoso incendio seguito nella Gran Città di Costantinopoli, metropoli dell'impero orientale a 5 settembre di quest'anno 1693* (Naples: appresso Domenico Antonio Parrino e Camillo Cavallo, 1693), USTC 1752421; *Nova e distinta relatione della Vittoria ottenuta dall'armi cesaree nel combattimento seguito sotto Giula, con fuga e rotta data a' Turchi* (Naples: appresso Domenico Antonio Parrino e Camillo Cavallo, 1693), USTC 1752422; *Vera e distinta relatione del terremoto accaduto in Napoli e parte del suo regno il giorno 8 di Settembre 1694. Dove si dà ragguaglio delli danni che il medesimo ha cagionato in molte parti del medesimo Regno e in particolare nelle 3 province di Principato, Citra Utra e Basilicata. Con il numero di morti e feriti che nelle medesime sono restati sotto le pietre* (Naples e Palermo: per Costanzo, 1694), USTC 1752440.

PRINT AND POLITICS

interesting to mention that several of these pamphlets can be found in multiple copies, such as it is the case for *Nuova distinta relazione della considerabilissima Vittoria, riportata dal Regio Esercito*, of which there are two copies in the Biblioteca della Società di Storia Patria and one in the National Library of Naples.[36]

Of course, most if not all of the news that was printed was of the celebratory kind. Victories over enemies, particularly over the French, were recounted with vivid details and often commemorated with reprints or further publication on the occasion of anniversaries. The USTC holds records for ca. 100 of such publications, printed by several different printers. This appears to be a further confirmation that a true monopoly of such material simply did not exist and in fact, the opposite appears to be true: the more important is the piece of news that they were printing about, the more printers were involved. The most notable demonstration of this is what happened with the Vesuvius eruption of 1636, as we will see in Chapter 4. This brings us to the second genre of political pamphlets: those published for purposes of commemoration. Besides military victories, marriages, funerals, investitures and royal visitations were joyous occasions for the city. And of course, every occasion such as these was used to showcase the splendour and grandeur of the Spanish crown, the devotion of its subjects and the political harmony and social prosperity of the city of Naples. Historians have largely ignored the role of public festivals organised by the Spanish court as an effective tool for bridging the gap between Spaniards and Neapolitans and building a more interwoven community. The prejudices held by Italian historians against Spanish rule led them to regard festivals and celebrations held by the Viceroy as something of interest only for the Spanish citizen, dismissing or not taking into account the considerable documentary evidence that speaks of a different reality, such as the numbers of pamphlets produced in this occasions and the fact that these were often referenced in the newspapers.[37] Besides the cyclical religious festivities, on any given year there were a number of occasions that warranted celebrations: from a visit of

---

36   [Anon], *Nuova distinta relazione della considerabilissima Vittoria, riportata dal Regio Esercito, comandato in persona dal glorioso nostro monarca Carlo Terzo Sopra quella de' Gallispani fortemente trincierato nelle vicinanze di Saragoza il dì 20 d'Agosto 1710 con la totale disfatta del medesimo. La cui nuova in cinque giorni è capitata qua a S. Em. Il Cardinal Grimani nostro Vice.Rè, e capitan Generale, la notte di giovedì 4 del corrente Settembre* (In Naples: per Domenico-Antonio Parrino e Camillo Cavallo, 1710) SNSP, CUOMO OP.2 SER 14.7; CUOMO OP.2 SER 14.8; USTC 1752423.

37   The bias with which historians have approached the history of the Spanish Viceroyalty in Naples, particularly in regard to this aspect, is rightfully pointed out by Gabriel Guarino, 'Spanish Celebrations in Seventeenth-century Naples', *The Sixeenth Century Journal* 37 (2006), pp. 25–41.

the Spanish sovereign to a marriage, from a funeral to the announcement of the King's recovery from illness. These were all events that the public needed to be made aware of, through processions and celebrations, and these needed to be recorded. Unsurprisingly, the pamphlets that can still be found in the collection of the various Neapolitan libraries are, for the most part, funerary.[38] These pamphlets usually contained a brief description of the mourning procession and those in attendance, some notes on the decor of the church, sometimes with accompanying engravings, and a transcription of the homily. The same structure and content can be found in the marriage pamphlets, but of those fewer exemplars remains in the libraries' collections.[39] The intent and purpose behind these celebrations, and the published accounts, was to show power, unity and the devotion of the Neapolitan subjects to the Viceroy and the Spanish crown. It was a subtle and understated political message. On other occasions, however, the full force of the printing press as a propagandistic tool was evident, stating in no uncertain terms the absolute control that the Spaniards had on Naples and the unwavering loyalty of the Neapolitan citizens.

The already tense situation between France and Spain caused by the participation of the two nations on opposite sides in the Franco-Dutch war (1672–1678) was further exacerbated when the French intervened in favour of the people from Messina when they rebelled against Spanish rule in 1675. These simultaneous conflicts occurred at the end of a long string of other conflicts that, throughout the seventeenth century, saw these two nations constantly opposing each other. As it is to be expected, these matters were often front and centre in political communications, both in the broadsheets and the newspapers. But the preferred media to address the conflict with the French soon became the pamphlet. A powerful and efficient tool to relay news of military manoeuvres and battles, the pamphlets were also used to steer public opinion. The pamphlets that were printed during the Franco-Iberian conflicts are an incredibly vivid and rich source for any historian, as we will see in the next chapter.

Already in 1647–1648, during Masaniello's rebellion and the brief experience of the Neapolitan Republic, it appears that the French had established the practice of having printed and manuscript proclamations posted around the city of Naples, with which they would encourage Neapolitans to rebel and free themselves from the tyrannical rule of the Spaniards. Neapolitans inevitably replied

---

38 Several examples can be found in the Bonazzi collection in the Biblioteca della Società di Storia Patria. The USTC lists 29 funerary pamphlets printed in Naples during the Spanish Vicerealm.

39 SNSP, Bonazzi 06.E.34.1 and 2; BNN SQ.25.K.44.10 Banco Napoli 01.D.30.

PRINT AND POLITICS

with declarations of devotion to their Spanish rulers and a list of all the misdeeds carried on by the French as proof of their untrustworthiness.[40] Almost thirty years later, the practice still continued. As Ludovico Cavallo reported on the issue of the *gazzetta* published on 10 December 1675, on 15 October a broadsheet encouraging the *Nobiltà e Popolo Napoletano* (nobility and the people of Naples) to rebel was printed in Paris and later distributed in Naples. Cavallo remarks how the political elite of the city had just printed a reply to that outrageous piece of French propaganda reminding all and sundry that every trouble that occurred in Italy, and particularly in the Kingdom of Naples, was and will ever be caused by the lies and treacheries of the French.[41]

3   The Cost of News

We have seen that at the beginning of their venture as licensed *gazzettieri* Parrino and Cavallo paid 520 ducats per year for the privilege: presumably, this was the same price that Ludovico Cavallo paid. Towards the end of their enterprise, the privilege cost them almost double, but when it moved to Antonio Bulifon he managed to obtain the same privilege for only 350 ducats per year, another bone of contention in the professional rivalry between Parrino and Bulifon.

But what do these prices signify? It is difficult to establish the price for a single issue of a newspaper, as this was not written into any contract and there is no surviving catalogue of Parrino's bookshop. The only indication in regard to the price of the avvisi can be found in an advertisement in issue 10, the last for the year 1693:

> We have already published the famous almanack by Chiaravalle and we will give a copy, as promised, to all those who subscribe to the *Avvisi* for the entire year for the price of 24 carlini, along with all the *Relazioni* and the Calendar both in Naples and throughout the entire Kingdom, where it will be our job to send [the Gazzette] to those who will have paid for the entire year in advance, and it will be more worthy than ever as the

---

40   We will see examples of these type of publications and discuss them more in depth in Chapter 3.

41   [Ludovico Cavallo], *Gazzette di Napoli* (Naples: Per Ludovico Cavallo, 10 December 1675). SNSP, S.G.B.1 vol. 1.

84   CHAPTER 2

Avvisi will be even richer with the most interesting news from all over the world.[42]

I do not believe it to be a coincidence that, of all the issues that I was able to examine in the Biblioteca della Società di Storia Patria, the only one that contains any reference to a price, or any attempt to advertise the newspaper itself, for that matters, is this one. We have seen that in September of that same year the yearly price for the privilege increased to 810 ducats and, although without any indications of the price for a yearly subscription in the previous years we do not know if Parrino and Cavallo increased the price accordingly, it is nonetheless safe to assume that they felt the need to increase the numbers of their subscribers, enticing them with free supplements and the promise of a new and improved version of the newspaper.

The currency in Naples was the ducato, a silver coin. Then there were tarì (1/5 ducato), carlino (1/10 ducato and 1/2 tarì), and grana (1/10 carlino, 1/20 tarì and 1/100 ducato). This means that Parrino and Cavallo had to sell 0.4 yearly subscriptions to earn a ducato (10 carlini = 1 ducato), and 337.5 subscriptions to cover the cost of the privilege. Considering a population of around 200,000 in Naples and the fact that they sold their newspapers across the entire Viceroyalty this is a more than reasonable number of subscribers. To give a sense of what kind of numbers we are talking about, the main Amsterdam newspaper had a print run of 2,000 issues, the Paris Gazette at the end of the seventeenth century published 12,000 copies while the average print run for the London Gazette was around 8,000, but could reach 15,000 for special numbers. Maintaining such a high number of weekly issues would involve the use of several printing presses, even more so if we consider that the newspapers were not the only thing that Parrino and Cavallo printed. However, with the exception of the occasional remark in regard to the use by Parrino of other printers' machinery, we do not have any information regarding the specific printing process of the newspapers.

It appears then that the price of the privilege was affordable for Parrino and Cavallo, particularly given the fact that the real profit was to be had through the sale of the publications that they advertised in the newspaper.[43] But was a yearly subscription of 24 carlini affordable? Once again, a conclusive answer is

---

42   [Domenico Antonio Parrino, Camillo Cavallo], *Gazzette di Napoli* (Naples: appresso Domenico Antonio Parrino e Camillo Cavallo, 24 December 1693). SNSP, S.G.B.1 vol. 4.

43   For a closer look to the marketing strategy employed by Parrino see: Nina Lamal, 'The first Advertisements in Italian Newspapers (1683–1700)', in Arthur der Weduwen, Malcolm Walsby (eds), *The book world of Early Modern Europe* (Leiden and Boston: Brill, 2022), pp. 455–480.

PRINT AND POLITICS

not easy to establish but to try and discern the cost of living in Naples one of the most useful sources is lease contracts.

In 1629 Domenico Maccaramo paid 65 ducats per year to rent two shops and three rooms (*due botteghe e tre stanze*).[44] With the exception of a decline immediately after the plague of 1656, rent prices remained pretty consistent through the seventeenth century. In the neighbourhood of San Lorenzo, many of the properties belonged to the monastery of S. Liguorio, that rented them for on average 60 ducats per year.

> To Adriano Scultore 12 ducats and from him to the Monastery of the nuns of S. Liguorio of this city to complete the sum of 33 ducats that he pays to repay the debt accumulated until 4 May 1686 for the rent of his house and shop located in the corner of S. Biagio of the booksellers where the aforementioned lives and that said Monastery rents to him for the sum of 66 ducats per year.[45]

This means that on average rent was 1.25 ducats (12.5 carlini) per week. A subscription for one year to the newspaper cost approximately twice the weekly rent. All things considered, I would say that a yearly subscription to the newspaper was something pretty affordable, that many even among the artisan class could afford. In comparison, the copies of proclamations that Egidio Longo sold for 5 grana each (0.5 carlini), as we have seen at the beginning of this chapter, were considerably less expensive even though they were aimed at a much more restricted audience. The books advertised in the newspapers could sometimes be a luxury item, but more often than not they were pretty affordable (the first volume of the Guerre d'Ungheria was priced at 8 carlini).[46] A sheet of paper cost c.0,5 grana, therefore Longo had a profit of twenty/twenty-five times what he spent in paper for each pamphlet. We can also calculate that Cavallo and Parrino spent around 2 carlini to buy the paper to print one year of the newspapers (52 issues), therefore they had a profit of twelve times what they paid for every subscription.

---

44   AFBN, BP, gc. 1647, 22 November.

45   AFBN, BP, gc. 1687, m. 874, d.12, 18 March. Further examples can be found in ASNA, Monasteri Soppressi, fs. 3350 (*Libro d'introito, ed esito dell'amministrazione dell'abbatessato della Signora Donna Lucretia Pignatelli dell'anno 1677, 1678 et 1679*).

46   "The diary of Negroponte, which includes a map, and was written by Sir Spinelli, general of the Malta wars, in his own handwriting, is now published and it is sold for 1 carlino." [Domenico Antonio Parrino, Camillo Cavallo], *Gazzette di Napoli* (Naples: appresso Domenico Antonio Parrino, 22 February 1689). SNSP, S.G.B.1 vol. 3. See also footnote 6.

→	Ducati	Tari	Carlini	Grana
Ducati	1	5	10	100
Tari	0.2	1	2	20
Carlini	0.1	0.5	1	10
Grana	0.01	0.05	0.1	1

↓	Ducati	Tari	Carlini	Grana
Ducati	1	0.2	0.1	0.01
Tari	5	1	0.5	0.05
Carlini	10	2	1	0.1
Grana	100	20	10	1

CHART 2.1   Neapolitan currency equivalence chart

We have seen in this chapter the multitude of ways in which political power interacted with printers, booksellers and the people of Naples, as well as the political and propagandistic use of cheap print. A pervasive and efficient communication strategy, one that allowed government officials to convey their messages to the broader possible audience in the least amount of time as well as swaying the public's opinions in their favour was of the utmost importance for the smooth running of the city, and never more so than during times of great political unrest, as we will see in the next chapter.

CHAPTER 3

Print in Times of Crisis

On 3 January 1647 [the government] started to collect the new fruit tax and to this effect, they started to send notice to all the stores in which the shopkeepers had dried fruit. The Viceroy granted this assignation to the Royal Counsellor Carlo Brancaccio, brother of the Cardinal with this same name, a Minister of good heart and sharp mind. He was a friend of the paupers and, in order to avoid disorders and frauds that could happen while collecting said taxes came up with a specific Regulation.

•••

The second reason [for the tension in the streets] was the fact that seditious and satirical writings were found around the various Seggi in the city. These writings threatened to exact an act of vengeance against the government and the ministry during the upcoming celebration of San Giovanni Battista if they would not stop the new fruit tax, and for this reason, the above-mentioned celebration was cancelled, given that, according to tradition, the Viceroy should have been seen on horseback across the city.[1]

∴

---

1   "Fu dunque a tre Gennaio 1647 cominciata a esigere la Gabella de' Frutti, pigliandosi a tal'effetto i manifesti da tutte le botteghe dove di già i bottegai avevano intromessi i frutti secchi. Ne commise il Vicerè la Delegazione al Regio consigliero Carlo Brancaccio, fratello del Cardinale di questo cognome, Ministro per altro di buona mente, il quale come amico de' poveri per evitare i disordini e le frodi che accader poteano nell'esazzione di essa, mandò fuori il seguente Regolamento.

...

Il secondo motivo fu l'essersi ritrovati alcuni cartelli sediziosi e satirici ne' dintorni de' Seggi, minacciantino nella prossima festa di S. Giovanni Battista voler fare vendetta crudele del governo e ministri se non si toglieva la Gabella de' Frutti, cosicchè fu prudentemente prohibita la suddetta festa, nella quale secondo costume si doveva portare il Vicerè in forma di cavalcata" Anon, *Sollevazioni dell'anno 1647* [Naples, Eighteenth century]. SNSP, ms XXII.C.6, leaves 139, 142.

The revolt of 1647 is undoubtedly the most famous of the Neapolitan rebellions against the Spanish crown but it is not the first. Rather, it represents the culmination of simmering tension between the Neapolitan people and their foreign government as well as one more act in the long-running conflict between the French crown and the Spanish Empire. Throughout the period of the Spanish Viceroyalty, traces of these conflicts and tensions can be found in the pamphlets and publications that circulated within the city, offering almost exclusively the perspective of Spanish supporters. That was the case until the situation exploded in 1647, and anti-Spanish sentiment (or, more accurately, the pro-French faction) briefly found its voice in popular print. The seditious and satirical writings mentioned above were probably manuscripts but it is also possible that some were indeed printed. Their existence and the reaction that they generated, the cancellation of the scheduled celebration which is particularly relevant given that we have seen in the previous chapter how important public celebrations were in maintaining order and control in the city, is proof that the written word that circulated among the streets of the city had a wide reach and that it influenced the actions of people and authorities alike.

The first conflicts between Naples and its Spanish rulers took place in the first half of the sixteenth century. In 1510 and again in 1547 the authorities tried to implement the Spanish Inquisition in Naples. These attempts were met with fierce resistance, so much so that they soon fizzled out and ecclesiastical jurisdiction remained solidly in the hands of the Roman office. Given the poor survival rate of archival evidence from the sixteenth century, we do not have many materials to study these instances, but Neapolitan historians have long agreed that these particular rebellions, although carried out with the participation of the lower classes, were born within the nobility and bourgeoisie.[2]

The first popular rebellion, popular because it was begun by the lower classes and carried on by them with little or no contribution from the nobility, occurred in 1585. Similarly to what would happen sixty years later with Masaniello's rebellion, the uprising of 1585 was brought on by economic factors, namely the increase in the price of bread within the city. Unlike the rebellion of 1647, however, this was self-contained. The anger was directed mainly toward the representative of the people of Naples (Eletto del Popolo), Giovan Vincenzo Starace (d.1585) viewed as responsible for the economic difficulties, and he was the one to pay the price ultimately. In the singular most important episode of the uprising, the people turned against their supposed delegate, lynched him and defiled his corpse. After this shocking display of violence and

---

2   Rosario Villari, *Un sogno di libertà. Napoli nel declino di un impero* (Milan: Mondadori, 2012), p. 29.

PRINT IN TIMES OF CRISIS

some looting of shops around the city, the increase in the price of bread was cancelled and everything went back to normal, although what happened was not forgotten.[3] It is worth mentioning that this particular revolt, although it failed to bring lasting changes and consequences, already exhibited evidence of anti-Spanish sentiment. The anger was directed toward Neapolitan government officials, judged as greedy, untrustworthy and corrupt, but similar opinions were directed against the Spanish government. Among the demands of the people for the cancellation of taxes on wheat, the middle class of professionals joined the revolt, demanding more rights within the public assembly and the right to choose the Eletto del Popolo, who from 1547 was instead appointed by the Viceroy and whose presence and power was basically rendered void by the stipulation that the delegates for the Sedili Nobili could deliberate without him. The chant of *abbasso lo malogoverno et viva la giustitia* (down with the bad government and long live justice) echoed in the streets of the city, all the way to the palace of the Viceroy and it was the same cry that sounded once again during the rebellion of 1647.

As was the case with Masaniello's rebellion, most information regarding this particular uprising comes from contemporary chronicles and histories, as well as ambassadors' papers. The role played by popular print in these events is not to be underestimated. Many anti-Spanish placards appeared on the streets, encouraging the people to rebel against the Spanish government and not to waste the opportunity to transform the uprising into a full-scale rebellion:

> O, stunned people, you started something and you did not finish it.
> On the day of the Corpus Christi [i.e. 20 June], every man be alert
> on the day of Saint Joanne [i.e. Saint John's day], every man leave their
>   comforts
> and pick up the weapons.[4]

---

3 On the ritualistic aspects of the murder of the Eletto del Popolo and its echoes during Masaniello's rebellion see Peter Burke, 'The Virgin of the Carmine and the Revolt of Masaniello', *Past & Present* 99 (1983), pp. 3–21; Peter Burke, 'A response,' *Past & Present*, 114 (1987), pp. 197–199; Rosario Villari, 'Masaniello: Contemporary and Recent Interpretations', *Past & Present*, 108 (1985), pp. 117–132.

4 "O populo storduto, hai incominciato et non hai fenuto./Al dì dello Corpo de Christo ogni homo sia listo, /al dì de Santo Joanne ogni homo lassa le panelle et piglia l'arme" in Fabio Mutinelli, *Storia arcana e aneddotica d'Italia raccontata dai veneti ambasciatori* (Venice: Pietro Naratovich, 1856), I, pp. 145–150.

   It is interesting to note that this particular poem became once again popular during the days of Masaniello's rebellion. I believe that this is due, beside the obvious similarities in the circumstances, on the fact that both in 1585 and 1647 the festivity of the Corpus Domini happened on 20 June. Given that St. John's day is on 24 June, a four days warning must have seemed enough.

This same medium was swiftly used by the authorities as well, firstly by printing, on that very same day, a broadsheet addressing the more immediate concern: the price of bread. Giving way to the demands of the people, the Viceroy Osuna established a political price for wheat of 1.5 ducats per *tomolo* (50.5 lt) buying a huge amount of wheat from Sicily, to be paid for by a new tax to be enforced not only within the city but in all the provinces as well, and a higher one for the provinces. This swift action served to placate the immediate demands and restore some semblance of order. It was so effective that the rebellion was not rekindled even when the punishments for the rebellion began to be dealt out, with a staggering number of trials and several particularly gruesome executions, all of which were communicated to Neapolitan citizens via printed proclamations. The specific broadsheets and proclamations printed around this event did not survive, as is the case with a lot of the seditious print, but we know of their content thanks to contemporary chronicles.[5] The final act of this brief rebellion took place on 4 December 1585 when the Viceroy Osuna published a pardon for all of those who were involved in the events of the previous June.

Despite the seemingly isolated nature of this particular riot and its fast resolution, underlying tensions kept simmering; the economic problems were not resolved and the echoes of social tensions and revolts throughout the Spanish Empire found their way to Naples, escaping censorship and stirring the pot. Between this event and the revolt of 1647 several other incidents occurred, none with any lasting effect. Meanwhile, the situation in the remainder of the Spanish Empire was fragile, and the citizens of Naples were very much aware of this.

Given its nature as a port city, as well as its role as a stronghold from which the Spanish crown regularly took money and men as reinforcements for its military campaigns, it should come as no surprise that Naples was one of the

---

Translation note: the word *listo* is one of the many Spanish words that were incorporated into Neapolitan dialect, maintaining the same exact meaning of being ready, being alert. *Panelle* is a traditional Neapolitan dish of sweet bread, and because of a metonymy it is also often used to indicated being cuddled. In the instance of this little poem I decided to use a mixture of both meanings.

5 The most relevant, besides the ones already mentioned, are: Tommaso Costo, *Giunta di tre libri al Compendio dell'Istoria del Regno di Napoli, nei quali si contiene quanto di notabile e ad esso Regno appartenente è accaduto dal principio dell'anno 1585 fino alla fine dell'Ottantasei* (Naples: Oratio Salviani, 1591); Gio Antonio Summonte, *Historia delle città e Regno di Napoli* (Naples: Giacomo Gaffaro, 1643); Giulio Cesare Capaccio, *Il forastiero* (Naples: Gio Domenico Roncagliolo, 1634); [Anon.] 'La morte di Gio Vincenzo Starace Eletto del popolo di Napoli, nel maggio 1585; racconto tratto da un ms. del secolo XVIII', *Archivio Storico per le Province Napoletane* I, 1 (1876), pp. 131–138; Nunzio F. Faraglia, 'Il tumulto napoletano dell'anno 1585. Relazione contemporanea', *Archivio Storico per le Province Napoletane* XI, 1 (1886), pp. 433–441.

PRINT IN TIMES OF CRISIS

places with the best information network. The constant flow of people and goods was accompanied by the same traffic in information, be it by word of mouth or in the form of printed works and manuscripts. It is important to stress once again that the dissemination of news and information was so thorough and widespread that it reached all strata of the population. During the events of 1585, for example, the mob was heard saying that the Viceroy would not dare to punish the killers of Starace nor those responsible for unrest because he would be wary of a repeat of what happened in Flanders during the Dutch Revolt when they lost all the northern provinces of the Netherlands.[6]

The Spanish government was very much aware of this situation and put particular effort into trying to put a stop to the circulation of information regarding revolts and rebellions in other provinces of the Empire. A prime example of this effort is the report detailing all the intercepted contacts between the Portuguese and Catalan rebels and the citizens of Naples, compiled and send to the king by the head of the Sacro Regio Consiglio and leader of the spy network, Antonio Pérez Navarrete.

> L. arrested a Catalan priest named D. Juan Forment, because he found in his possession some manuscripts and books printed in Barcelona against His Majesty and he also carried several broadsheets printed in big letters in which it was said 'As I have done, so shall you do', referring to the city of Barcelona and Naples, and he had to put those up in Naples. He was imprisoned in the Castle of Baya where he died.[7]

One thing is certain: both the government and the would-be agitators were very well aware of the huge impact of popular print as a medium capable of conveying in a swift and efficient manner political messages and the potential it had in swaying public opinion. Both parties tried their hardest to use this tool in the most effective way. In the months and days immediately before Masaniello's revolt, the future revolutionaries put all their energies into stirring up political and social tension, while simultaneously encouraging the people of Naples to rebel, providing them with countless examples and reassurance of what they had to gain. A prime opportunity for this strategy came

---

6   Fabio Mutinelli, *Storia arcana*, p. 145.

7   "L. Carcero à un Clerigo presbitero Catalan, llamado D. Juan Forment, y le hallò en su poder algunos escritos, y libros estampados en Barcelona contro S.M y traya diversos carteles de letra grande, que en uno dellos dezia: Quem ad modum ergo fecis, et ita vos faciatas. Ablando Barcelona co la Ciudad de Napoles, que tenia para poner por Napoles. Se carcero en el Castillo de Baya donde se muriò" [Antonio Navarrete], *Breve relaciòn de los servicios hechos a su Magestad por el Doctor D. Antonio Navarrete, Cavallero del Avito de Sant Tiago, Decano y Propresidente del Sacro Consejo de Napolès* (s.n, [1601]), p. 15.

92   CHAPTER 3

from neighbouring Sicily. In the month of May, the city of Palermo rebelled against the Spanish government, and for a while, it actually appeared that their uprising might succeed. On 21 May 1647, the Viceroy of Sicily published two proclamations with which he cancelled all taxes on basic food necessities as well as granting a pardon to all of those who took part in the rebellion and the felons that had escaped from prison. Immediately, several copies of these proclamations were printed and circulated in Naples, so much so that 'almost everyone had a copy'.[8] It was a not-so-subtle way of saying that a rebellion was not only possible, but indeed advantageous, because it was the only way to obtain change, and it was also relatively risk-free, as the two Sicilian proclamations proved.

One cannot say that these particular pieces of print were the deciding factor in what would happen a few days later, nor would I consider it to be the proverbial straw that broke the camel's back. Rather, it was a combination of political and economic factors that built a very volatile situation that reached boiling point on 7 July 1647; the masterful use of popular print as a political and propagandistic tool served as more kindling for a fire that was already smouldering.

1   Masaniello's Revolt

The episode that sparked the revolt was a controversy between tax collectors and fruit merchants from the provinces concerning the proper amount that

---

8   "And then the courage grew, and with the courage the envy that was brought on by news of the success of the revolt of Palermo and the majority of Sicily, with the exception of Messina. With force and weapons they obtained from His Excellency the Marquess of Los Velez, Viceroy of Sicily, the cancellation of every tax and the general pardon for all of those who were in prison, be they guilty of breaking into the prison, of murder, of robbery and of all every other crime, including those of escaping the prison during said rebellion. And both of these broadsheets circulated and ended up into everyone's hands". (Crebbe poi l'ardire, e con l'ardire l'invidia all 'udito successo della rivolution di Palerno, e di buona parte della Sicilia, fuorche di Messina per lo sgravamento à forza d'armi ottenuto dall' Eccellentissimo Signor Marchese de Los Velez Vicerè di quel Regno, di tutte le Gabelle, e per l'indulto anche generale di tutti gl'eccessi di frattura di carceri, di homicidi, di furti, di armamenti in campagna, e di tutti i delitti, compresi l'ultimo della fuga di detti carcerati nel tempo di detta revolutione, andando attorno ambidue bandi per le mani di tutti del tenore seguente). Alessandro Giraffi, *Le rivolutioni di Napoli descritte dal Signor Alessandro Giraffi. Con pienissimo ragguaglio d'ogni successo, e trattati secreti e palesi* (Naples: s.n., 1647), p. 12. On this particular source see Silvana D'Alessio, 'Un'esemplare cronologia. Le rivoluzioni di Napoli di Alessandro Giraffi (1647)', *Annali dell'isitituo italiano per gli studi storici* 15 (1988), pp. 287–340; Id., 'Una nuova aurora. Su un manoscritto de "Le rivolutioni di Napoli" di Alessandro Giraffi', *Il pensiero politico* 32, 3 (2000). pp. 383–403.

they needed to pay for the fruit tax. From Piazza del Mercato, the mob that immediately formed, led by Tommaso Aniello, better known as Masaniello, began to march through the city toward the Royal Palace, where they gained entry and caused the Viceroy to flee for the safety of the convent of St. Luigi. The immediate aim of the rebellion was not to rid the city of the Spaniards but rather to obtain more political rights for the lower classes as well as alleviate economic and fiscal pressure. That is why in the first days of the rebellion the objects of the people's wrath were mainly the properties of tax collectors and warehouses of rich merchants, those regarded as guilty of having profited from the misfortune of the people of Naples. In this initial phase of the rebellion, Masaniello's phase, the city remained loyal to Spanish rule. Masaniello even met with the Viceroy, who gave in to every demand. It is only after Masaniello's death on 16 July, killed by his own supporters after having shown signs of erratic behaviour that the revolt began to assume more anti-Spaniards traits.[9] There are many popular legends with respect to Masaniello's last days; his increasingly weird actions, which went from throwing a knife into the crowd of people below his window to the deranged idea of transforming the Market Square into a harbour completed with a bridge to connect Naples to Spain, were rumoured to be caused by a poison that was administrated to him during a feast with the Spanish rulers with the specific purpose to discredit him.[10] Despite the extremely brief role that Masaniello had in the rebellion and everything that came after, he has always been hailed as the true protagonist (along with his hidden counsellor Giulio Genoino), so much so that the event is known as Masaniello's rebellion.[11] This is particularly due to the pro-French writings of the time, but even more so by the resurgence of

---

9   This is an extremely brief and concise recap of the main point of the rebellion in order to provide some context. For a proper account of the events as well as historiographical interpretations see: Vittorio Conti, *La rivoluzione repubblicana a Napoli e le strutture rappresentative (1647–1648)* (Florence: Centro Editoriale Toscano, 1984); Silvana D'Alessio, *Masaniello. La sua vita e il suo mito in Europa* (Rome: Salerno, 2007); Rosario Villari, *La rivolta antispagnola a Napoli. Le origini (1585–1647)* (Bologna: Laterza, 1967); Rosario Villari, *Un sogno di libertà* (Milan: Mondadori, 2012).

10 Specifically in regard to Masaniello's lunacy and its causes see Aurelio Musi, *La rivolta di Masaniello nella scena politica barocca* (Naples: Guida Editori, 1989).

11 I will not analyze here the historiographical controversy surrounding the role of Genoino in the rebellion. A frequent and prominent character in the majority of contemporary chronicles, often heralded as the real mastermind behind Masaniello's action, recent historiography casted doubts on this interpretation. See Nicola Napolitano, *Masaniello e Genoino. Mito e coscienza di una rivolta* (Naples: Fausto Fiorentino Editore, 1962); Neil Ritchie, 'Genoino, Masaniello and the 1647 Revolution in Naples', *History Today* 30, 6 (1980). pp. 27–32; Villari, *Un sogno di libertà*.

FIGURE 3.1　Micco Spadaro (1609–1675), *La rivolta di Masaniello* (post 1647/1660). Naples, Museo di Capodimonte

Note: Micco Spadaro (1609–1675), was a painter of the Neapolitan baroque. Extremely attuned to the current events, he is the artist that illustrated the majority of pivotal events of the seventeenth century, such as the one here depicting the circumstances that kicked off Masaniello's rebellion in Piazza del Mercato. This is not the only painting that he made during and about the rebellion, but rather the first in a series. He painted a portrait of Masaniello and one of Gennaro Annese, as well as the "Lynching of don Giuseppe Carafa" and the "Punishment of Thieves during Masaniello's reign". With the same emotional impact and attention to detail he captured the Vesuvius eruption in 1631 as well as the tragedy of the plague epidemic of 1656. Known for his masterful use of color and its propensity for not shying away from the more macabre aspects of life, Spadaro's paintings offer us an extremely realistic and vivid account of what was happening during the more arrowing events of the seventeenth century, effectively communicating the misery, violence and frenzy that these circumstances generated. For an in-depht analysis of history painting in Naples see: Wendy Wassyng Roworth, 'The Evolution of History Painting: Masaniello's Revolt and Other Disasters in Seventeenth-Century Naples', *The Art Bulletin* 75, 2 (1993), pp. 219–234.

pro-French sentiments in the nineteenth century. This canonised a perception of Masaniello as a martyr for freedom from the oppressor as well as a true patriot and champion of Neapolitan independence. This role, in reality, should be attributed to Gennaro Annese, who took on the leadership of the rebellion after Masaniello's death and who turned it into an anti-Spanish revolution.

He was the one who can be credited for driving the Spaniards out of the city after months of violent fighting as well as for the foundation of the Neapolitan Republic under the French tutelage on 22 October 1647. Particularly after Juan José de Austria fired upon Naples from the ships that were stationed in the Gulf of Naples, he was the one who took it upon himself to write to both the Pope and the French Duke of Guise asking for their aid and protection against the Spaniards.

There is one thing on which every chronicle and every historian agree: during the days of the revolt, the printing presses were extremely busy. Between the official proclamations and the countless anonymous broadsheets and pamphlets, a significant amount of popular print was published, but unlike what happened with publications regarding the eruption of Vesuvius in 1631, the majority of which survived to this day, as we will see in the next chapter, the same cannot be said for documents concerning the rebellion.

Very few of the printed materials that were produced during Masaniello's rebellion survive today, both because of their heavily political and potentially controversial messages and because of the turbulent and frantic nature of the days of the rebellion. This is somewhat opposite to what happened in regards to sources from other famous European rebellions, such as for example the Dutch Revolt or the French Revolution, where people were very aware of the importance of what was happening around them and for this reason, they strived to get their hands on and preserve as much as possible of what was printed on the subject. The majority of what we know of the events of the rebellion and the brief experience of the Neapolitan republic come from manuscripts, written mainly during the seventeenth century and heavily influenced by the personal political view of the writers. While many of them were published anonymously, it is immediately clear whether the author is a Spanish supporter, quick to dismiss the rebellion as nothing more than the misguided action of poor people wrongfully stirred by traitorous noblemen, or a French sympathizer, praising Masaniello as a martyr for freedom. Even the few printed items published once the dust settled follow this same scheme. This is hardly a surprise. In the case of an event as disruptive as a revolution, one that overturned the status quo, it is incredibly difficult to find unbiased narratives.

There is one surprising exception to the general lack of contemporary documents in regard to Masaniello's rebellion: the printed broadsheets and proclamations. In contrast to their general low survival rate, the number of broadsheets and proclamations printed between 1647 and 1648 that survive today is incredibly high: for the timespan between October 1647 and April 1648, the period of the Neapolitan Republic, we have no fewer than 250 surviving proclamations, the majority of which can be found in the Library of the convent of San Martino, which now forms part of the collections of the National Library of Naples, and in the Library of the Società di Storia Patria.[12]

The relationship between print and manuscript is especially relevant in the context of Masaniello's rebellion. Comparing the sources available from the days of the revolt with the sources produced during other times of crisis during the seventeenth century, specifically the eruption of Vesuvius of 1631 and the plague epidemic of 1656, demonstrates immediately a huge difference in the type and quantities of printed materials available. In both these instances, we have many sources, written and printed while the events were unfolding.[13] People felt the need to publish their versions of what was happening, their explanations, their suggestions and possible solutions. For the eruption of Vesuvius, we have hundreds of pamphlets. The documents available about the plague, while fewer in quantity, are still varied enough in nature, with pamphlets, broadsheets, laws and chronicles, all of which will be discussed at length in the next chapter. Masaniello's rebellion, taking place squarely in the middle of these two other calamitous events, offers a much narrower range of sources. Glaring and obvious is the lack of narratives of the event written while it was taking place. But is this shortage due to the natural passing of the centuries and the general state of Neapolitan archives or by design?

When it comes to narrating natural calamities, it is easy to recount what was happening, and although political and religious explanations were abundant, it is still possible to write an impersonal, objective rendition of the facts. Writing about a revolution while it was happening is an entirely different matter. Because of the nature of the event itself, there is no such thing as an impartial account. Writers either supported the revolution and therefore were pro-French and against the Spanish government, or were firmly against it, steadfast in their support of the legitimate authorities and firm in their condemnation of the rebels and the French government. It is not unreasonable to suggest, then, that given the already tense political and social climate, particular attention was paid to what was printed and circulated in the streets of Naples. When the rebels succeeded in their goals of ridding themselves of the Spanish government and pledging their allegiance to the French, the last thing they would have wanted was to have pro-Spanish publications spread freely throughout the city. Likewise, when the brief experience of the Neapolitan

---

12   The proclamations of the Neapolitan Republic are edited in Vittorio Conti, *Le leggi di una rivoluzione. I bandi della Repubblica Napoletana dall'Ottobre 1647 all'aprile 1648* (Naples: Jovene Editore, 1983).

13   For the media landscape of Naples during the revolt see Davide Boerio "News from Naples (1647–1648): communicative Effects, Public Spaces and the Media Landscape." in Caputo (eds), *Tales of two cities.*

PRINT IN TIMES OF CRISIS

Republic came to its inevitable end and the Spaniards regained control of the city, mending the rift and presenting the city as once again united was of the utmost importance, thus the need to ensure that any and all writings supporting the now failed rebellion and disparaging the Spanish crown were kept out of the public eye.

Manuscripts, however, were more difficult to control and censor than printed works.[14] This applies particularly to those manuscripts that were written for personal use, such as diaries, or authors' copies of printed texts. Thus, while printed books and pamphlets written during the time of the rebellion are relatively rare, the same cannot be said for manuscript chronicles.

2   French Propaganda in the Neapolitan Republic

Unlike what we have seen in the previous chapter, the proclamations and broadsheets that were printed in Naples under the control of Gennaro Annese and the Duke of Guise, and in general those printed during the Neapolitan Republic, are all propagandistic in tone. From prosaic everyday provisions for stockpiling gunpowder to heartfelt calls to arms the tone used by the French and the revolutionaries was always political, one more way in which they could emphasise the difference between themselves and the Spaniards. One of the main concerns of the Republican government was to maintain public order. While before the revolution this was done more subtly with ordinances about carrying weapons within the city limits and the use of carriages, war was not a time for delicacy.[15] Already busy enough fighting against the Spanish to maintain control over the Kingdom of Naples, the revolutionary authorities could not afford tension within the city and taking the chance of having to fight on two different fronts, therefore everything that could even remotely be perceived as a threat against public order had to be dealt with immediately. Such is the case, for example, of problems with the administration of public justice, which we can find addressed in two different broadsheets regarding very different circumstances.

Apparently, keeping up with the regular administration of justice amidst the chaos of war was a demanding and difficult task, one rendered even more arduous by the intervention of other interested parties. But a working, efficient

---

14   For a detailed list of the manuscripts about the revolt held in the Neapolitan libraries see: Saverio di Franco, 'Le rivolte del Regno di Napoli del 1647–1648 nei manoscritti napoletani', *Archivio storico per le province napoletane*, 125 (2007), pp. 326–457.

15   See previous chapter.

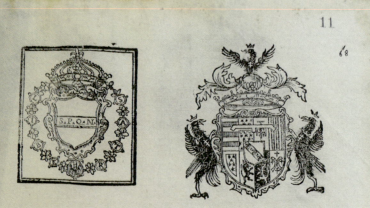

HENRICO DI LORENA
DVCA DI GVISA, CONTE D'EV' PARI DI FRANCIA,&c.
Defensore della Libertà, DVCE della Sereniſſima, e Real Republica
di Napoli, e Generaliſſimo delle ſue Armi.

*BERNARDO SPIRITO V. I. D. Auditor General dell'Eſercito
di queſta Sereniſsima Republica.*

Erche n'è venuto à notitia, che molte Perſone ſotto Nome di Scriuani, vadano per queſta Città, ſuoi Borghi, e Caſali ſenz' ordine alcuno pigliando Informationi delli Delitti, che alla giornata ſuccedeno, & ſenza darne parte à Noi procedeno à far ciò, che li piace concordandonoſi con le parti, occultando la Giuſtitia in diſſeruitio di N. S. Iddio, & graue danno del publico. Perciò volendomo rimediare. Hauemo fatto lo preſente Bando, con lo quale dicemo, & ordinamo, & in nome di S. A. S. comandamo, che neſſuna Perſona di qualſiuoglia ſtato, grado, & conditione ſi ſia da hoggi auanti ſotto pena di falſo,& altra ad arbitrio di S.A.S.ardiſca poner mano à pigliar Informatione di Delitti, che ſuccederanno da Soldati, & in perſona di eſſi, mà quelle ſi debbiano pigliare dalli Scriuani daNoi deputati, & alliſtati per il ſeruitio di queſta Generale Audienza. Et acciò li delitti, che per lo paſſato ſon ſucceduti non reſtino impuniti,ordinamo ſotto la medeſima pena à dette Perſone,che ſi ritrouano hauer pigliato Informatione di quelli,che frà termine de 24. hore doppò la publicatione del Preſente, quello originalmente debbiano portare auanti di Noi acciò ſi poſſino dare li ordini neceſſarij, auertendoli, che eſſendono renitenti ad eſequirlo ſi pigliarà contro di loro Informatione, & ſaranno puniti come falſarij. Datum Neap. die 7. Ianuarij 1648.

Berandrus Spiritus Auditor Generalis Exercitus.

Franciſcus Napolionus Secret

IN NAPOLI, Per Secondino Roncagliolo Stampatore di
queſta Sereniſſima Real Republica 1648.

FIGURE 3.2 Broadsheets by Henry of Lorraine, Duke of Guise, SNSP, ms XXIX.E.2 f.11r Naples, Biblioteca della Società Napoletana di Storia Patria

HENRICO DI LORENA

DVCA DI GVISA, CONTE D'EV', PARI DI FRANCIA, &c.

Difensore della Libertà, DVCE della Sereniſſima, e Real Republica di Napoli, e Generaliſſimo delle ſue Armi.

BERNARDO SPIRITO V. I. D. *Auditer General de tutti l'Eſerciti di queſta Sereniſſima Republica.*

PErche S.A. Sereniſſima del Duca di Guiſa, Duce di queſta Sereniſſima Real Republica mediante publico Banno, hà ordinato, che nel paſſare de noſtri ſoldati alli Quartieri occupati da Spagnoli, non ſi douesſe dare ſacco, ı è altra moleſtia alle caſe, e beni de' Cittadini, et habitanti in eiſi, ſotto pena della vita, et à ſua notitia è peruenuto, ch'alcuni ſoldati, nell'auanzare il Borgo de Chiaia, habbiano pigliate robbe d'alcune caſe di detto Borgo di Chiaia ſotto titolo di beni di ribelli, et con tale occaſione ſiano ſtati danneggiati alcuni Cittadini, et habitanti in detto Borgo; S. A. S. per rimediare à tali diſordini, ha inuiato Noi, perche vſando il condegno caſtigo contro de detti ſoldati, che hanno fatto tal contrauentione, procuraſſimo per ogni mezo poſſibile la recuperatione di detti beni per quelli reſtituire alli veri padroni. Perciò ſtante che in poter noſtro ſono ſtati eſibiti, tutti argenti, gioie, denari, et beni mobili preſi in detta occaſione, dopò d'hauermo vſato il douuto rigore della giuſtitia contro li delinquenti; per il preſente Banno, ordinamo à tutte, e qualſiuoglia perſone le quali in detta occaſione del ſudetto Borgo di Chiaia; haueſſero perſe, denari, gioie, argenti, mobili, et qualſiuoglia altra coſa, frà il termine de quattro giorni, debbiano comparire auanti di Noi, ò vero in qualſiuoglia meglior modo, farci nota la perdita di dette loro robbe, à fine, che precedente legitima recognitione ſe le poſſa fare la douuta reſtitutione di eſſi, altrimente elaſſo detto termine, s'intendano tutte dette robbe incorporate à beneficio di queſta Sereniſſima Real Republica, come beni de ribelli, et acciò venga à notitia de tutti, ordinamo il preſente Banno ſe publichi per tutto detto Borgo di Chiaia, et altri luochi ſoliti. Datum nella noſtra Reſidentia della Generale Audienza. Nel Vomaro li 18. di Gennaro 1648.

Bernardus Spiritus Auditor Generalis totius Exercitus.
Vidit Salonus Fiſcus.   Franciſcus Napolionus eſt Secr.

In Nap. Per Secondino Roncagliolo, e riſtampato nella Stampa del Nucci. 1648.

FIGURE 3.3 Broadsheets by Henry of Lorraine, Duke of Guise, SNSP, ms XXIX.E.2 f.24r. Naples, Biblioteca della Società Napoletana di Storia Patria

100   CHAPTER 3

justice system was an indicator of strong leadership, and the French authorities were determined to ensure that things ran smoothly. The broadsheet was designed to put an end to undue interferences in cases of criminal proceedings.

> It has come to our knowledge that many people who present themselves as scribes roam this city, its districts and suburbs without any authority, gathering information about the crimes that are committed every day and, without asking our permission, doing whatever they want, agreeing with the parties, concealing Justice against God's law and causing harm to the community. Wishing to rectify this situation, we have issued this ban by which we affirm, order and, in the name of His Most Serene Highness, command that from this day no one of any class, rank or condition, on penalty of being equated with those accused of perjury and condemned to the corresponding punishments and all those established at the discretion of His Most Serene Highness, may collect from the soldiers (or from those on their behalf) information concerning the crimes committed since such information must be collected by the scribes deputed and enlisted by us for this purpose in the service of this Generale Audienza. And in order that the crimes committed in the past may not go unpunished, we hereby order under the same penalties those persons who have gathered information in this regard to present themselves before us within 24 hours of the publication of this ban and deliver [said information] into our hands, so that justice may be properly administered. We hereby also warn them that, should they fail to comply with this order, they will be prosecuted and condemned as forgers [as in, because they are spreading false information]. Promulgated in Naples on 7 January 1648.[16]

---

16   "Perchè n'è venuto a notizia, che molte persone sotto nome di scrivani, vadano per questa Città, suoi Borghi, e Casali senz'ordine alcuno pigliando informationi delli Delitti che alla giornata succedono & senza darne parere a Noi procedono a far ciò che li piace concordandosene con le parti, occultando la Giustizia in disservizio di N.S. Iddio, & grave danno del pubblico. Perciò volendomo rimediare Havemo fatto lo presente Bando con lo quale dicemo & ordinamo, & in nome di S.A.S. comandamo che nessuna Persona di qualsivoglia stato, grado & conditione si sia da hoggi avanti sotto pena di falso & altra ad arbitrio di S.A.S. ardisca poner mano à pigliar le informationi di Delitti che siccederanno da Soldati, & in persona di essi, ma quelli si debbano pigliare dalli Scrivani da Noi deputati & allistati per i servizi di questa Generale Audienza. Et acciò li delitti, che per lo passato sono succeduti non restino impuniti, ordinamo sotto la medesima pena à dette Persone che si ritrovano haver pigliato Informationi di quelli, che fra termine de 24 hore dopo la pubblicazione del Presente, quello originalmente debbano portare avanti di Noi, acciò si possino dare li ordini necesari, avvertendoli, che essendono renitenti ad esequirlo

PRINT IN TIMES OF CRISIS   101

The second broadsheet is very different. At the beginning of January 1648, the neighbourhood of Chiaia, a notoriously Spanish one, was ransacked by soldiers of the Republic, who were later accused of having robbed homes and possessions of innocent citizens under the guise of seizing rebel properties. The French authorities intervened with a proclamation, primarily affixed in the affected neighbourhood, offering apologies and four days to reclaim possession of the stolen goods, before they became the official property of the Republic.

> His Most Serene Highness the Duke of Guise, commander of this Most Serene Royal Republic, has issued a public proclamation ordering our soldiers not to plunder or otherwise damage the houses and property of citizens and inhabitants when they cross the districts occupied by the Spaniards, on penalty of death. However, [His Highness] has received news that some soldiers, advancing through the Chiaia neighbourhood, have taken possession of goods present in some houses of the said neighbourhood, believing them to belong to rebels, and that, on this occasion, damages have been caused to some citizens and inhabitants of the said neighbourhood. His Most Serene Highness, in order to remedy these disorders, has instructed us [i.e. Bernardo Spirito] to administer a suitable punishment against the soldiers who have transgressed orders, and to do everything possible to recover this property and return it to the rightful owners. Therefore, since we have regained possession of all the silver, jewels, money and movables lost on this occasion (after having exercised the rigour of justice against the offenders), we hereby order anyone in the Chiaia neighbourhood who has lost money, jewels, silver, furniture or anything else on the said occasion, to come before us or to give us notice of the loss of their property within four days, so that, after due investigation, we may proceed with the restitution. At the end of this period, ownership of the said goods shall automatically pass to the Most Serene Royal Republic as goods belonging to rebels. In order that these provisions may be known to all, we order that this ban be posted throughout the Chiaia neighbourhood and in the usual places. Promulgated in the Residency of the Generale Audienza in the Vomero neighbourhood on 18 January 1648.[17]

---

si piglirà contro fi loto Informatione e saranno punit come falsari. Datum Neap. Die 7 Ianuarij 1648" SNSP, ms XXIX.E.2 f.11.

17   "Perchè S.A.S del Duca di Guise, Duce di questa Serenissima Real Repubblica mediante pubblico Banno ha ordinato che nel passare de nostri Soldati alli Quartieri occupati dalli Spagnoli no si dovesse dare sacco, né altra molestia alle case e beni de Cittadini & habitanti in essi sotto pena della vita & a sua notizia è perveuto ch'alcuni soldati, nell'avanzare

102   CHAPTER 3

This second proclamation has a slightly different tone because besides chastising the perpetrators of these unauthorised actions and explicitly addressing them as soldiers, it also raised the issue of the plunder being perpetrated for personal gain rather than to aid the cause of the Republic. The proposed solution was to require soldiers to notify Vincenzo d'Andrea, a functionary within the palace of justice, of any suspected enemy of the Republic. The government could then proceed to seize the incriminated properties and recompense the notifying soldier with a fourth of them, rather than subject him to a fine and possible jail time for carrying on unauthorised raids.

Besides the broadsheets and proclamations, an extremely vivid source for the political propaganda during Masaniello's revolt is offered by the countless pamphlets, both printed and manuscript, that could be found in the streets of Naples, alternatively advocating for the French or the Spaniards and listing all the horrific and dishonourable actions carried on by their opponent.

It is particularly interesting to note that these two seemingly separate media were in reality not separate at all. The ideas and arguments that were present in the pamphlets were echoed in the official broadsheets, and not only that but the pamphlets were explicitly mentioned in the broadsheets, proving that the same propagandistic effort, if not the same people, were behind both. This is demonstrated by a little edict issued by the Duke of Guise on 3 February 1648, addressing the state of the war in general. Echoing the argument that they came to Naples moved only by a desire to help, a common response to the even

---

il Borgo di Chiaia, habbiano pigliate robbe d'alcune case di detto Borgo di Chiaia, sotto titolo di beni di Ribelli & con tale occasione siano stati danneggiati alcuni Cittadini & habitanti di detto borgo; S.A.S per rimediare a tali disordini, ha inviato Noi, perché usando il condegno castigo contro de detti soldati, che hano fatta tal contravvenzione, procurassimo per ogni mezzo possibile la recuperazione di detti beni per quelli restituire alli veri padroni. Perciò stante che in poter nostro sono stati esibiti tuti argenti, gioie, denari & beni mobili persi in detta occasione, dopo d'havermo usato il dovuto rigore della giustizia contro li delinquenti, con il presente Banno ordinamo a tute e qualsivoglia persone le quali in detta occasione del suddetto Borgo di Chiaia havessero perso denari, gioie, argenti, mobili & qualsivoglia altra cosa, frà il termine di quattro giorni debbano comparire avanti di Noi ovvero in qualsivoglia modo farci nota la perdita di dette loro robbe à fine che precedente legittima recognitione se possa fare la dovuta restitutione di essi. Altimenti elasso detto termine, s'intendano tutte dette robbe incorporate a beneficio di questa Serenisima Real Repubblica, come beni di Ribelli, & acciò venga a notizia de tutti ordiniamo il presente Banno se pubblichi per tutto detto Borgo di Chiaia & altri luoghi soliti. Datum nella nostra Residentia della Generale Audienza nel Vomero li 18 di Gennaro 1648" SNSP, ms XXIX.E.2 f.24. A proclamation with the same exact text and imprimatur but with a different layout and characters can be find at ibid f.25. The problem of unauthorized raid against so called rebel properties was not a new one and it is addressed in various broadsheets, see for example SNSP, XXVI.C.1 f.95 and 96; SNSP, XXIX.E.1 f.94.

PRINT IN TIMES OF CRISIS

more common accusation flung by the Spanish of the French being moved only by greed and their hunger for power, the Duke of Guise expressed anguish and regret that it was necessary to use deadly force while administering justice. The blame for it should be laid squarely on the Spaniards, guilty of deceiving the good people of Naples with falsehoods and empty promises. But now was not the time to be led on by them, but rather the time to rally and rid the Republic of the Spanish plague once and for all.

> We have declared through all printed works that our coming here was prompted solely by the genuine desire to give up our blood and our life in the service of these most faithful people and the Serenissima Real Repubblica and in doing so doing good for everybody. We are pleased to believe that our actions up to this day have served to prove our intentions.
>
> This all means that we exercise the hard duty of the law with a heavy heart. We cannot comprehend how some can be tempted by the empty promises of the Spaniards to act against their own home, against everything that we have accomplished in the service of the freedom of this Serenissima Real Repubblica and even the freedom of the whole of Italy. How [are they tempted] to act against themselves, their houses, their relatives and friends when have we not already discovered the frauds of the Spaniards? They, who can count as their greatest gift deceit? They, who do not know the concept of loyalty nor what it means to hold true to their word; they who have destroyed this kingdom in ways big and small and they have always done so, even when the entire world was watching them while they were at the height of their fortune? Now is the time for them to pay the price, now that they are weak and losing everywhere, now that they are losing even the Kingdoms in their own empire and there is nothing they can do. They can do what they want, lie to their hearts' content because the Heavens are fighting with us and we, made strong by this most glorious and miraculous assistance, will laugh at the futility of their deceit while crying, with bloodied tears for those poor fools that believed them and for this were hanged. From our palace, on 3 February 1648.[18]

---

18   "Habbiamo pubblicato sù tutte le Stampe non haver havuto il venir nostro altro fine, che quello di spargere generoso la vita el sangue in servitio di questo Fidelissimo Popolo, e Serenissima Real Repubblica, ed insieme di giovare a tutti indifferentemente. Ci giova anche di credere haver fin hora le nostre ationi corroborata la rettitudine di questa intentione. Confessiamo anche di più quel desiderio di sempre beneficare purchè si possa essere puro prorito del Genio habituato per tutti gl'anni dell'età nostra. Tutto ciò vuol dire, che esercitiamo li rigori della giustizia con una ripuglianza non mai la maggiore. Né

104   CHAPTER 3

Once again a broadsheet that deals primarily with concerns of public order,
this echoes the tone and grandiloquence of various other calls to arms printed
during the revolutionary period, even before the French actually arrived in
Naples.[19] It is of course impossible to be able to affirm with any certainty to
which writings the Duke of Guise was referring, or even if he was referring to
a particular one or was talking more in the general sense. This does not mean
that we lack possible candidates, rather the opposite is true. The argument that
the French were prompted to take action in the Neapolitan revolt because of
a love for freedom and a genuine desire to help it is the one most frequently
used in French propaganda. As we have seen in the previous chapter, slanderous writing and publications were not a novelty in the contest between
French and Spaniards, but their frequency increased to an all-time high during Masaniello's revolt. *Manifesta il Re Christianissimo* was a pretty common
title for many pamphlets printed in favour of the French, while *Risposta del
Fedelissimo Popolo Napoletano* was the preferred title for the equally popular
answer provided by the Spaniards.

    Although with minor differences in length, tone, address and content, the
central argument of every pro-French pamphlet was the same, whether they
were printed in Naples or Paris. The French protested repeatedly that they
only intervened in other countries' conflicts to aid their respective legitimate
government, and were never prompted by greed or the urge to expand their
own domain; in Italy, they view themselves as the last defence against the
Spanish tyrant and that was the only reason why they decided to intervene in

---

        sappiamo perché alcuni si lascino ingannare dalla vanità delle promesse Spagnole contro
        la propria Patria, contro quello che tanto compie al buon servitio della libertà di questa
        Serenissima Real Repubblica, anzi della Libertà d'Italia tutta, contro se stessi, contro le
        proprie Case, Parenti e amici e forsi non si sono scoperte le frodi de Spagnoli? Quelli, che
        vantano di loro gran requisito l'inganno? Quelli, che non intendono ciò che sia fede, non
        che ciò che importi la fede data, quelli che hanno scortitcato il Regno in generale e in par-
        ticolare e che l'hanno sempre fatto, mentre che il Mondo gli'osservava al sommo delle loro
        fortune? Si faccia la conseguenza, per li tempi presenti, mentre si vedono ridotti ad un
        estremo di debolezza, che perdono da per tutto, che perdono i Regni in casa propria senza
        poter dare segno né meno di risentimento, ma facciono quanto fanno, ingannino quanto
        possono, che il Cielo combatte per Noi, e Noi sempre vigorosi sotto l'auspici felicissimi di
        questa miracolosa assistenza, ci rideremo della leggierezza de loro Arteficii e piangeremo
        questo sì con lagrime di sangue quei meschinelli ingannati che si fanno impiccare. Dal
        nostro Palazzo, li 3 Febbraro 1648" SNSP, ms XXIX.E.2 f.37. Other Fench calls to arms can
        be found in the same volume at f.7, f.36.

19   For example, a proclamation issued by the Duke of Guise promising his imminent
        arrive in the city which, according to Donzelli prompted a new wave of propaganda and
        attempted bribery to take place in the Spanish quarters in order to sway the inhabitants
        to the French cause. BNN, bib. San Mart. 69 f.186, 187.

PRINT IN TIMES OF CRISIS

the Neapolitan rebellion, to free the good Neapolitan people from the slavery in which they were kept by the Spaniards and make them free to choose their own king or government.[20]

The explicit connection between the proclamations and the pamphlets provided evidence of a cohesive and coordinated propagandistic effort; indeed, one gets the impression that the French authorities were greatly invested in this, perhaps even as much as in the actual war effort. Further proof of a keen understanding of the role of popular print as a political and propagandistic tool can be found in the efforts directed to control these particular media. When talking about strategies to control printing the first thing that always comes to mind is censorship. We have seen in the previous chapters that both state and church censorship existed in Naples during these times but that it was not always efficient. The laws and regulations in regards to print were definitely still in place during the time of the rebellion and subsequent Republic, as is evidenced by the double imprimatur for Donzelli's work as well as several proclamations granting different kinds of printing privileges to various printers.[21] We lack any kind of documentary evidence in regards to the practice of censorship during these times, so it is impossible to say whether it was effective or not, with the exception of a proclamation specifically addressing what censorship regulation would be put in place in the Republic.[22] The proclamation from 15 November 1647 is straightforward in its provision: it once again declared that every printer needed to obtain permission from the specific office before printing anything 'even just one page'; it specified the subsequent pecuniary penalty for those who refused to abide by this rule. What I find to be extremely interesting, however, is the introduction that precedes the actual provisions, because it emphasised how aware the authorities were of the importance of the printed word, specifically how it could be used to spread false information.

---

20 There are many pamphlets making the same arguments, including [Maffei], *Manifesta il Re cristianissimo le ragioni dell'armi sue incaminate nel regno di Napoli.* Paris, per Pietro Rocoler stampatore, [1648]. USTC 6005897.

21 See for example the privilege granted to Lorenzo Gaffaro to print every broadsheet and proclamation [Duke of Guise], *Si ordina con il presente et espressamente comanda ...* (Naples: per Lorenzo Gaffaro stampatore di S.A. Serenissima, 1648). BNN, ms. XV.D.36 (54).

22 The section of the State Archive containing the majority of documents dealing with censorship and permissions issued to printers was destroyed during World Word Two. As far as ecclesiastical censorship is concerned, a manuscript catalogue of the *Fondo Sant'Uffizio, Congregazione Libri Proibiti* available at the Archivio Storico Diocesano shows the presence of documents from the years of the rebellion, but access to these is currently not permitted due to their state of conservation.

In order to avoid all sorts of problems that can be caused by print, both against God and against these most Faithful People, given that many things are printed without our knowledge, and without the name of the printer, or the place or the date in which these are printed; given that [those who do this] do not care about the penalty of 1,000 ducats to be paid [for this offence] nor about the forfeiture of the print run, given that some put on their publications the name of other printers; given that others re-print already published books, and in their doing so they add or remove something, changing the meaning of the works; given that all of this can in the future cause great heartaches to these most Faithful People because of the trickery and ill-will of their enemies; given that we know the importance of the printed words and the credibility that these have with the world. In order to avoid all that we have said before shall come to pass, we decided to issue the following proclamation.[23]

Furthermore, we have proof of a marked and decisive interest from the authorities in monitoring what circulated on the streets of Naples, given that this specific topic is addressed in two different broadsheets, one dated 11 September 1647 and one from 23 November of the same year.

Francesco Antonio Arpaia *Eletto* of the Most Faithful People of Naples.
    In these days placards have been found in some districts of this most faithful city, affixed by some sons of iniquity to continue fomenting tumults and clashes and disturbing the general peace. Therefore, we proclaim and order that whoever will deliver us one of the culprits, in whatever state and condition they may be [i.e. dead or alive], will be given a reward of two thousand ducats. Similarly, a pardon and a two thousand ducats reward will be granted to persons already tried and judged, and to

---

23   "Per obviare a gl'inconvenienti, che dalle stampe possono soccedere, in disservitio di Dio, e di questo Fidelissimo Popolo, stante, che si stampano molte cose senza nostra saputa, e senza porvi il nome del Stampatore, né il luogo dove è stata stampata, né la data del millesimo, non curandosi delle pene per il passato imposte di docati mille, e perdita delle stampe, e così anco altri pongono il nome di Stampatore forastiero, et altri ristampano, e col ristampare accrescono, e diinuiscono parole, o dittione, che puole mutar senso, i contraria intelligenza, il che può apportare, in futurum, qualche danno, secondo l'intelligenza delli inimici, e mal'affetti di questo Fidelissimo Popolo. Però considerando Noi di quant'importanza siano le cose stampate, e di quanta credenza appresso il Mondo tutto; et acciò non si caschi per l'avvenire nelle cose suddette, ci è parso di fare il presente Banno" [Gennaro Annese], *Per obviare a gl'inconvenienti ....* (Naples: per Secondino Roncagliolo Stampatore di questo Fidelissimo Popolo, 15 Novembre 1647). BNN, ms. XV.D.36 (59).

PRINT IN TIMES OF CRISIS

accomplices, but not to the principal perpetrator. Promulgated in Naples, 11 September 1647.[24]

Gennaro Annese *Generalissimo* of the Most Faithful People and the Kingdom of Naples.

Some daredevils have had the temerity to affix placards in which our officers and other persons are slandered in order to disturb and undermine the efforts made for the common freedom and peace recently obtained. By such means, orchestrated by our enemies, attempts are being made to create havoc among the most faithful people. Therefore, we proclaim and pledge our word that a reward of two hundred ducats will be granted to any person who, upon verification of guilt, turns over to us the person guilty of creating and affixing the said placards. We also promise and give assurance that the accomplices of this crime will be granted a pardon [should they hand over the main perpetrator].

Naples, 23 November 1647.

To be printed and published by our printer.[25]

---

24 "Francesco Antonio Arpaia Eletto del Fidelissimo Popolo di Napoli.

Perché in questi giorni si sono ritrovati alcuni Cartelli affissi in alcuni Quartieri di questa Fidelissima Città, il tutto solamente operato d'alcuni fifli d'iniquità, per mantenere li tumulti & turbolentie, & inquietare la commune Pace; per tanto Noi vi diciamo, & ordiniamo, che qualunque persona, che ci darà in mano uno di questi tali di qualsivoglia stato, grado e conditione si siano, se li daranno di taglione docati duemilia; del che se ne possa similmente indultare qualsivoglia persona etiam sorgiudicati di sentenza, e tutti quelli che si fussero ritrovati l concerto, eccettuatene però il principale, à quali se li daranno similmente li sopradetti docati due milia di taglione. Datum Neap. Die 11 Septembris 1647."

[Francesco Arpaia], *Francesco Antonio Arpaia Eletto* (Naples: per Secondino Roncagliolo Stampatore di questo Fidelissimo Popolo, 1647) SNSP, MS. XXIX.E.1 f.64.

25 "Gennaro Annese Generalissimo di questo Fideliss. Popolo e Regno di Napoli.

Perché alcuni temerarij hanno preso ardire affiggere Cartelli, dicendo male di Nostri Officiali, et altre persone. Il tutto per intorbidare l'impresa per la commune libertà, e quiete incominciata, cercando con questi mezzi machinati da nemici mettere disturbo fra il Fidelissimo Popolo; per tanto dicemo, e promettemo sotto la nostra parola dare docati ducento a qualsivoglia persona, che verificherà, e darà in mano nostra la persona di quello, che haverà fatti, et affissi detti Cartelli, promettendo anco indulto ad uno delli complici di tal delitto, assicurandoli della osservanza.

Nap. li 23 Novembre 1647.

Si stampi e si pubblichi per il nostro stampatore."

[Gennaro Annese], *Gennaro Annese Generalissimo di questo Fideliss. Popolo e Regno di Napoli* (Naples: per Secondino Roncagliolo Stampatore della Sereniss. Real Republica di Napoli, 1647) SNSP, MS. XXIX.E.1 f.130.

The importance of these documents is twofold. They prove the existence of voices of discontent that found their space in public places and also acknowledge the difficulties that the authorities had in dealing with this phenomenon and controlling it. It is particularly interesting to note that I have not found anything similar from the pre-revolutionary time. This does not mean that there were no contrary opinions toward the Spanish authorities, but rather that in their effort to present a strong face to the world, they declined to acknowledge them publicly. Furthermore, both of these documents are from the very early days of the Republic when strict control over public opinion was absolutely necessary, but the authority to enforce such control was not yet sufficiently strong, thus the need to acknowledge the seditious writings and try to inhibit them in a different way. With the passing of time and the strengthening of the Neapolitan Republic, these kinds of responses became less necessary, while different concerns in regard to public order rose to the forefront of public communications.[26] Unfortunately, the exact nature and content of these seditious fliers are unknown to us, given that none have survived. Official provisions such as the two mentioned above, however, can serve as proof of the existence of such publications, and presumably of the intensity and frequency of the phenomenon given that the authorities felt the need to address it.

Moreover, they serve as proof of a deep understanding of the enormous psychological impact of the printed word on the mind of the people. Printed broadsheets were viewed as something official, with wide dissemination, something that demonstrated the force and control of the government over its citizens. This is why the Neapolitan Republic produced as many printed proclamations as possible, in a show of force and control that went beyond what was evident in practice; the proliferation of proclamations, and their high visibility, was a tangible demonstration of the strength of the regime. This is also the reason why even the opposing faction, which would have been smarter to rely on the more elusive and untraceable word of mouth, chose to take on the risk of discovery by making their presence known in a more impactful way, through printed and posted documents. The fact that this particular kind of document does not survive does not signify a lack of evidence advocating for the Spanish cause.

---

26   The concern for seditious print became once again subject of a proclamation toward the end of the Neapolitan Republic. With the Spanish troops gaining ground and the aggravated military conflict, maintaining a strong control over the circulation of news within the city of Naples became once again a primary concern. See [Duke of Guise], *Conoscendosi, che in qualche cattivo spirito ...* (Naples: per Lorenzo Gaffaro Stampatore di S.A. Serenissima, 3 March 1648). SNSP, ms XXIX.E.2(49).

PRINT IN TIMES OF CRISIS

3   The Pamphlet War

As we have seen through the broadsheets threatening retribution, the Spaniards were not silent spectators during the revolt and its aftermath. To every volley launched by the French, they responded with one of their own both in the military conflict and in the pamphlet war. Even before the rebellion, both French and Spaniards did not pull back when it came to trying to sway public opinion in their favour. Already in 1636, we can find libels printed about the Franco-Spanish war, the only purpose of which is to present the adversary in the worst possible light, and themselves as saviours. In a miscellany in the National Library of Naples, we can find two examples of these sorts of publications. In 1636 Egidio Longo published a *Manifesto delle giustificate ationi della corona di Spagna*.[27] It is a small treatise first published in Spain and later in the same year translated into Italian and printed in Naples. With the official declaration of war between France and Spain the previous year and the economic efforts that the war demanded, it should not come as a surprise that the Spanish authorities put some effort into painting the conflict as something inevitable, and the French as power-hungry conquerors drove by greed and the selfish will to gain more territories and riches. This is the core of the Spanish argument, and it is presented in various ways through all the pamphlets, broadsheets and libels addressing the Franco-Spanish conflict. In this same collection, the second pamphlet represents the French side.[28] Under the guise of expressing his faithfulness and respect for the French king, the anonymous author puts together a defence of the action of the French, based on the same arguments that we have seen before: a love for freedom and the genuine desire to help others.

Observing these two publications side by side, one thing is immediately clear. The intended readership is vastly different. The Spaniards wrote mainly to their own people and were more focused on slandering their enemy. Particularly when addressing their own subjects, the messages could not be any clearer: you know us, you love us, we do not need to waste time in telling you how good we are but rather we will prove it to you through our actions, and defending you from a vile enemy. The French, for their part, did not address their own people but rather their enemy's subjects; while we see the occasional

---

27   [Anon.], *Manifesto delle giustificate ationi della corona di Spagna, e delle violenze della corona di Francia. Tradotto dalla lingua castigliana all'italiano* (Naples: per Egidio Longo stampatore regio, 1636); BNN 26.D.21.3 USTC 4011105.

28   [Anon.], *Discorso sincerissimo fatto da un'umile e affettuoso servitore della Corona di Francia al (per se stesso) Pio, Giusto, Magnanimo e Cristianissimo Ludovico XIII re di Francia* (Macerata and Naples: s.n., 1636); BNN 26.D.21.4 USTC 4011106.

reference to the adversary's faults, the main focus of their agenda is to present themselves in a favourable light, thus hoping to convince their intended audience to switch side. Once again, the subtext is clear: you do not need us to tell you how bad the Spaniards are, as their subjects, you already know; we are simply reminding you of this, while simultaneously reassuring you of our good and pure intentions.

With the progression of the conflict between the two nations, instances and references to pamphlets and manifestos printed in France and posted in Naples, urging the city to rebel against the Spaniards, became more and more frequent, as did the subsequent Spanish responses. The high point of this pamphlet war was of course during the period of Masaniello's rebellion and the Neapolitan Republic. This is one other instance in which the relationship between print and manuscript became manifest. Printed copies of the broadsheets posted in Naples by French agents rarely survive, but manuscript copies can be found in the collection of the National Library, particularly in the collection from the Library of St Martino.[29]

In this manifesto, the French king addressed the people of Naples, stating that he heard their pleas for help and that he will answer, sending his soldiers under the command of the Duke of Guise to help them rid themselves of the unbearable tyranny of the Spaniards. On the following page, the same hand diligently copied a pro-Spanish answer of the Neapolitan people. Once again, this was the transcription of a broadsheet that was plastered throughout the city of Naples. As we have already mentioned, there are several publications titled *Risposta del Fidelissimo Popolo*, and all are fairly similar in their content.[30] In this, the Neapolitans reiterated their unwavering allegiance to the Spanish crown and firmly rebuffed any offer of help from the French, stating that they did not need it and that in any case, any help that was brought to them by the French only caused them grief and trouble in the past.

Even once the particular episode of the Neapolitan Republic reached its conclusion and the ongoing war came to a temporary resolution (in 1648 the French became more preoccupied with their internal problem and the Fronde, to the great delight of the Spaniards, who published a detailed account of these events), the slanderous publications continued on both sides.[31] We can find

---

29   [Anon], *Manifetso ritrovato di mattina affiso in una piazza di Napoli stampato in Aix et risposta* (1648) BNN, Bib. San Martino, ms 253 (ex 244).

30   The most likely candidate is [Anon.], *Risposta al manifesto del Christianissimo Re di Francia, nel quale espone le ragioni dell'armi sue incamminate al Regno di Napoli, impresso in Parigi a 26 Aprile 1648* (Naples: per Domenico Maccaramo, 1648); USTC 4020306.

31   [Anon.], *Relatione del tumulto seditioso di Parigi e regno di Francia. Principiato nel mese di Maggio 1648* (Naples: per Egidio Longo stampatore regio, 1649) BNN, SQ.25.K.44.(8), USTC

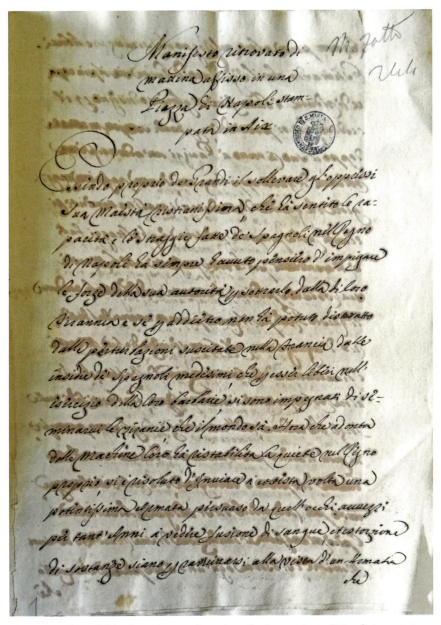

FIGURE 3.4 [Anon], *Manifetso ritrovato di mattina affiso in una piazza di Napoli stampato in Aix et risposta* (1648). BNN, Bib. San Martino, ms 253 (ex 244). Naples, Biblioteca Nazionale

references to these types of publications as late as 1685, for example, when this situation was addressed in the newspaper.[32] The main preoccupation of the *gazette* was to address the spread of false news by the French, as we have seen in the previous chapter, but it is nonetheless worth mentioning that, despite the newspapers being printed forty years later than the pamphlets discussed up until now, the arguments offered by both parties employed the same communication strategy.

4 The Spanish Side of the Argument

When the Neapolitan Republic came to an end and the Spaniards regained control over the Kingdom of Naples things quickly got back to how they used to be. It is particularly interesting that, even before they actually won the war, we can find various different broadsheets promising grace and forgiveness to those who fought for the rebellion and the Republic.

On 31 January 1648, Juan José de Austria wrote a defence, printed and distributed in Naples in the same month by Francesco Antonio Orlandi, in which he promised not to exact vengeance nor punish the people of Naples for the damage done while fighting for the Republic.[33] The broadsheet of the Duke of Guise in which he issued his warning against those who were gullible enough to fall for the promises of the Spaniards was published only three days after this, proving that despite the city being under French control, the Spaniards still had ways to ensure that their own broadsheets and proclamations reached a wide audience.

It is worth mentioning that the tone of every communication addressed from the Spaniards to the Neapolitan citizens is never one of reprimand, but rather extremely paternalistic, almost as one of a father speaking to a child. The rebellion is almost seen as a tantrum, and the main focus is the treason that the people committed allying with the French, but even in this circumstance, they will be the ones who will regret this, because they were now slaves to French tyranny.[34] The same paternalistic tone and communication

---

4019539 . In this same volume can also be found four other pamphlets written in reply to French seditious broadsheets.

32   [Domenico Antonio Parrino], *Gazzette di Napoli* (Naples: Per Domenico Antonio Parrino, 17 Settembre 1686). SNSP, S.G.B.1 particulalry vols. 1 and 2.

33   [Giovanni D'Austria], *Il Baronaggio, e nobiltà di questa Città* ... (Naples: per Francesco Antonio Orlandi stampatore Regio, 1648). SNSP, ms. XXIX.E.2 (45), USTC 4047356.

34   [Anon], *Avvertimenti al popolo di Napoli per la chiamata del Francese* SNSP, MS XX.C.24.

PRINT IN TIMES OF CRISIS

strategy can be found in the broadsheets issuing the royal pardon, once the rebellion ended

> [Taking into consideration] the swiftness with which these Most Faithful People returned to their due obedience, & the love and care that they always showed in the service of His Majesty, giving up their own blood and possessions to help him keep His Royal Crown; taking into consideration that the riots and uprising that recently came to pass were brought about by the action of malicious people, enemies of the Crown, and of the public Peace, that with many different and false inventions and accusations seduced the minds of the Most Faithful People of this City and Kingdom in order to lure them into committing such serious excesses; because it is our Will to prove how magnificent is the love, goodwill and Kindness that our Lordship the King has for this Most Faithful Kingdom, and His Royal mercy with which in every time he receive all of those who came at His Royal presence, [because he] wants that everyone can enjoy the same peace and comfort that they had previously. We hereby grant General Pardon, & Clemency for everyone, and for all the people that were guilty of all kinds of crimes because of the aforementioned disturbances and riots happened in this Most Faithful City and Kingdom from the seventh of the past month of July of the past year 1647 up until today, without anyone being excluded, no matter how big the crime, even if they were guilty of *laesae Maiestatis in primo capite* both in this Most Faithful city, and its provinces and its villages and in all the Kingdom itself, and even if they were the Heads of the Revolutions, and in the aforementioned Riots they were accomplices, instigators, participants, or in whatever capacity they were involved in those; we order and command to all the above-mentioned [Government officials and Provinces governors] to warn everyone under their jurisdiction, without any right to object or do otherwise; nor for these same reasons can anyone be arrested or persecuted but everyone shall have to benefit from this Pardon, even if they [the officials] had received information regarding a crime and began a trial against someone, if he was jailed because of the said crimes, he has to be released immediately. Such we declare, and so shall be done, and not otherwise.
>
> Datum Neapoli die 8 mensis Aprilis 1648.[35]

---

35 "... la prontezza con la quale questo Fidelissimo Popolo è ritornato alla debita obedienza; & l'amore, & finezza con che ha sempre accudito al servitio di Sua Maestà, spargendo il sangue, e l'havere per mantenimento della Sua Real Corona; e considerando, che li

Once again the message was very clear: in order to return to the *status quo*, the blame for everything that had happened was placed solely on the French and their deception. The citizens of Naples were always faithful but temporarily led astray by deceptions and lies; now the proper order of things was restored. The attempt to present themselves as compassionate and loving rulers was carried even further by a broadsheet issued only days after the general pardon, promising to extend the pardon not only to those who were guilty of crimes related to the failed revolution but in a much broader sense to all those who were currently in jail, no matter what their crimes had been.[36]

Maintaining the appearance of control remained one of the central features of Spanish political communication. During and after the experience of the Neapolitan Republic continuity and coherence can be found in their proclamations, a continuity given human form in the career of royal printer Egidio Longo, who never ceased to sign his imprimaturs as the royal printer. The years 1647 and 1648 were particularly complex for the Spanish Empire and the beginning of a season of rebellions throughout Europe. Between the revolt in Portugal and Catalonia, the pressure of the Dutch in the West Indies, the loss

---

tumulti e revolutioni passate sono state causate per opra d'alcuna gente maligna inimica della Corona, e della pubblica quiete, che con diverse e false inventioni sono andati seducendo l'animi del Fedelissimo Popolo di questa Città, e Regno per farli cadere in eccessi così gravi; volendono Noi dimostrare quanto sia grande la benignità, affetto, & amore, che il Re nostro Signore porta à questo Fedelissimo Regno, e la sua Real clemenza, con la quale in ogni tempo abbraccia tutti quelli, che vengono alli suoi Reali Piedi; desiderando che per tutto si goda della pace, e tranquillità, che per l'adietro si è goduto. Ci è parso far la presente, con la quale Indultamo, e concedemo General Perdono, & Indulto à tutti, e qualsivogliano persone che hanno commesso qualsivoglia delitto per causa delli Passati rumori, & tumulti successi in questa Fidelissima Città, e Regno dalli sette del passato mese di Luglio dell'anno passato 1647, per tutto hoggi, senza eccettuarne nessuno, per enorme che fusse, ancorchè siano di crimen laesae Maiestatis in primo capite tanto per questa Fidelissima Città, suoi Borghi, e Casali, quanto per tutto il presente Regno, etiam che fussero stati Capi delle Rivolutioni, e tumulti predetti, loro complici, fautori, consultori, ò che in qualsivoglia modo havessero cooperato in essi; ordinadomo e comandadomo à tutti li sopraddetti, e chiascheduno di loro insolidum unicuique in sua iurisditione, che così lo debbiano permettere, osservare & eseguire inviolabilmente, senza replica né contradditione alcuna, né per tal causa debbiano molestare, né far molestare le dette persone, ma le debbiano far godere del presente Indulto, ancorchè se ne fusse presa informatione, e incominciato a procedere contro di essi, & ritrovandosi carcerato alcuno per dette cause lo debbiano subito escarcerare, e cossi s'esequa, e non altimenti.

Datum Neapoli die 8 mensis Aprilis 1648." [Conte D'Ognatte], *A tutti e Singoli Officiali ...* (Naples: per Egidio Longo Stampatore Regio, 1648) SNSP, ms XXIX.E.2 (90), USTC 4046785.

36 [Giovanni d'Austria], *Avendo noi conceduto indulto Generalissimo ...* (Naples: per Francesco Antonio Orlando Stampatore Regio, 20 aprile 1648) SNSP, ms XXIX.E.2 (94), USTC 4046783.

of Brazil to Portugal and the revolts in Italy, the cracks and stress brought on by decades of wars began to show, especially in those sections of the Empire that bore the financial burden of the military expenses. However, despite this and despite the attempts from their enemies to exploit the situation to their advantage, the Spanish crowns showed remarkable resilience. In Naples in particular, although some forms of punishments and repercussions were meted out on the more prominent rebels, the general impression given was that Masaniello's rebellion never happened at all and that the strength of the loyalty of the Neapolitan citizen toward the Spanish crown never wavered. And for the most part, this strategy worked. Of course, nothing was truly forgotten, and the phantom of the rebellion and punishment was once again brought up nine years later when Naples was struck by the plague. Nevertheless, besides the fact that the spectre of Masaniello was still very much alive, what the plague served to prove was that the Spanish leadership was stronger than ever and that in a time of crisis, it was to the established public rituals of the Spanish authorities that the people turned, as we will see in the next chapter.

CHAPTER 4

Print and Natural Disasters

Many have been the consequences of this fire, both natural, supernatural and moral. And first and most miserable were the natural ones, which means that the threatening horrors of the nearby fire caused the inhabitants of the mountainside to flee for their life.[1]

•••

Posterity, be horrified and take these last swindlers of a Realm, that I am now entrusting to the care of the centuries.[2]

• •
•

During the seventeenth century, Naples and its Kingdom were the theatres of a series of shocking events. We have already discussed Masaniello's rebellion in the previous chapter, but this popular unrest was preceded by a violent volcanic eruption and several earthquakes (1631–1632) and followed by a devastating plague that ravaged the Kingdom and killed between 240,000 and 270,000 people (1656). These circumstances left deep wounds in the minds and souls of Neapolitan peoples and were often discussed, even by contemporaries, as one long event.[3] The unique character of these catastrophes is clearly reflected by the sheer number of narratives that were produced around them, both in

---

1 "Molti sono stati gli effetti di tanto incendio, e naturali e soprannaturali, e morali. E prima miserabili sono stati i naturali, conciosia che gli horrori minaccevoli del vicino incendio sollecitavano alla fuga gli habitatori della falda del monte." [Anon.] *Nuove Osservationi fatte sopra gli effetti dell'incendio del Monte Vesuvio* (Naples: per Lazzaro Scoriggio, 1632) SNSP, *Sismica*, 06.B.16(3), USTC 4011940.
2 "Posterità, inhorridisci, e prendi questi, che consacro all'interesse de' secoli, estremi deliqui d'un Regno." Pasquale Nicolò, *A posteri della peste di Napoli e suo Regno nell'anno 1656, dalla redentione del mondo* (Naples: per Luc'Antonio di Fusco, 1668) SNSP, *Sala* A.05.D.12 USTC 1708080.
3 This is especially true for Masaniello's rebellion and the plague, that are often linked together in the narratives of the times. As we will see later in this chapter, many situations used to describe the locations and people affected by the plague closely resemble the discourse around the popular rebellion of 1647 that we discussed in previously.

© KONINKLIJKE BRILL BV, LEIDEN, 2025 | DOI:10.1163/9789004549401_006

manuscript and print. In this chapter, we will discuss the different narratives of the eruption of Vesuvius and the plague in popular print and the role of this kind of publication in helping the people of Naples understand what happened, come to terms with it, and rebuild a functioning society. But before going into that, analysing what was an extraordinary amount of print and discourse generated by a single natural, scientific event, it is worth briefly discussing the state of scientific publication in Naples during the seventeenth century, particularly where cheap print was concerned.

What kind of publication was 'scientific'? Considering that we are discussing a time before the epistemological paradigm advocated by figures such as Galileo Galilei and Francis Bacon was universally acknowledged and adopted, there was no distinct difference between science and belief. Everything that was part of an organised, systematised corpus of knowledge, even if derived from *a priori* assumptions, was considered science. Lynn Thorndike (1882–1965) was the first to use the expression 'experimental science' in the historical-scientific field, to distinguish between the modern idea of science and what could fall under that definition up to the early modern period (this was experimental as in tentative, based not only on trial and error, yet constantly corroborated by the authority of a textual tradition).[4] A pamphlet discussing the position of a comet as a foretelling of future catastrophes would not be considered a scientific publication today, but astrology was without a doubt a science in the mind of authors and readers of the time.

Alongside experimental science, we can find, sometimes overlapping the first, the concept of *magia naturalis*. This was a philosophical system based on the interpretation of natural forces as something living and innate to everything that existed within nature. Ideas borrowed by this philosophy were so diffused not only to the point of being assimilated into popular culture but could also be found in medical treatises and scientific works. Falling somewhere between these two we have on one side natural events with a supernatural explanation, like for example monstrous births and the literature that such events would generate and, on the other, the books of secrets. This last editorial genre was one of the most popular in Italy during the sixteenth century and with its scientific and technical approach functioned as a bridge between elite and popular culture.[5]

---

4   Prior to the scientific revolution and the diffusion of the scientific method, for something to be considered science it needed to be done according the principle of *auctoritas*. See Mark A. Waddell, *Magic, Science, and Religion in Early Modern Europe* (Cambridge: Cambridge University Press, 2021).

5   William Eamon, 'Science and Popular culture in Sixteenth Century Italy: the Professors of Secrets and their books', *The Sixteenth Century Journal* 16, 4 (1985), pp. 471–485; Id., *Science*

The person who, in Naples, better represents this mixture of science, magic and popular beliefs is Giovan Battista della Porta (1535–1615). He is one of the most famous and fascinating figures when it comes to the history of science and in particular when it comes to the study of the relationship between science, magic and the Inquisition. Despite this, even in the most recent historiography on the subject, the main reason that led to him being questioned and ultimately condemned by the Inquisition remains a mystery. However, during my research, I was able to find some precious evidence that will shed light on this question as well as demonstrate the complexity and various layers of the "scientific thought" in Early Modern Naples. It is known that Della Porta found himself under the scrutiny of the Inquisition already in October 1577, and I believe that I have found a complaint lodged against Della Porta which probably was the main evidence used against him in his trial. In the document I found Della Porta alongside two of his friends, Giovanni Capocefalo, who was a physician, and Giovanni Antonio d'Andrea, was charged with taking part in a necromantic ritual. At the time of the complaint, this term was used to refer to magic that was conducted with the help of ghosts, spirits or dead things. And it appears a fitting charge given that in the document it was described how these three were seen burying a skull with fava beans in the eye sockets and how later Capocefalo came back to harvest the beans. It is then said that he was seen putting said beans into his mouth and speaking in front of a mirror. This was because the entire thing described here is a ritual, although Della Porta would have considered it an experiment, to attempt to become invisible. The importance of this document in the legal trial of Giovan Battista della Porta is tied with another document that I was able to find, which contains a detailed list of forbidden books that Della Porta had in his home and the complaint previously described is proof of the fact that Della Porta not only had such books but he actively studied them and used them in his scientific pursue.[6] This entire proceeding is relevant to our investigation because demonstrates how the lines between popular culture, magic, science and popular belief were virtually non-existent.

One of the things that we need to take into consideration when dealing with popular print is the survival rate of these publications. These were texts printed on cheap paper, with low-quality ink, whose primary objective was to pass on information, to communicate something, to be read and ultimately

---

   and the Secrets of Nature. Books of Secrets in Medieval and Early Modern Culture (Princeton: Princeton University Press, 1994).

6 An article on Della Porta's trial and the scientific relevance of this experiment is currently being written with Dr. Leonardo Anatrini.

PRINT AND NATURAL DISASTERS 119

discarded. This appears to be particularly true when dealing with the popular version of scientific publications. Books of secrets, charlatans' lists of remedies, apothecaries' recipes and so forth, were texts with a practical purpose, that were used often and frequently within households and therefore are unlikely to have survived until today. Pamphlets recounting a comet sighting, a monstrous birth, a volcanic eruption, or whatever weird and magical event that occurred within the Kingdom of Naples or elsewhere and that struck the fancy of authors and readers alike, were also the kind of texts intended for immediate consumption. Almost no one would have wanted to hold on to a pamphlet telling the story of the comet of 1680 unless they had a specific interest in the subject, no more than any of us today would hold on to every single issue of a local newspaper. But if that is the case, where do one can look to find evidence of such publications? The overall state of Neapolitan archives and the general survival rate for materials from the Spanish Viceroyalty leaves gaps in the available sources, which requires that alternative source materials need to be brought into question.

Chronicles and diaries of the time are particularly useful sources. Especially in times of crisis, whether they were caused by political unrest as we have seen in the previous chapter or by natural causes, a greater number of accounts than usual can be found, both in their original manuscript forms or in later printed editions, usually from the nineteenth century. Besides the fact that the authors themselves often referred to a particular publication, I believe it reasonable to assume that they could not have possibly witnessed in person every single thing that they talk about, and therefore they had to have alternative means of collecting information; one of those could very well be printed pamphlets. Particularly for documents concerning the Neapolitan plague of 1656, which we will analyse later in this chapter, De Renzi's work is an invaluable source.[7] Written in 1867, his book is a collection of documents produced in Naples in 1656 on the topic of the plague, both manuscripts and printed, most of which are unfortunately no longer available in archives, or at least not accessible. It is apparent that when it comes to massive events we can consider ourselves lucky because we can actually read a great number of publications which provide authentic witnesses; for the other categories of cheap print that we are going to talk about in this chapter, we often can only find references to their existence but not the publications themselves. Such is the case, for example, of a monstrous birth that occurred in Naples on 13 September 1660:

---

7   Salvatore De Renzi, *Napoli nell'anno 1656. Ovvero documenti della pestilenza che desolò Napoli nell'anno 1656, preceduti dalla storia di questa tremenda sventura narrata* (Naples: tipografia di Domenico de Pascale, strada Anticaglia n ° 35, 1867).

The past week in the street near the church and convent of the Spanish nuns of Solitude, called Strada Nova, a woman, wife of a servant to the cadet family of the Viceroy Count of Pignoranda, gave birth to a monster that had a human body but head, neck, hands and feet were that of a camel. He was blind in his only eye and had two horns on his head and lived a very short time. And although I have not seen this with my own eyes, nonetheless several notable people witnessed this and one of them told me that a fine nobleman of the realm had written of this to a friend outside Naples and he had read this news. Others would not want to believe it and said that it was not true. But I was talking about curiosities and strange things with a textile merchant who was at the Armieri and he confirmed all of this from the mouth of one of his workers who lives in that same street and that witnessed the event and so I talked with him in the Strada Nova alla Solitaria and he confirmed that once news of this reached the Palace, they managed to stop the publication of any news on this event.[8]

It could seem counter-intuitive but cheap print was actually one of the preferred means to disseminate 'scientific' information. The squares of any port city of the Early Modern period were a bustling hive of activities where many different people could come together and cross paths. This inevitably included charlatans, doctors, pedlars, and street vendors. Charlatans would perform in the same square where itinerant pedlars were selling lists of remedies. Printers and booksellers had their stalls or stores nearby from which they would print and sell the same pamphlets that the others would then perform and sell. Among the best-sellers, books of secrets played a prominent role. A long-lasting Neapolitan bestseller was *I secreti della Signora Isabella Cortese*,

---

8 "La passata settimana nella strada vicino la chiesa e monasterio di monache spagnole della Solitaria, detta la Starda Nova, una donna, moglie di un servitore della famiglia bassa del conte di Pignoranda viceré, partorì un mostro di corpo umano, però a testa era col collo, mani e piedi di camelo, con un occhio cieco e due corna in testa e visse poco spazio; e benchè io non l'abbia visto, nondimeno venne affermato da diverse persone di intendimento e con questi uno mi disse che un cavaliero titolato l'aveva scritto ad un suo corrispondente fuori di Napoli, e che lui aveva letto questo avviso; altri non volevano crederlo anzi lo negavano che non era vero però io casualmente discorrendo di curiosità con un mercante di drappi dell'Armieri, quale l'affermava per bocca di un suo tessitore ch'habitava in detta nominata strada, ch'era presente, e l'intesi da lui che stava in detta Strada Nova alla Solitaria e che, sapitosi in Palazzo, si operò di maniera che non si pubblicasse." Fuidoro, *I giornali di Napoli*, vol. 1 pp. 54–55.

PRINT AND NATURAL DISASTERS

with over twelve editions printed between 1561 and 1677.[9] A remarkable example of the genre, this particular book offers us a great number of recipes for many different uses and situations. Along the cosmetic and beauty tricks we can find, among other things, remedies to eliminate freckles, dye your hair red or blond, preserve oneself from the plague, cleaning suggestions, a remedy for sore gums, several indications on the proper way to treat wounds and even some useful suggestions against male impotence. With its wide array of helpful remedies that embodied the technical and scientific knowledge of the time, this, as well as the other books of secrets, was the embodiment of a culture that appealed to all levels of the literate public. It is not scientific, magical, or even entirely rooted in superstitions but it is actually all these things together and therefore the perfect example of popular print.[10]

When talking about scientific publications in Naples one cannot fail to mention the numerous *Accademie* that rose in the city in the seventeenth century. Centred around influential and prominent figures of intellectual and political life, these were the circles where scientific knowledge advanced. The most notable was the *Accademia de' Segreti*, established by Giovan Battista della Porta in 1560 which lasted only twenty years; also the *Accademia degli Oziosi*, founded in 1611 and the *Accademia degli Investiganti*. The *Investiganti*, established in 1663, was probably the more progressive, with members interested in everything from astrology to chemistry, including mathematics, alchemy and botany. It was an intellectual bridge between Renaissance tradition and the modern Cartesian theory, but sadly it was short-lived: in 1668 authorities shut down the Accademia, citing public disorder, since its members had the

---

9   [Isabella Cortese], *I secreti della Signora Isabella Cortese, ne' quali si contengono cose minerali, medicinali, artificiose e alchemiche, e molte dell'arte profumatoria, appartenenti a ogni gran signora* (Venice: Giovanni Bariletti, 1561). Although the first edition was printed in Venice, it was reprinted in several cities throughout Italy and it has been suggested that the author behind the pseudonym was none other than Girolamo Ruscelli, known author of others book of secrets and that he probably wrote the majority of this during his Neapolitan stays, as it suggested by the fact that several recipes similar to those in this particular books can be found in others "secretarii" such as Fioravanti's *Compendio de' secreti rationali*, always with the designation "*a la Napoletana*" (in the Neapolitan way).

10   A couple of other titles of book of secrets printed in Naples, although not as near as famous as Isabella Cortese's one, are Orazio Bonadonna, *Tesoro di sanità, nel quale si contengono secreti mirabilissimi, per sanare quanti mali possono venire alle persone & stroppiar quanti sani siano al mondo* (Naples: per Domenico Maccarano 1628), USTC 4004695; and Cinzio d'Amato, *Nuova, et utilissima prattica di tutto quello ch'al diligente barbiero s'appartiene, cioè di cavar sangue medicar ferite, et balsamar corpi humani. Con altri mirabili secreti, e figure* (Naples: Ottavio Beltramo, 1632), USTC 4011020. Both are more focused on medical remedies, but they do contain the odd housekeeping recipe.

122   CHAPTER 4

tendency to get into public brawls with those who disagreed with them.[11] Although the writings produced by members of such circles were usually for other members and therefore complex and definitely not popular, sometimes they would indulge in more popular pieces, as we will see when discussing the eruption of Vesuvius.

1   The Vesuvius Eruption of 1631

In 1631 a volcanic eruption shook Naples. On 16 December, Vesuvius woke up after 500 years of inactivity with a massive pyroclastic eruption; the volcano's activity lasted for several days and eventually came to a halt on 4 January 1632. The lava flow did not reach the city itself but caused great destruction in the villages nearby, reaching the sea after having laid waste to Torre del Greco and Torre Annunziata though it stopped before reaching the city at Portici. This was one of the most impressive and destructive eruptions of Vesuvius in modern times and it definitely made an impression on the mind and souls of the contemporaries, stimulating a massive outpouring of publications.

Over 240 different texts were printed between the end of 1631 and 1632 about this particular eruption, and most of them can be found in the Biblioteca della Società di Storia Patria, within the Maschio Angioino in Naples, in the collection called *sismica* (about earthquakes and volcanic eruptions).[12] This number refers just to works printed in Naples immediately after the eruption and it is a clear indicator of the importance of the event in the eyes and minds of Neapolitans. The *Sismica* collection is a part of the private library of Alexis Perrey (1807–1882), a French seismologist and collector of works relating to earthquakes and volcanic activity. The section of his personal collection about Naples was bought by the Italian Alpinism Club and donated to the library of the Società di Storia di Patria. The fact that the biggest collection of cheap print on the eruption of Vesuvius of 1631 could be found within a private collection of someone with a specific and professional interest in the matter is further

---

11   For a detailed account of alchemy in Naples and its connections with the intellectual elites and Accademie see Antonio Emanuele Piedimonte, *Alchimia e medicina a Napoli. Viaggio alle origini delle arti sanitarie tra antichi ospedali, spezierie, curiosità e grandii personaggi* (Naples: Intra Moenia, 2014).

12   The interest was such that already in 1632 the editor Vincenzo Bove added to a pamphlet about the eruption a list of 32 other publications on the same subject. See Gioseffo Normile, *L'incedij del Monte Vesuvio, e delle stragi e rovine, ch'ha fatto ne' tempi antichi e moderni, infino a 3 di Marzo 1632* (Naples: per Egidio Longo. Si vende all'insegna del Bove, 1632). SNSP, Sismica, 06.B.16(8).

PRINT AND NATURAL DISASTERS

proof of the ultimate volatile nature of these publications, that managed to survive to this day only because of the foresight of an individual collector.[13] Besides *Sismica*, another collection that has proven to be extremely useful for this research is the *Cuomo*, a private collection put together by Abbot Vincenzo Cuomo (1770–1814) and donated after his death to the city of Naples. It is a collection of pamphlets and small books, only a part of which has been catalogued online, of various subjects, including lives of saints, the Neapolitan plague, politics, society and the eruption of Vesuvius.

Many of these publications were what we can call popular print. They were addressed to a wide audience, fairly short, printed on low-quality paper and often structured to facilitate the reading of them out loud. We witnessed an immediate commercialisation of the event, with printed accounts published while the eruption was still happening. This clearly paid well for printers and publishers; people both in Naples and outside were curious and eager for news on this extraordinary eruption, as it is testified by the presence of several of these publications in libraries across the world and by the ten different editions in less than a month of Vincenzo Bove's account.[14] The fact that almost all the pamphlets that we will mention in this chapter in regard to the eruption of 1631 survived in multiples copies that can be found not only in Naples but across Europe, particularly in Spain and France, provides a clear indicator of the fascination that this event had on contemporaries. The USTC was invaluable in collecting these data and establishing this pattern. Printers like Ottavio Beltrano, Egidio Longo, the Roncagliolo's family, Domenico Maccarano, Francesco Savio and Lazzaro Scoriggio latched on to this business opportunity, and it is reasonable to postulate some kind of arrangements between them because of the specialisation in the type of publication that each of them printed, and because of the presence of the same printer's device, usually depicting a stylised version of Vesuvius with the top surrounded by smoke and flames, on publication printed by many of them.

These kinds of printed works can roughly be sorted into three different categories; we have poems and songs, those which opted for a chronicle approach

---

13   For further information on how this collection came to be in Naples, see Loredana Esposito, 'Il fondo Sismico della Società Napoletana di Storia Patria', *Archivio storico per le province napoletane* 125 (2004), pp. 597–601.

14   Vincenzo Bove, *Nuove Osservationi Fatte sopra gli effetti dell'incendio del Monte Vesuvio, Aggiunte alla Decima Relatione dello stesso incendio già data in luce. Di nuovo rivista, e ristampata per Vincenzo Bove* (Naples: per Lazaro Scoriggio, 1632) SNSP, *Sismica*,06.B.15(18), USTC 4011046.

124   CHAPTER 4

and those which provided a more historical and scientific narration.[15] For any
of these categories, we can find important names from the printing industry
but also the Neapolitan cultural elite, many of whom published across all three
main genres.[16] I will examine here notable and curious examples.

The majority of poems and ballads dealing with this event chose to do so
in an epic tone, clearly taking inspiration from Greek mythology. Vesuvius is
portrayed like a Titan, the city of Naples like the fair Partenope and the mighty
and glorious St Gennaro like a hero of old, coming down to save the city. Such
is the case of the *L'afflitta Partenope per l'Incendio del Vesuvio al suo Glorioso
Protettore Gennaro*, a poem in which, as the author explains in the introduction:

> We pretend that the beautiful Queen Partenope, saddened, wanders
> through the night, along with many handmaidens (these represent the
> unfortunate lands that were destroyed), crying her sorrowful tale to the
> lonely fields. A wild man (the author) hears her and suddenly runs toward
> the voices, asking her who she might be and why she looked so miserable.
> When she told him about herself and her sad tale she also prayed him to

---

15   Medical, ecclesiastical, and popular is a division put in place by David Gentilcore while
      analysing the history of medicine within the kingdom of Naples. To some extent, we can
      adopt this same model of categorisation when looking at "scientific" cheap print, particu-
      lar those dealing with the eruption of Vesuvius and the plague. On the medical side we
      can find the more objective and scientific ones, for the popular we have both supersti-
      tious recounts and remedies as well as gossips and chronicles while for the ecclesiastical
      one we have the religious and or esoteric interpretation of such phenomena. Of course,
      such categorization is one established by historians to better define the object of their
      research but back then the lines were way more blurred and many if not the majority
      of publications could actually fall into alle three of the above-mentioned categories. For
      further analysis on the subject see David Gentilcore, *Healers and Healing in Early Modern
      Italy* (Manchester: Manchester University Press,1998), especially Chapter 1.
16   The fascination with the Vesuvius and its eruption was not limited to the years immedi-
      ately following it, but it generated a lot of discourse and publications up to this day. For
      an overview of the publications on this subject from 1631 to 1897 see Federigo Furchheim,
      *Bibliografia del Vesuvio. Compilata e corredata di note critiche estratte dai più autorevoli
      scrittori vesuviani* (Naples: ditta F. Furhheim di Emilio Prass editore, 1897). This bibliog-
      raphy lists over 2500 between books, articles, journal and pamphlets in eleven different
      languages. Despite the incredible amount of work that went into the redacting of this
      bibliography, it is not a comprehensive one; for the eruption of 1631 for examples only
      144 publications are listed. For further information on the influx of publications on the
      subject see also Luigi Riccio, 'Nuovi documenti sull'incendio vesuviano dell'anno 1631
      e bibliografia di quella eruzione', *Archivio Storico per le Provincie Napoletane* 14 (1889),
      pp. 489–555; Alfonso Tortora, *L'eruzione Vesuviana del 1631. Una storia moderna* (Rome:
      Carocci, 2014).

consecrate the printed pages (i.e. the pamphlet itself) to her protector St Gennaro, so as to obtain his mercy.[17]

Giovanni Lotti pushed the mythological references even further, in a mixture of epic and mundane, of poetical licence and true-to-life descriptions. Born in Tuscany, he was a poet with strong ties to the Neapolitan and Roman cultural elites. His membership of the Neapolitan *Accademia degli Erranti* secured him a mention in the catalogue of illustrious men of Naples compiled by the Archivist of the Regia Camera della Sommaria, Niccolò Toppi.[18] The lyrical tones and allegorical references are abundant when it came to describing the eruption itself, albeit with a sort of scientific accuracy, as Vesuvius is being described as Janus, given the fact that the eruption caused a second crater to appear. The author also added to his narration an element of observation, leaving behind the Grecian inspirations in order to describe the processions with the relics of St Gennaro and their role in putting a stop to the eruption.[19]

---

17 "Si suppone che la bella Reina Partenope afflitta per l'incendio del Vesuvio accompagnata da molte ancelle (significate per esse le misere Terre distrutte), sen vada di notte, per solitarie campagne, piangendo le sue sventure; quale udita da selvaggio habitatore, accorrendo alle voci, la dimandò quale ella si fusse, e perché sì sconsolata viveva; quale datale contezza di sé, non che delle sue sventure, lo prega che quelle impresse, con segni di grazie voglia, al suo Protettore Gennaro consecrare." [Anon.], *L'afflitta Partenope per l'incendio del Vesuvio al suo Glorioso Protettore Gennaro. Dell'Insensato Accademico Furioso* (Naples: nella stampa di Secondino Roncagliolo, 1632) SNSP, *Sismica*, 06.G.062(8), USTC 4010884. The *Accademia degli Insensati* was founded in Perugia in 1561 and it was a literary and linguistic society. Within this institution the sopriquet *Furioso* belonged to Leandro Bovarini. As there are no traces of an Accademia with this name in Naples it is plausible to assume that the author of this poem was indeed Bovarini but without further information it is impossible to make a definitive attribution.

18 [Giovanni Lotti], *L'incendio del Vesuvio in ottava rima di Giovanni Lotti Accademico Errante* (Naples: per Gio' Domenico Roncagliolo, 1632) SNSP, *Sismica*, 06.062.13(3), USTC 4010881. Niccolò Toppi, *Biblioteca napoletana et apparato à gli huomini illustri in lettere di Napoli, e del Regno* (Naples: Appresso Antonio Bulifon All'insegna della Sirena, 1678), p. 316. For further information on Lotti and his poetic works see Nadia Amendola, *La poesia di Giovanni Pietro Monesio, Giovanni Lotti e Lelio Orsini nella cantata da camera del XVII secolo* (PhD book, Beni culturali e Territorio, Università di Roma "Tor Vergata", Johannes Gutenberg-Universität Mainz, 2016/2017).

19 "Godea Napoli altera, e tutta intesa/ A lusingar del cor le voglie infide,/ E tanto cieca più, quanto più illesa/ Del periglio comun restar si vide./ Ma mentre insiste a la Divina offesa,/ E scherza, e burla, e balla, e gioca, e ride,/ O del braccio Divin potenza estrema/ Ecco il lampo, ecco il tuono, ascolta, e trema./ Era Argo il Cielo, e Polifemo il Mondo,/ L'un cieco in sonno, e l'altro occhiuto in stelle,/ E de Fraterni Rai mancava il biondo,/ Ch'illuminava ancor l'Indie novelle,/ E quel gran Chiostro, ch'è d'Atlante il pondo,/ Apria lassù mille dorate celle,/ Per farci fede, e dimostrarci appieno,/ Che 'l Monastico Chiostro è un ciel terreno./ Questo felice, hor miserabil monte/ Duplicata cervice al ciel sublima,/

126   CHAPTER 4

The epic undertones were not confined only to the more poetic narrative. Giovanni Apolloni in his pamphlet compared the eruption of Vesuvius to the opening of Pandora's box, which let out *un postribolo di furie horribili* (a horrific rampage of Furies) while the mountain itself was usually Olympus but, in the moment of the explosion, became Hydra, a multi-headed monster unpredictable in its fury that spews flames, ashes and rocks from many different apertures.[20]

A recurring theme across almost all the narratives is a religious aspect. The people of Naples put their faith in the patron saint of the city, St Gennaro, to save them from catastrophe. The Viceroy ordered all the lights in the churches to be kept on and all the relics to be brought out, to show the city's devotion. And when the eruption finally ceased and the city was safe again this was attributed solely to the work of San Gennaro. The ritualistic aspect of the processions, both those that featured penitents and flagellants and those that carried the sacred relics and were led by the Viceroy, is something that is mentioned in almost every pamphlet published on the subject. Based on the political affiliation of both authors and printers, the spotlight could be on the Viceroy leading the procession or on the saint himself. According to some chronicles, the relics of St Gennaro, his head and the vial containing his blood, were merely exposed; others talked about them being carried through the city by the Viceroy but both sides agreed on the results: the Saint's blood became liquid again and in the face of such miracle the fury of Vesuvius ceased.[21]

   Si che sembra mirar Giano bifronte,/ Che qual mitra lunata apre la cima./ La destra parte hà ripida la fronte,/ Ma la sinistra opposita alla prima,/ Ch'elevando pian pian le sparse membra,/ Nel gran tempio terren cupola sembra. /S'estrasse dal Tesoro il gran Gennaro/ Quegli, che con la testa esague avviva,/ E del volgo, e del clero il gregge amaro/ Con mesto ossequio il suo Pastor seguiva./ Ma già la notte e 'l negro fumo al paro/ Estinta havean del dì la lampa estiva,/ Notte, che fù in funtion supplici, e pie/ Più frequente, e operosa assai del die./" Giovanni Lotti, *L'incendio del Vesuvio in ottava rima di giovanni lotti, accademico Errante* (Naples: per Gio domenico Roncagliolo, 1632) SNSP, Sismica.06.G.62(3), USTC 4010881.

20   Giovanni Apolloni, *Il vesuvio ardente di Giovanni Apolloni all'Illustrissimo Signor Conte Mario Carpegna* (Naples: per Egidio Longo, 1632) SNSP, Sismica, 06.G.15(7), USTC 4011033. We do not have much on the author. According to a descriptive catalogue compiled in the Eighteenth century Giovanni Apolloni was a knight from Arezzo; he could be the theatre author and librettist Giovanni Filippo Apolloni, the lyrical tones and descriptive images are certainly there, but it is impossible to say for sure given that most of the modern biography put his birth in 1635, although we do not have any certainty in that regards.

21   Some examples are: [Giovanni Orlando Romano], *Dell'incendio del monte di Somma. Compita relazione di quanto è successo infino ad hoggi. Pubblicato per Giovanni Orlando Romano alla Pietà* (Naples: per Lazzaro Scoriggio, 1632) SNSP, *Sismica*, 06.B.15(10), USTC 1752436; [Vincenzo Bove], *Il Vesuvio acceso . Descritto da Vincenzo Bove per l'Illustrissimo*

FIGURE 4.1 Micco Spadaro, Processione di San Gennaro per l'eruzione del 1631 (1656/1660). Naples, Museo di Capodimonte

Everyone in Naples was firmly convinced of this, as is evident by the written testimony as well as the numerous works of art depicting St Gennaro stopping the volcano that were produced in the years immediately following the event.

For outsiders, things were probably more ambiguous; an author described as a gentleman living in Naples was sceptical of the so-called miracle of San Gennaro and recounted this with a healthy dose of scepticism, finishing his narration with 'but the city of Naples will be always safe because of the miracle of St Gennaro (or so they will believe).'[22] His was the only sceptical voice.

Signore Gio.Battista Valenzuela Velazquez, Primo Reggente per la Maestà Cath. Nel Conseg. Supremo d'Italia (Naples: per Secondino Roncagliolo, 1632) SNSP, *Sismica*, 06.B.16(4), USTC 4011047.

22 [Marc'Antonio Padavino], *Lettera narratoria a pieno la verità dei successi del Monte Vesuvio detto di Somma, seguiti alli 16 di Dicembre fin alli 22 dello istesso mese. Scritta da un gentilhuomo dimorante in Napoli a uno di questa corte* (Rome: appresso Francesco Cavalli, 1632) SNSP, *Sismica*, 06.B.15(4), USTC 4011030. The author was living in Naples as an emissary of the Venetian Republic, the last in a long string of diplomatic assignments that had seen him travel across Europe for more than twenty years. He compiled this report for the Venetian senate.

128   CHAPTER 4

Abbot Flavio Ruffo, linking the eruption of 1631 to all the other known eruptions of Vesuvius, went as far as crediting the miraculous apparition of San Gennaro's blood and head for the ending of the eruption narrated by Pliny, the one that destroyed Pompei and Ercolano in 79, while Geronimo Favella emphasised how it was divine intervention that saved the city not only from the fire but also from the falling ashes.

> I cannot avoid saying how I witnessed, near Torre del Greco, a small farm belonging to a poor old man, that the other day was trimming the grapevines, being spared by flames and fires, while all around him they brought the greatest destruction. And it is impossible to describe the infinite Mercy that Our Lady of Constantinople, St. Gennaro the Glorious and all the other Saints that protect us granted to this City because at the beginning of this most terrible eruption Vesuvius threatened ruination but on that first night only a little ash fell here and as soon as they [the Saints] appeared the ash vanished, and was carried north by a great wind and by the sirocco but then was pushed back by the tramontane and led towards Sardinia and the Barbaria. As little as what could be carried on the point of a knife fall onto this City because the Hellish Mountain could not, as he so wished to do, pour it onto us because God Almighty so wished.[23]

---

23   [Flavio Ruffo], *La ristampata lettera con aggiunta di molte cose notabili, del Signor Abbate D. Flavio Ruffo. Nella quale dià vera & minuta relazione delli Segni, terremoti e incendi del Monte Vesuvio, cominciando dalli 10 del mese di Dicembre 1631 per infino alli 16 Gennaio 1632* (Naples: appresso Lazzaro Scoriggio, 1632) SNSP, *Sismica*, 06.B.16(2); Flavio Ruffo was the second son of Carlo Ruffo, Duke of Bagnara, and Antonia Spatafora. Born in Messina, his mother sent him to Naples to become a clergyman, where he acted as advisor for both his mother and his younger brother, the much more famous Antonio Ruffo. His role within the family was to build and reinforce the ties and connections of the family in Naples, while the others concentrated their efforts in Messina. He was very successful in his endeavour, as it is proven by the great presence of Neapolitan art in the family art gallery.
      [Gieronimo Favella], *Abbozzo delle ruine fatte dal Monte di Somma, con il seguito infino ad hoggi 23 di Gennaro 1632. All'infinita cortesia, rara gentilezza & unica generosità del Sig. Paolo Ruschi Gio Gieronimo Favella offerisce, dedica e dona* (Naples: nella stampa di Secondino Roncagliolo, 1632), USTC 4011050 SNSP, *Sismica*, 06.B.15(6). Geronimo Favella is one of the many characters of the Neapolitan scene to have had close ties to the theatre; he married an actress and with her set up his own theatre company. His acting career was unsuccessful and short lived but enabled him to get in contact with the Viceroy Monterrey, who appointed him as one of the first authorized *gazzettieri* of the Kingdom of Naples. Although we have nothing left of his work as a journalist, the theatre background is evident in the dramatic tones and images used to describe the Vesuvius eruption in the pamphlet above.

The religious dimension, particularly in the interpretation of such events as a sign of divine wrath, was present even in the more scientific descriptions.[24] Giovanni Forleo Leccese wrote an eminently scientific observation on what could possibly be the cause of such an eruption and the accompanying earthquakes, describing the event itself with none of the lyrical and tragic excess of the works analysed up until now. However, on the *verso* of the front page, there is a miniature of St Gennaro, to whom this pamphlet is dedicated, and Forleo concluded his work by saying that earthquakes and eruptions are perfectly natural things but that 'many times the Almighty God, as we said in the beginning, uses them as an instrument of our suffering, to remind us always to obey to His goodwill and His sacred laws, as to not repel Him with our sins.'[25]

As we have previously explained, the kind of publications that we could refer to as scientific in 1631 was very different from what we consider to be science today. Filippo Finella wrote and published a fairly popular treatise dedicated to the Viceroy in which he clearly linked the eruption to the position and influence of the astrological constellations and planets in the sky in the months leading up to the event, particularly the solar eclipse that took place in October 1631.[26] In this same pamphlet, he also commented on the effectiveness of the intercession of St Gennaro and the Virgin Mary in stopping the eruption and he also provided a fairly technical and precise description of the event itself, detailing the kinds of earthquakes and collateral events that accompanied the eruption.

Once again we can see how the lines and definitions between scientific, religious and superstitious belief were very blurred and how all of these concepts

---

24   For the relationship between science and faith in regard to the Vesuvius see also Jane E. Everson, 'The Melting Pot of Science and Belief: Studying Vesuvius in Seventeenth-Century Naples', *Renaissance Studies* 26 (2012), pp. 691–727.

25   [Giovanni Forleo Leccese], *Meteorico discorso sopra i segni, cause, effetti, tempi & luoghi generalmente di tutti i Terremoti & incendi di diverse parti della terra* (Naples: per Secondino Roncagliolo, si vendono all'insegna del Bove, 1632) SNSP, *Sismica*, 06.F.43 USTC 4014038. The same concept can also be found in [Giovanni Giannetti], *La vera relatione del prodigio novamente successo nel Monte Vesuvio, con la nota di quante volte è successo ne' tempi antichi, con una breve dichiarazione di quel che significa* (Naples: per Gio. Domenico Roncagliolo, 1632) SNSP, Sismica, 06.B.15(9), USTC 1752433.

26   [Filippo Finella], *Incendio del Vesuvio del Lanelfi* (Naples: appresso Ottavio Beltramo, 1632) SNSP, Sismica, 06.G.15(16). Born in Naples presumably in 1584, Finella was a man of letters with a deep interest in *magia naturale* and the esoteric, as it was common for those who were followers of Della Porta. He was a member of the *Accademia degli Incauti*, play-writer and scientist, especially famous for his writings on the subjects of astrology, alchemy, palm-reading, and physiognomy. I assumed this was a popular publication as there are seven known surviving copies, four in Italy, two in France and one in the U.K. (USTC 4011026).

Quanto al tempo, dico, che per caufa naturale, è proceduto dall'Eclifſe antecedente del Sole, che fù à 24. Ottobre 1631. à hore 18. e min. 20. dopò mezo giorno. Et acciò V. E. con ragione naturale poſſa congetturar l'effetti, ponderi col ſuo ſano giuditio la figura nel tempo dell'Eclifſe.

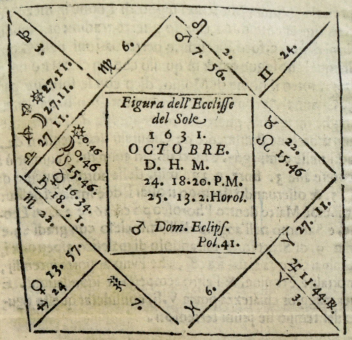

Queſto Eccliſſe è dominato da Marte, perche la Luna, & il Sole ſono in congiontione nel primo grado di Scorpione; & ben che il Sole ſia nel ſuo proprio decano, Marte è grandemente offeſo da i luminari, da Saturno, e da Mercurio, con li quali ſi mira di quadrato; e perche ſe ne ſta detto Marte nel mezo Cielo in Leone con gradi 7. e min. 56. & i luminari in aſcendente ambi peregrini, mi fan-

A 3   no

FIGURE 4.2 The constellations in October 1631; SNSP, Sismica 06.G.15(16). Naples, Biblioteca della Società Napoletana di Storia Patria

FIGURE 4.3
The constellations in December 1631. SNSP, Sismica 06.G.15(16). Naples, Biblioteca della Società Napoletana di Storia Patria

were often intertwined; even more so when it came to discussing how to prevent such occurrences and how one could save oneself from the volcano's fury. Such pamphlets were not very common. Unlike as it was the case with the plague, as we will see shortly, very few authors would risk trying to offer a remedy for a volcanic eruption. This was because, although both the plague and the eruption of Vesuvius were seen as acts of God, the length and scope of the plague were such that people were desperate to try any solutions to save themselves and their loved ones. The eruption was different; it started suddenly and just as suddenly would cease, and because of its immediacy and brevity it would have felt much more inescapable than the plague. Nonetheless, there were a couple of authors who tried their hands at figuring out a remedy against the earthquakes and eruptions, using a mix of popular superstitions, scientific beliefs and Christian devotion.

132   CHAPTER 4

Giovanni Orlandi, in his *Nova e compita relatione dello spaventevole incendio del Monte di Somma*, after a brief discussion of the previous eruptions and a more detailed description of the events of 1631, suggested a solution to his readers (and all of this in just sixteen pages):

> Cardinal Baronio told us, in the year of the Lord 528, that the city of Antiochia was greatly plagued by earthquakes and it was revealed to a most devoted servant of the Lord that if we would put the above-mentioned words above the doors and windows of houses they would remain free because the earthquake brought great ruin upon cities and farms and houses and only those places that had the words written upon were spared. We now tell this to all those who believe, for the benefit of everyone.[27]

Giovanni Orlandi was a prolific editor and engraver. Born in Rome, he began his career in Naples as a pedlar, with a small stall near la Pietà. At some point around 1635–40 he probably opened a proper shop near his house, which he left to his son after his death in 1649. It is interesting that his production as an editor specialised in disaster narratives, both of the natural kind (he curated at least four different pamphlets on the eruption) and those caused by wars and battles. He was also the author of one of the most famous engravings of the 1631 eruption of Vesuvius. There are two interesting things to note about Orlandi's remedy. On the one hand, it is for earthquakes, but it is written as the closure of his pamphlet on volcanic eruptions. This is because in the mind of contemporaries the two events were linked and often one and the same. On the other hand, this small piece of advice is the perfect demonstration of both the strong interconnections between faith, science and beliefs and of the principle of *auctoritas*, that ruled any kind of speculative thought at least up to the Scientific Revolution, and often even after that. The formulation of this remedy closely resembled a spell, both for the placement of the words and their rhythm; but it was a spell made in the name of God, by a devoted Christian, and that makes it a prayer. It is a kind of apotropaic magic based on the recourse to the salvific protection of Christ, that comes from Christ himself, while the attribution to a cardinal that lived centuries prior lends it authority in the name of a tradition.

---

27   [Giovanni Orlandi], *Nuova, e compita relatione del spaventevole incendio del Monte di Somma detto il Vesuvio, dove s'intende minutamente tutto quello che e successo fin'al presente giorno, con la nota di quante volte detto Monte si sia abbrugiato. [...] aggiuntovi un remedio devotissimo contro il terremoto* (Naples: per Lazzaro Scoriggio, 1632) SNSP, Sismica, 49.9 USTC 4011083.

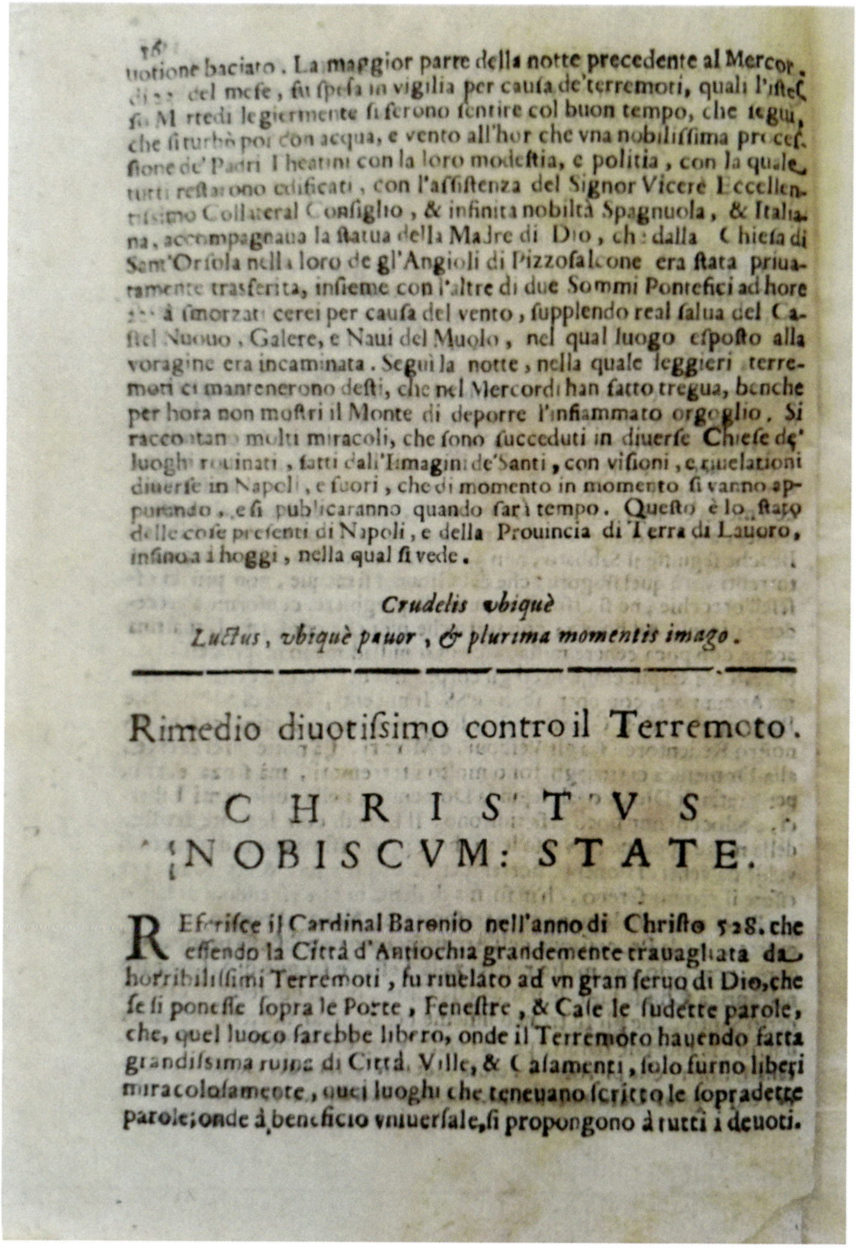

16

uotione baciato. La maggior parte della notte precedente al Mercor.
di 22 del mese, fù spesa in vigilia per causa de'terremoti, quali l'istef,
fù Mrtedi legiermente si ferono sentire col buon tempo, che segui,
che si turbò poi con acqua, e vento all'hor che vna nobilissima procef.
sione de'Padri Theatini con la loro modestia, e politia, con la quale,
tutti restarono edificati, con l'assistenza del Signor Vicerè Eccellentissimo Collateral Consiglio, & infinita nobiltà Spagnuola, & Italia.
na, accompagnaua la statua della Madre di Dio, ch: dalla Chiesa di
Sant'Orsola nella loro de gl'Angioli di Pizzofalcone era stata priua-
tamente trasferita, insieme con l'altre di due Sommi Pontefici ad hore
··· à smorzati cerei per causa del vento, supplendo real salua del Castel Nuouo, Galere, e Naui del Muolo, nel qual luogo esposto alla
voragine era incaminata. Segui la notte, nella quale leggieri terremoti ci mantenerono desti, che nel Mercordi han fatto tregua, benche
per hora non mostri il Monte di deporre l'infiammato orgoglio. Si
raccontano molti miracoli, che sono succeduti in diuerse Chiese de'
luoghi rouinati, fatti dall'Imagini de'Santi, con visioni, e riuelationi
diuerse in Napoli, e fuori, che di momento in momento si vanno ap-
purando, e si publicaranno quando fara' tempo. Questo è lo stato
delle cose presenti di Napoli, e della Prouincia di Terra di Lauoro,
insino a i hoggi, nella qual si vede.

Crudelis vbiquè

Luctus, vbiquè pauor, & plurima momentis imago.

Rimedio diuotifsimo contro il Terremoto.

CHRISTVS
NOBISCVM: STATE.

REfrifce il Cardinal Baronio nell'anno di Christo 528. che
essendo la Città d'Antiochia grandemente trauagliata da
horribilissimi Terremoti, fu riuelato ad vn gran feruo di Dio, che
se si ponesse sopra le Porte, Fenestre, & Case le sudette parole,
che, quel luoco sarebbe libero, onde il Terremoto hauendo fatta
grandissima ruina di Città, Ville, & Casamenti, solo furno liberi
miracolosamente, quei luoghi che teneuano scritto le sopradette
parole; onde à beneficio vniuersale, si propongono à tutti i deuoti.

FIGURE 4.4 [Giovanni Orlandi], *Nuova, e compita relatione del spaventevole incendio del Monte di Somma detto il Vesuvio* (1632). SNSP, Sismica 49.9. Naples Biblioteca della Società Napoletana di Storia Patria

And just in case the strong ties with religion were not clear enough, the pamphlet was once again dedicated to St Gennaro, with an icon of the saint and a hymn in his name on the verso of the front page.

The same solution is provided by Michel'Angelo Masino.[28] While describing the various calamities caused by the Vesuvius, he placed a particular emphasis on the role of churches, relics and penitents procession in comforting people and providing respite from the tragedy, before repeating *verbatim* Orlandi's remedy and quoting the stubbornness of sinners as the reason why this solution was not as effective as it should have been. This brief exploration into the accounts printed about the eruption of Vesuvius proves once more that the differences between interpretations were not as clear cut. Making a clear distinction between rational and religious interpretations offered to such events it is an oversimplification that does not reflect the mindset of seventeenth-century people.[29]

The scale of this eruption was so large that news about it did not remain confined to Naples, nor even Italy but reached far and wide in Europe. The *Gazette de Paris*, for example, kept its readers updated on the situation in Naples, even reporting some exquisitely local bits of folklore, such as the fact that prostitutes in the city of Naples were renouncing their profession. "The penance of Neapolitan people visibly contributed to diminishing the earthquake that threatened to swallow them, and this earthquake greatly contributed to their salvation. As further proof of this, once this maelstrom ended, 25 lascivious young girls and women converted within a day and were now living in a very honest manner."[30] This was apparently seen as something of extraordinary relevance since it was reported in almost every pamphlet that described the event more in the manner of a chronicle. The details were marginally

---

28 [Michelangelo Masini], *Distinta relatione dell'incendio del Vesuvio, Alli 16 di Decembre 1631 successo. Con la relatione dell'incendio della città di Pozzuoli, e cause delli terremoti, al tempo di Don Pietro da Toledo Vicerè in questo regno nell'anno 1534* (Naples: per Gio Domenico Roncagliolo, 1632) SNSP, Sismica, 6.B.16(9), USTC 4012327.

29 The strict dichotomy between science and faith in the interpretation of natural disasters has been suggested, among others, by Alwyn Scarth, *Vesuvius: A biography* (Oxford : Oxford University Press, 2009), pp. 135–137.

30 "La Penitence des Neapolitains a visiblement contribuè à la diminution du tremblement de terre qui menaçoit de les engloutir, & ce tremblement à leur salut. Pour prevue dequoy cet orage a cesse, & 25 filles & femmes debauchées s'y sont converties en un jour, qui vivent à present fort honnestement". (Gazzette du Paris, 6.11.1632). For an in-depth analysis of the network of news between Naples and Europe and what could possibly have been the source for the French Gazette see Carlos H. Caracciolo, 'Natural disasters and European Printed News Network', in Joad Raymond, Noah Moxham (eds), *News Networks in Early Modern Europe* (Leiden: Brill, 2016), pp. 756–778.

PRINT AND NATURAL DISASTERS

different from version to version but the gist of it remained the same: prostitutes in the city of Naples, whether a few or all of them depending on who was writing, were renouncing their profession and their wicked ways. This is perfectly coherent with the general feeling of being punished by God through the eruption; people sought comfort in churches and relics, particularly those of St Gennaro, and hastened to repent and seek forgiveness for their sins, be it by public penitent processions or leaving an immoral job to rejoin the ranks of pious Christians.[31]

But what was the role of the political elites in all of this? According to one source, the conversion of the prostitutes was initiated by a Viceroyal decree:

> Around the hour of 2 AM, twelve drums accompanied by town criers went through the city announcing that by order of the Viceroy it was now forbidden to sleep with women of the streets, under penalties of jail.[32]

In many of the relations, particularly those printed by Egidio Longo (which is unsurprising considering his role as the royal printer) we can find a more nuanced account of the actions taken by Viceroy Monterrey to ensure the safety of the city and its inhabitants. These emphasises his efficiency in this time of crisis as well as his selflessness in deciding to remain in the city and forbidding nobles to leave.[33] But besides the more obvious actions such as issuing orders and decrees, the political and propagandistic use by the civic authorities of events such as this is evident in more subtle ways. The Viceroy was the one to declare that the churches should stay lit after dark and we can find

---

31 This can be found, besides the works mentioned up until now, in [Anon.], *Novissima Relatione dell'incendio successo nel monte di Somma a 16 Decembre 1631. Con un'avviso di quello che è successo nell'istesso dì nella città di Cattaro, nelle parti d'Albania* (Naples: per Egidio Longo, 1632), p. 25 "Many courtesans hardened by sins and grown old in sins converted and abandoned the luxuries and lewdness. Some of them took husband while others chose to change their life by closing themselves in convents."; SNSP, Sismica, 06.B.15(5), USTC 4011031.

32 "All'ore due della notte li banditori andarono per la città e per ordine del Vicerè era proibito dormire con donne di malaffare, sotto pene de la galera." [Giulio Cesare Braccini], *Relatione dell'incendio fattosi nel Vesuvio alle 16 di Dicembre 1631. Scritta dal Signor Abbate Giulio Cesare Braccini da Gioviano di Lucca in una lettera diretta all'Eminentissimo e Reverendissimo Signore il sig. Girolamo Colonna* (Naples: per Secondino Roncagliolo, 1631), p. 14; SNSP, Sismica, 06.B.15(6); USTC 4011032.

33 See for example [Frat'Angelo de Eugeni], *Il maraviglioso e tremendo incendio del monte Vesuvio; detto a Napoli la montagna di Somma nel 1631* (Naples: per Ottavio Beltramo, 1631) SNSP, Sismica, 06.B.15(14), USTC 4011023. "Having His Excellency decided that it was better to die than to leave his citizen, he declared that everyone had to stay and no one could leave Naples" (p. 4).

136   CHAPTER 4

him leading several processions, carrying the sacred relics of St Gennaro and
kissing the vial with his blood. The eruption of 1631 gave the Spanish rulers the
perfect opportunity to showcase their respect and adherence to Neapolitan
popular devotion, to present themselves not as foreigners but as an integral
part of the community and the recounting of their presence in every publication on the matter only served to strengthen their public image.[34]

Of course, this does not mean that there were not any contrary voices and
that the sentiment toward the authorities was overwhelmingly positive. Not
surprisingly, however, traces of this anti-Spanish sentiment do not appear in
the printed production; to find them, we need to turn our attention to Messer
Padavino once again, but instead of his printed relation concerning the catastrophe, we need to look at the dispatches that he sent to Venice.[35] According to
his letters, several copies of a broadsheet appeared in the streets of Naples on
6 January 1632. These broadsheets, printed just in time for the return of the
Viceroy from Pozzuoli, featured a pasquinade entitled *Dell'Incendio del Monte
di Somma* and attributed the eruption of Vesuvius to the greed and misgov-
ernment of the Spaniards, going as far as comparing the Viceroy to Vesuvius.[36]
Another testimony to anti-Spanish sentiment in the city can be found in a
manuscript chronicle of the time by Ferrante Bucca.[37] He reported a rumour
that framed the eruption of Vesuvius as a consequence of St Gennaro's anger
against the Spanish rulers, particularly the Infanta Maria Anna of Spain who
allegedly behaved badly during her visit to the city's cathedral, insisting on
defying protocol to favour herself and her Spanish companions.[38]

It is improbable that these were the only dissenting voices: it is more likely
that others were silenced before leaving a testimony, even though the frequency with which publications on the eruption appeared undoubtedly made
censoring them difficult. Nonetheless, these critical publications constituted
an exception. The fact that dissent was largely absent in the print production
and confined to manuscript chronicles and ambassadors' papers is proof of a
deliberate and precise use of print by the authorities, both civic and religious;
it was not by chance that the established narratives that made their way into
print focused on the positive role of the Viceroy and the ecclesiastical authorities during this time of crisis. It was instead part of a propagandistic effort

---

34   On the political use of Neapolitan religious believes by the Spanish authorities, see
      Dauverd, *Church and State* (2020), pp. 103–147.
35   ASV, *Dispacci Ambasciatori Veneziani a Napoli*, 51 n 156.
36   There are no surviving printed copies of this poem, but a manuscript version can be
      found in BNN, *Ms. Branc.* III D.
37   Ferrante Bucca, *Giornali Historici.* BNN, Ms. X B.51.
38   Ibid, fol. 48ᵛ–55ʳ.

PRINT AND NATURAL DISASTERS

aimed at portraying the ruling class as a solid presence, able to maintain control and re-establish public order, in which print played a fundamental role.

Lastly, it is worth mentioning the publication of several pamphlets recounting this same event in Spanish, printed in Naples. It appears that both the magnitude of the event and the opportunity for political propaganda were such that it was important to make sure narrations of it were available also for the Spaniards.[39]

2 The Plague of 1656

Shortly after the eruption of Vesuvius, the city's equilibrium was once again disrupted by the popular rebellion led by Masaniello, and then, before Naples and its inhabitants had time to regain their footing, a terrible plague struck the Kingdom. Being the third world-shattering event in a relatively short period of time, it is unsurprisingly that both in the narratives of contemporaries and in later historiography the Neapolitan plague is rarely addressed on its own. It is always linked to the two previous calamities, and it is a connection that travels both ways. The plague is seen as a consequence of what happened in the past and the accounts of the past are framed in a new light that makes them portents and omens for the plague itself. Riaco, for example, viewed the plague as a form of Judgement Day and he sustained his argument not only by means of astrological computation but also by explaining how there had been many portents, such as earthquakes, volcanic eruption and even the coming of the Antichrist, in the form of none other than Masaniello.[40] The same opinion is shared by Carlo Morexano, who compared the plague to the Great Flood, 'even more so when we compare the year, as in that one took place in the year 1656 after Creation and this one in the year 1656 after Incarnation.'[41] He was also sure that the constellations and the sky had indeed foretold the plague because, according to a libel known as *Le cifre celesti*, 'Saturn was in the corner of the seventh house along with Venus and the head of the Dragon, which

---

39   See SNSP, Sismica,06.B.017 that contains, among others: Francisco Grande de Lorenzana, *Brebe compendio del lamentable ynzendio del Monte de Soma* (Naples: por Giovanni Domenico Roncagliolo, ad instanzia di Giovanni Orlandi, 1632) SNSP, Sismica,06.B.017(11), USTC 401162; Simon de Ayala, *Copiosissima y verdadera relacion del incendio del monte Vesuvio donde se da cuenta de veinte incendios que ha auido sin este ultimo* ... (Naples: per Ottavio Beltramo, 1632) SNSP, Sismica, 06.B.017(10), USTC 4012272.

40   Carlo Francesco Riaco, *Il giudicio di Napoli. Discorso del passato contagio rassomigliato al Giudicio Universale* ... (Perugia: per Pietro di Tommaso, 1658) SNSP, Capasso, 03.F.16. The author was a priest and a theologian.

41   [Carlo Morexano], *Torchio di osservationi della peste di Napoli dal Dottor Carlo Morexano Messinese* ... (Naples: per Sebastiano di Alecci, 1659); SNSP, Capasso II AA 42 p. 9.

138   CHAPTER 4

meant sudden deaths with many poisons.'[42] Morexano was a physician from
Messina who came to Naples as the epidemic was getting underway, having
been invited by the same doctor who would be the first one to speak of plague,
Agostino Baratto. Finding himself a prisoner in the city he applied his medical
expertise to help the sick. He survived the plague and was able to return to
Messina.

In the words of one more author:

> When in the year 1631, on 16 December the famous eruption of Vesuvius
> occurred, it foretold His Almighty power against the sins that were tak-
> ing over the realm. With those awful rumbles and sounds like the echo
> of a Divine trumpet this ambassador of destruction warned us, with the
> thunderbolts that he threw, with the flames that he spewed, he declared
> the Divine Wrath. In the womb of the volcano, he was telling the story
> of the tragic birth of an entire century: with the earthquakes the rebel-
> lions in the Provinces, with the steel and fire inside it the weapons and
> flames of the Popular Rebellion of 1647 (when, in a time that I dread to
> recall, in a single instant the lives of notable people and with them the
> noblest and richest spirits of the Realm fell victim to such violence). In
> the hot rivers of fires that he spewed [he foretold] the rivers of blood, in
> the open mouth [of the volcano] the famine, in the putrid air the plague,
> in the sulphur the fake remedies.[43]

The plague first appeared in Naples in January 1656, but nobody talked about
it until at least March and the government refused to acknowledge the serious-
ness of the problem until May. This delayed response from the authorities and
the fact that the firsts hotspots for the plague were popular neighbourhoods,
particularly Mercato and Lavinaio, at the centre of Masaniello's rebellion nine
years before, fostered rumours of a conspiracy to punish through poison and
disease those who had rebelled. There are no surviving copies of broadsheets,
pamphlets or *avvisi* spreading these rumours (and it is debatable if such things
even existed or if the rumour mill was fed only by words on the streets and
hearsay) but diaries and chronicles written by contemporaries do not shy away
from them.

When we talk about communications regarding the plague that ravaged the
streets of Naples in 1656 we need to be aware that we are talking of two very
different and separate aspects of things. On the one hand, we have damage
control, all the efforts that were made by the government to ensure the safety

---

42   Ibid, p. 16.
43   Pasqaule Nicolò, *A' posteri della peste*, p. 3.

FIGURE 4.5 Micco Spadaro, Largo mercatello durante la peste a Napoli (1656). Naples, Museo di Capodimonte

and health of the citizens, establishing and disseminating rules and regulations. On the other hand, we have everything else, what we could consider as behind-the-scene publications: gossip, chronicles, diaries, libels looking for a scapegoat and the counter-information strategies used by the government to manoeuvre the public opinion to its favour.

Because of the extreme stress that an event like a plague would have put both on citizens and the government, one needs to be extremely careful in approaching the contemporary documents, and take them *cum grano salis* as:

> It is true that around this event we have many stories and many written at the time; but the writers, still fearing for their possible imminent death, suffering from the loss of friends and family and shocked by the public tragedy tend to be more prone to hyperbole than storytelling, do not care for the scientific fact that could explain such tragedy but focus every attention on miracles and in general, they emerge from this horrendous catastrophe more fearful than knowledgeable, more slave of their prejudices than in possession of accurate information.[44]

Although De Renzi talked specifically about chronicles, the same caution needs to be applied to ambassadorial despatches as well as any pamphlets or

---

44   De Renzi, *Napoli nell'anno 1656*, p. 11.

140   CHAPTER 4

foglio volante published in that year. We will try here to provide examples from each of these sources both to showcase the wide range of publications on the plague and to apply, where possible, a direct comparison between the different narratives from different voices. We will once again encounter some very familiar names from the printing trade.

We should not be surprised to find the Viceroy committed to providing scrupulous instructions to his citizens, such as removing from the streets all pigs and dogs suspected to be responsible for the spreading of the disease, and at the same time for him to be the first in line, with sacks of earth on his shoulder, to try to appease God, according to the foretelling of a nun, Suor Orsola Benincasa.[45] As Gentilcore and many after him rightly pointed out, the fact that we as historians tend to apply categories to our subject of study does not mean that these categories were entirely distinct and separated throughout history. Particularly the boundaries between religion and superstition, medical practice and ecclesiastical remedies, popular knowledge and official medicine were very flexible, and never more so than during a time of utter chaos and confusion such as an outbreak of the plague.[46]

The first example of official communication on the matter is relatively late, on 30 May 1656. It is a broadsheet signed by the Deputati della Salute in which there are indications of the procedure to be used to try and contain the disease, separating sick people from the healthy in every house, family and neighbourhood.[47] The government ignored the problem for as long as possible, conscious of the impact that a plague would have not only on the spirit and morale of the citizens of Naples but also on the economy of the Kingdom. The fact that the plague probably arrived in Naples with a ship from Sardinia (where the plague was already raging) that did not observe the proper quarantine protocols and had a fabricated health certificate was probably another reason for the delay. Both could easily explain why the first doctor who mentioned the word was not believed and was instead jailed; he later died from the plague.[48] But soon the number of deaths became too high to ignore:

---

45   A. Rubino, 'Anno 1656: peste crudele in Napoli', *Archivio Storico per le Province Napoletane* 19, 4 (1894), pp 696–710.

46   Gentilcore, *Healers and Healing*, p. 102.

47   Salvatore De Renzi, *Napoli nell'anno 1656*, p. 169.

48   "There was a doctor, called Giuseppe Bozzuti, who after having observed the sick above-mentioned, said to Donato Grimaldi, a former Eletto del Popolo, that this sickness was the plague. But this observation cost him dearly because once the fact that he was publicly telling of a plague in Naples reached the ears of Alonso d'Angelis, Eletto del Popolo, and of the Viceroy, instead of accepting his counsel and open their eyes on such a grievous matter, they locked the poor doctor in a dark dungeon. He became very sick with the plague and they granted him a pardon so he could die in his home" Domenico

PRINT AND NATURAL DISASTERS

His Excellency Lord Count of Castriglio, at the time Viceroy, commanded the nature of the disease to be discussed among the most competent physicians of the city. And so on 12 May, they gathered in the house of the most prudent Francesco Liotti, at the time royal physician and General Protomedico, after many discussions, they concluded the sickness was the plague. And so, His Excellency the Viceroy established a tribunal to decide on the matter of health (i.e. Deputazione di Salute) and as its director, he chose Messer D. Emanuel de Aguiar, Knight of the order of St James and at the time rector of the Royal Court of the Vicaria. And they chose two representatives for every noble seat and two for the people's seat, alongside the Eletto del Popolo, to take the necessary step to maintain order and health.[49]

Despite this late start, once the government decided to confront the problem they proceeded fairly rapidly: the Viceroy instituted a committee for public health (*Deputazione per la salute pubblica*) with the task to organise and coordinate the city's response to this menace, and they relied liberally on print to get their message spread throughout the city. It is also interesting to note that while accounts like the one from Giulio Spinola, the Papal ambassador in Naples and therefore anti-Spanish, refer to a general lack of control in the management of the pestilence, with sick people left free to roam or completely abandoned to their deaths without anyone checking on them, the proclamations issued by the Cancelleria tell a different story.[50] The second edict issued by the Tribunale della Salute ordered that for every street of every neighbourhood the captain should nominate a person *timorata di Dio* (extremely pious) to go door to door and register the sick in every home, carrying them to the Lazzeretto or putting the house in quarantine.[51] Payment to the royal printer Egidio Longo for such publications is an indication that these dispositions were more than just words on paper.[52]

The importance, in the mind of the government's officials, of a pervasive communication strategy is clear from financial documents issued in favour of Egidio Longo by the *Deputazione di Salute*. Although the majority of Longo's

---

Antonio Parrino, *Teatro eroico, e politico dei governi de' Vicerè del Regno di Napoli dal tempo del Re Ferdinando il Cattolico fino al presente* (Naples: nella nuova stampa del Parrino e del Mutii, 1694) vol III pp. 34–35.

49   Carlo Morexano, *Torchio di osservationi*, p. 34.

50   Giulio Spinola (1612–1691) was a cardinal and had the role of *nunzio apostolico* in Naples from 1658 to 1665. ASV, *Nunziatura di Napoli*, F.54, f. 359 e seg.

51   Salvatore De Renzi, *Napoli nell'anno 1656...*, p. 157.

52   AFBN, Banco del Santissimo Salvatore, Giornali copiapolizze 62: foglio (1656 giugno. 09).

142   CHAPTER 4

commitments during this time were for his role as *Capitano dell'ottina* of San Biagio (we can find payment for the organisation of the disposal of infected bodies, collection of white cloth to make shrouds and uniforms for the *Bianchi*), he was still the royal printer as well and as such it fell to him to print all sorts of broadsheets and communications.

> To the Deputati della Salute [we give] 100 ducats and from them [we give them] to Egidio Longo for printing these proclamations: 150 for the deputies of St Gennaro's lazaretto, 100 broadsheets on stretcher-bearers, 100 proclamations for the undertakers, 900 about the distributions of doctors, surgeons and barbers in the various neighbourhoods, 700 doctors' reports with the suggested remedies and therapies, 150 prohibitions to exports goods outside of Naples, 150 instructions for landlords and merchants, 100 proclamations for the stretcher-bearers to carry bells around their legs, 150 prohibitions for those who are currently sick with this malady to leave their houses, 150 on the subject of pigs and dogs, 1,000 purges from the *protomedico*, 600 prevention techniques also from the *protomedico*, 3,000 vows made to the Holy Conception of the Saint Virgin Mary.[53]

> To the Deputati della Salute [we give] 75 ducats and from them [we give them] to Egidio Longo for having printed about 1,500 sets of instructions on how to visit patients, apply purges and enforce the quarantine. 1,250 of those were printed on a single sheet bound as a booklet, and 250 in two separate broadsheets that were posted through the streets of this city for 5 *grana* each and [we give him this money] for the paper on which he printed them.[54]

---

53   "Alli deputati della salute D. 100. E per loro a Egidio Longo per aver fatto stampare l'infratti banni cioè: 150 per li ministri del lazzaretto di San Gennaro, 100 banni circa li seggettari, 100 banni delli beccamorti, 900 banni quali con il ripartimento delli medici fisici, chirurgici e barbieri nelle ottine, 700 consulte di medici ed il preservativo et modo di curare, 150 banni che non escano robbe da Napoli, 150 banni d'alloggiatori e mercaturie, 100 banni che li seggettari portano le campanelle alle gambe, 150 banni che l'infermi del corrente male non escano dalle loro case, 150 delli porci e cani, mille vomicatori del protomedico, 600 preservativi dell'istesso, 3000 voti fatti alla Santissima Concettione di Maria Santissima Vergine." AFBN, Banco del Santissimo Salvatore, Giornali copiapolizze 62: foglio (1656 lug. 03).

54   "Alli deputati della salute D. 75. E per loro a Egidio Longo per la stampa e carta di 1500 istruttioni per la visita, spurga e quarantena, quali cioè 1250 stampate in foglio a modo di libro e 250 in due fogli reali grandi, che si sono affissi per le strade di questa città a grana 5 l'una." AFBN, Banco del Santissimo Salvatore, Giornali copiapolizze 63: foglio (1656 ott. 30).

PRINT AND NATURAL DISASTERS

Of these thousands of printed documents, as far as we can establish, scarcely any survive. Although as historians we naturally mourn their losses, at the same time we cannot be too surprised by this. Despite the considerable number of copies produced, we are still looking at cheaply made products intended to be of immediate use, not to be preserved. Moreover, the survival rate of printed pamphlets produced in times of civil and social unrest, such as during an epidemic plague, is even lower than usual, because clearly there were greater concerns than preserving copies of public ordinances. What little we do have, we owe to the efforts of those individuals that took painstaking care to transcribe these documents, be it because it was their job as public functionaries or because they intended to write a chronicle or diary. Thus, even though we cannot read the original publications, we are still able to discern their content.[55]

One of the main concerns for the people of Naples was how to cure themselves and diverse opinions on this critical question were ventilated: 'everyone was waiting with surety for the antidote ... those who wanted to print it however knew that the remedy for the plague that had been left by Angelucci and it will soon be printed and that said remedy was scorpion's oil'.[56] Angelucci was one of the many doctors and charlatans (the line was never so blurred as it was during the plague), who offered remedies and cures from the plague. Once again, the Viceroy took action with the help of Egidio Longo, who along with the report on the autopsy performed by doctors appointed by the Viceroy on two victims of the plague printed a list of official, authorised remedies.[57] Among the approved, official remedies we can find instructions to fumigate the infected air by burning rosemary, incense, laurel and juniper and of course the never failing *teriaca* and Mitridate's pills. These remedies were considered true and effective because they were found written 'in his own hand in his sanctuary' (Mitridate's pills) or because they were used in a similar plague that hit the city the previous century, once again reaffirming the principle of *auctoritas* that ruled all scientific beliefs of the time.

---

55   It is worth mentioning that, given the poor conservation state of Neapolitan archives and the even worse cataloguing of their collection, it is far easier to find manuscript chronicles in the libraries collection than searching for printed ordinances in the Archives, particularly because the majority of archival documentations from the Spanish Viceroyalty was destroyed during World War II.

56   Giuseppe De Blasiis, 'Relazione della pestilenza accaduta in Napoli l'anno 1656', *Archivio storico per le province napoletane* I, 1 (1876), pp. 323–357. This is the printed version of BNN, Ms. Br. III.E.9.

57   [Marco Aurelio Severino, Felice Martorella], *Consultatio medicorum praevia sectione cadaverum pro praeservatione et curatione pestis* (Naples: per Egidio Longo, 1656). A transcription of the text can be found in De Renzi, *Napoli nell'anno 1656*, pp. 187–192.

The quest for a remedy was indeed very important for both the suffering population and the authorities; every conceivable substance was regarded as a remedy for the plague, and many obtained some sort of licence, before revealing themselves to be a complete hoax. Doctors, physicians and even charlatans were compensated for their services by the Deputazione della Salute. Remedies were paid for with public money, and the same can be said for the ingredients needed to prepare the remedies; thus the authorities had a marked interest, even on the economic side of things, in finding and funding an efficient cure. 'To the Deputati della Salute [we give] 8,830 ducats and from them [we give them] to Gasparino del Negro because he spent them when buying many things to make liniments and other antidotes for the health of everyone.'[58] Morexano talks at length about charlatans and their remedies:

> Among the numbers of those unlicensed physicians, there was one, that up to that time was known for selling used household items. He went through the city bragging about having a *secret* to cure the plague and he gained so many followers and so many gullible people believed him that he obtained a licence to sell it. His secret was nothing more than a mixture of preserved roses with antimuonium grains, crudely mixed, and given to be drunk along with six ounces of barley water. In the two days that it took him to sell all his medicine, they said he gained more than 2,000 *scudi* but it was not a happy circumstance because all those who had believed him and taken the vile concoction died. And not long after he was justly punished for his treacherous ways by death, and not even his secrets could save him. Because having himself contracted the same plague that afflicted the people that flocked to his door, day and night in their thousands, he miserably died in just a few days.[59]

Alongside various recipes such as the one here described, Morexano reveals alternative means of staving off the plague such as amulets with Saint's effigies and spells written on them. The relationship between the authorities and charlatans was a complex one: the authorities were desperate enough to try any kind of cure or remedy, no matter where it came from, but at the same time,

---

58   "Ai Deputati della Salute 88,30 ducati e da loro a Gasparino del Negro per averli spesi nel comprare molte cose per fare linimenti e altri antidoti per la salute di tutti." AFBN, Banco del Salvatore, giornale copiapolizze, matr. 63 (28 Luglo 1656). For further analysis of the relationship between authorities and charlatans in a time of plague see David Gentilcore, 'Negoziare rimedi in tempo di peste: alchimisti, ciarlatani, protomedici', *Roma moderna e contemporanea* 14 (2006), pp. 75–91.

59   Carlo Morexano, *Torchio di osservationi*, pp. 27–28.

PRINT AND NATURAL DISASTERS

they were perfectly aware that the unprecedented crisis was the perfect opportunity for schemers and conmen to make a fortune selling dubious powders that could do more harm than good.

As had happened when Vesuvius erupted, the Neapolitan people turned to their faith and rituals to find comfort and solace in the new nightmare that was the plague. Although every physician and man of science denounced this as a bad idea that would only serve to spread the contagion further, many processions took place, with and without the sacred relics. It is interesting that although Morexano, Gatta and Parrino shared the opinion that these processions were doing more harm than good because 'it gave the last necessary push to the spreading of the disease and now there were no neighbourhood nor house that was safe from the plague', they also agreed that the situation was so desperate that only God could now save the city.[60]

This view was shared by the Florentine emissary in Naples. Present in Naples during the plague, which would eventually claim his life, the frequent letters that he sent to Florence offer an interesting external perspective on the Neapolitan situation. Overall, he is extremely critical of the way in which the authorities were dealing with the sanitary emergency. In his opinion, the measures that were put in place to contain the plague were not strict enough, and the people of Naples were not scared enough to obey them even if they were. He constantly reports people violating the quarantine measures and resisting the officials when they tried to enforce the royal decrees in regard to the burning of clothing and mattresses that belonged to people who were sick or died of the plague. Furthermore, he accused those who recovered from the plague of creating further problems in a city already on the brink of collapsing by indulging in all sorts of antics in the belief that having survived the plague they were now invulnerable and immortal. As if all of this was not enough, the Spanish authorities worsened the situation by refusing to listen to the Comitato della Salute, the medical and professional experts on the subject, and staging unnecessary and dangerous religious processions:

> The gentlemen of the Deputazione della Salute wanted to maintain a quarantine throughout the city but both His Excellency the Viceroy and the Consiglio Collaterale were in agreement that not only it was not necessary but the Viceroy himself removed from their tasks the above-mentioned gentlemen Deputati ... His Excellency and his Consiglio

---

60   Ibid., p. 25. The same is said by Geronimo Gatta, *Di una gravissima peste che nella passata primavera e estate dell'anno 1656 depopulò la città di Napoli* (Naples: Luc'Antonio Fusco, 1659) p. 198, and Domenico Antonio Parrino, *Teatro Eroico*, p. 245.

146   CHAPTER 4

Collaterale, having listened to the opinion of twelve doctors, decided not
only to declare void and null every broadsheet issued by the Deputati
della Salute in regards to the quarantine but also to issue an order declar-
ing that the city was once again healthy and that because of this the can-
nons of the city would be fired and the Te Deum sang to celebrate the
mercy of God.[61]

The idea that the plague was a punishment was present in every chronicle and
manuscript account of the time. Of course, for anti-Spanish authors, the punishment was being dealt out by the Spaniards themselves to make the people
pay for the rebellion of 1647, but at the time of the plague these were minority
voices: this sentiment only gained support and popularity later in the century.
For the majority of authors, the punishment was from God, and therefore only
by appeasing Him could the city be saved. This sentiment was shared by the
authorities and reinforced and shared through public edicts. One published on
28 September 1656, once the plague had reached its peak and was now gradually receding, opened with an acknowledgement of God's role in the remission
of the plague. 'God Almighty has already, in His infinite Mercy and thank to
the intercession of the Immaculate Conception of the Holy Virgin Mary, of the
Glorious St Gennaro and of the Protector Saints of this most faithful city of
Naples, alleviated the rightful punishment that he brought upon this city for
our sins and that is why we have lately seen an improvement in the state of the
plague, although it is not yet vanquished.'[62]

The city vowed to uphold and defend the glory of the Immaculate
Conception, commissioning frescoes with biblical scenes to be painted above
the seven main city gates, thus fulfilling a vow that was actually made during

---

61   "Li signori Deputati della Salute volevano si facesse una quarantena generale, però il
        s. Vice Re sia il Coll[ateral]e vi concorre, onde non solo non haverà effetto ma di più il
        med[esi].mo s. V[ice]. Re ha sospeso alli detti signori Deputati il possere [?] procedere
        nella criminalità, perché sono tutti sollevati e malicontenti.
              ... è stato resoluto da S[ua]. E[ccellenza]. et suo Coll[ateral]e consiglio, precedente
        prima un collegio di dodici medici, non solo distaccare ogni trattato hauto la deputazione
        della Salute di fare una quarantena generale per tutta la città, ma di publicare in essa
        q[uel].lo med[esi].mo giorno la recuperata salute con esservi cantato il Tedeum et sparate
        tutte le castella, in rendim[en].to di grazie, q[ua].le piaceria al s. Iddio di concederne".
        ASF, *Mediceo del Principato*, 4117, n.n. (19 September 1656) The letters from September
        and October all relates to the Neapolitan Plague. These were sent to the Segretario di
        Stato granducale Giovan Battista Gondi (1589–1664) from Curzio Dazi, the secretary of
        the Florentine emissary in Naples Vincenzo de' Medici, who died from the plague on
        20 July 1656 (vd. *Mediceo del Principato*, 4116, n.n., 25 July 1656).
62   Salvatore De Renzi, *Napoli nell'anno 1656*, p. 202.

PRINT AND NATURAL DISASTERS

the plague epidemic in 1556–57.[63] They also commissioned a print run of ex-votos in the name of the Virgin Mary, as we have seen from the payment order to Egidio Longo.[64] But the biggest show of popular devotion, an event that involved the Viceroy himself, was the construction of the Suor Orsola Benincasa's hermitage, following a prophecy made by the nun herself. She was the last child of a very pious and devout Neapolitan family and proved to be interested in religious life since childhood; she was also prone to episodes of religious exaltation during which she claimed to receive visions from God. Her popularity was such that people would queue outside the hermitage in which she lived, and later the church that she built, just for a chance to hear her visions. She even started a religious order for nuns near the Sant'Elmo convent. After her death in 1618, it was said that she continued to perform miracles because her body immediately turned into a relic, bleeding so profusely that all the witnesses could collect some of her blood.[65] But her popularity reached its peak during the plague, when, as Celano narrates:

> In the year 1656, in which Naples was ravaged by the most horrendous plague, some pious men, I do not know who had printed a prophecy that it was believed to have been made by this most faithful servant of God [i.e. Nun Orsola Benincasa] in which it was said that the nunnery should be built amidst a great calamity that would happen in the city [to save it]; Neapolitan people, eager to assuage the Divine wrath that so horrendously was punishing them, all came out, both the sane and the sick and those that had been cautious until now, and around the middle of the month they all went to the convent of Nun Orsola, and some were carrying rocks on their shoulders and others had woods and beams for the construction, some were leading donkeys carrying limestone and other were excavating the ground and in all the city there was not a single piece of wood or plank left in the stores and all of the merchants and builders and their assistants went to work without demanding money. It was so large and important that the Viceroy Count of Castriglio himself went there and in a show of devotion with his own hand, he excavated and carried twelve baskets of earth.[66]

---

63   [Francesco Castellano], *Conclusione degl'illustri signori eletti della città* (Naples: s.l.,1657) BNN, San Martino LIX.7.1.54.

64   Cf. note 53.

65   Giovanni Bonifacio Bagatta, *Vita della Ven. Serva di Dio Orsola Benincasa* (Rome: per Francesco de Lazzeri, 1696). Giulia Calvi, 'L'oro, il fuoco, le forche: la peste napoletana del 1656', *Archivio storico italiano* 139, 3 (1981), pp. 405–458.

66   Celano, *Notitie del bello*, V, p. 47.

The problem of the plague spreaders was a real one. Even among doctors, there were those who actually believed that the plague could indeed be caused by some sort of venomous powder that was maliciously spread on food and water. Once the rumour started, it proved impossible to contain. Soon the city was ablaze with talk of *untori* and whoever had the misfortune to be caught in suspicious activities would immediately find himself in jail, if the angry mob did not happen to reach them sooner than the authorities. As we have already noted, there was a strong connection in the mind of contemporaries between Masaniello's rebellion and the plague. It therefore should not come as a surprise that some of the people who were involved in the uprising chose this occasion to riot once again, pointing their fingers at the Spaniards as being responsible for the plague, not only in some metaphorical, biblical sense but in a tangible way: the Spanish soldiers were in possession of infected powders and they were spreading them in the populous neighbourhoods to punish the people for what had happened nine years prior.[67] The Spanish authorities were quick to intervene. Realising that it was impossible to eradicate belief in the existence of plague spreaders, they shifted the blame, arresting and torturing a confession out of a Portuguese soldier and a French merchant, both known enemies of Spain.[68] They also quickly imprisoned those who were trying to use the situation to incite a new rebellion. Not surprisingly, no records of any of these events have survived in print. Battling the plague was not only a medical emergency but a political one and maintaining public order, particularly through strict control of information, was of the utmost importance.

The situation in Naples gradually improved from August onward and by the end of the year, the city was officially plague-free. The official announcement was held with all the appropriate fanfare on 8 December 1656, a day dedicated to the Virgin Mary, and by the beginning of 1657 life was returning to normal. A broadsheet published in February marked this, lifting the travel restrictions that had been in place since March 1656 and once again offering thanks to God for having spared the city:

> Given that, thanks to the Mercy of Our Lord Saviour and through the intercession of his Sainted Mother and the Saints Protector, in this city we are now living healthy and without any suspicions of contagious disease, we have decided with approval and counsel of the Royal Consiglio Collaterale, that always assist us, to issue the following proclamation. With this, we command all government officials, Mayors, Eletti, and

---

67   Carlo Morexano, *Torchio di osservationi*, p. 38.
68   Carlo Celano, *Notitie del bello*, v, p. 56 .

Health officers of this city that if any person that comes from this city with the appropriate health certificate should happen to pass through their territories, they should give them free access as was done before the plague.[69]

We have seen ample proof that the situation in Naples during the plague was as is to be expected, tense and fraught. People were literally dying in the streets, and rumours as to who was at fault were rampant. The plague quickly became not only a health concern but also a problem of public order. Authorities had to preserve the citizens of Naples from the plague while at the same time guarding themselves against new insurrections and maintaining morale. Few documents survive that can tell us what the day-to-day life in the city ravaged by the plague was like, but thanks to De Renzi's effort, chronicles and subsequent texts printed on the events we can obtain a vivid impression. Up to an extent the authorities managed to keep health concerns separated from the effort made to maintain public order, allowing these two different problematics to blend together only when it came to the topic of religion.

The people of Naples were very much aware of and exposed to both of these narratives. They bore witness to the Viceroy and other official powers taking part in apotropaic rituals to save the city from this calamity and at the same time, they would have seen or heard the broadsheets scattered in every street, *piazza* and market listing practical rules and provisions to deal with the plague. They would have had access to doctors and practitioners as well as dubious remedies discussed on the streets (which often were ones and the same). Among the practical rules, we have the obligation for stretcher-bearers to wear a bell, the prohibition on selling water because the water-sellers would let sick and healthy people drink from the same vessel, the prohibition on dogs and pigs roaming the streets, the prohibition on leaving the city, the obligation for those who were sick to remain quarantined in their houses, and the list of rules and regulations to be observed inside the *lazzeretti*. Several of these were also printed in Spanish, and at the bottom of every one of these proclamations we can read the usual warning 'And to make sure that everyone received this news, we will post this broadsheet in all the usual places in the city'.[70]

The dual nature of the fight against the plague is visible in the cheap print as well, once again proof of the incredible value of this media as a mirror of society; a mirror so much more accurate because the nature of the texts themselves reflects the society in its entirety, including the masses. There is a trend,

---

69 De Renzi, *Napoli nell'anno 1656*, p. 223.

70 De Renzi, *Napoli nell'anno 1656*, pp. 195–201.

not only within historiography but also according to common wisdom, to see Naples as the theatre of a constant conflict between the illiterate, angry mob of Neapolitan people and the evil foreign rulers, and this is particularly true when it comes to the Spanish Viceroyalty and times of social unrest. However, as Domenico Cecere rightly stated, and as I hope I have illustrated in these last two chapters: 'There was not a clear contrast between the authorities and their subjects, most of all because the latter were not passive receivers of political and religious messages produced elsewhere .... On the contrary, the narratives of disaster that occurred in the seventeenth century can be read as representing one of the spheres in which different authorities and social forces competed to strengthen their own power and prestige.'[71]

---

71 Domenico Cecere, 'Moralising Pamphlets: Calamities, Information and Propaganda in Seventeenth-Century Naples', in Domenico Cecere et al. (eds), *Disaster Narratives in Early Modern Naples. Politics, Communication and culture* (Rome: Viella, 2018), pp. 129–145.

CHAPTER 5

Print and Religion

Annibale di Capua Archbishop of Naples etc.
The Sacred Council of Trent adopted more than adequate precautions in regard to those books that booksellers can carry and sell, and the execution [of the Tridentine decrees] has been enforced in this city many times .... Despite this, due to negligence, disregard and sometimes even by evil design, booksellers are still selling forbidden books, forbidden both because they were declared so in the *Index* and the public ordinances and because some of them need to be amended. For this reason, this is what [we command] to help those who are in need, in order to compensate and protect both booksellers and whoever should find himself in possession of such books: with this decree, we order the booksellers of the city of Naples to prepare, within a month of the publication of this decree, a catalogue in alphabetical order of every single [book] they own, and even those they have ordered and to bring this catalogue to us so that we easily ... describe all of the books that we receive every day .... We declare this, so that the bookseller cannot, nor should believe that they can, sell or hold books without giving prior notice to us, and because they can keep [those books] for which they have received our written approval. This we have decided, under penalty of the requisition of books and an excommunication *latae sententiae* against the transgressors, which could only be lifted by us.
Naples, in the Archbishop Palace, 21 July 1592.
A[nnibale]. Archbishop
[Giovanni Camillo] Prezioso, Notary [of the Archbishopry].[1]

∴

---

1 "Annibal de Capua Archiepiscopus Neapolitanus etc.
     Satis ac sufficienter per Sacrum Sanctum Concilium Tridentinum fuit provisum circa libros vendendos per librarios et detinendos, idque executioni in hac Civitate multotiens demandatum [...] et nihilominus et incuria et negligentia et aliquoties hominum malitia aliqui retinentur et vendentur per bibliopolas libri qui sunt prohibiti et per indices ac edicta publica, et aliqui correctione egentes. Hinc est quod Nos indemniati et saluti cum biblio

The relationship between print and religion is a complex one. Similarly to what we have seen in regard to print and the state, this is a relationship that is marked by a balance of control, censorship and propaganda.

In recent years many scholars have recognised that, unlike what was the prevalent view for the longest time, the Catholic Church was very aware of the power of the printed words. Of course, whenever we think about the Church and books the thought immediately goes to the Inquisition. To censorship, to book burnings, to the mighty pen of a zealous censor slashing across the pages of Giordano Bruno's work. And while all these things existed and of course, ecclesiastical censorship was a powerful tool employed by the Church, the reality of the relationship between books and religion is more complex than that. The awareness that ecclesiastical authorities had of the importance and power of books shaped the approach that the Church took in dealing with this medium. It was an approach that was multifaceted and layered. Even when it came to censorship itself, the work done by those who were tasked to control the circulation of information and ideas through books was something that went further and beyond a mere work of destruction and cancellation. Ecclesiastical censorship rewrote, modified, altered, and promoted. Saved as well as destroyed.[2] Not only that, but the Catholic Church used print and printed books in a proactive manner to spread its version of truth, to recruit, persuade, convince and convert people.

When it comes to the Spanish Viceroyalty of Naples, only one aspect of the complex relationship between the Catholic Church and books has been investigated, the censorship angle. Censorship here is intended merely in its bleakest aspects of control, suppression and destruction. In this chapter, we

---

polarum, tum etiam omnibus aliis, ad quos libri pervenire possunt, providere et consulere satagentes, huius mandati serie iniungimus bibliopolis Civitatis Neapolis a die publicationis seu intimitationis presentis nostri mandati, quatenus infra mensem debeant inventarium et notam omnium et singulorum […] existentium adeo ordinatum et alphabeticum confectum et penes Nos presentasse, ut de facili et […] describere omnes libros qui ad manus […] in dies perveniendos, quos ut nullo modo vendere nec retinere possint nec debeant, prohibemus, absque eo quod notitiam dederint prius Nobis, ut decepta approbatione nostra in scriptis declarante illos venales, et posse detinere, et hoc sub pena ammissionis librorum ac excommunicationis latae sentente contra inobedientes, quam absolutionem Nobis expresse reservamus.

Datum Neapoli in Archibiscopali Palatio die 21 Julii 1592. A. Archiepiscopus Pretiosus Actuarius" ASDN, *Carte del card. A. di Capua*, unnumbered ms. The missing words in the transcription are due to the deterioration of the document.

2   On this particular aspect of ecclesiastical censorship in Early Modern Italy see Marco Cavarzere, *La prassi della censura nell'Italia del Seicento* (Rome: Edizioni di Storia e letteratura, 2011); Giorgio Caravale, *Libri pericolosi. Censura e cultura italiana in Età moderna* (Bari: Laterza, 2022).

PRINT AND RELIGION

will discuss some interesting cases of censorship as well as the relationship between printers and the Church. But we will also look at what other strategies the Church applied to control the print trade and what was printed and circulated in Naples.

1 Religious Censorship

For the longest time, the cultural landscape of Spanish Naples has been regarded as a wasteland. The tyrannical control exerted by the Spanish authorities combined with the iron fist of ecclesiastical censorship created a hostile environment in which printing was a failing business, printers were few and books printed in Naples were generally cheap editions of little relevance. We have already disproven most of these assumptions in the previous chapters, and it is important to reiterate that in recent years the historiography on the subject has been gradually changing.

When it comes to the topic of ecclesiastical censorship, however, the predominant opinion among Neapolitan scholar is still pretty bleak. The *Sant'Uffizio* archival collection in the Archivio Storico Diocesano of Naples is currently for the most part not available for public view, due to the poor state of conservation of many of the documents. However, simply looking at the catalogue edited by Giovanni Romeo we can immediately see instances in which printers and booksellers were brought in front of the authorities of the Sant'Uffizio because they were accused of holding or selling prohibited books.[3] The work done by Pasquale Lopez on the topic of ecclesiastical censorship, extensively based on this same archival collection, has been used as further confirmation of the inescapability of religious censorship and its negative impact on the printing industry.[4] Nevertheless, once we look at the practice of

---

3   Giovanni Romeo, *Il fondo Sant'Ufficio dell'Archivio Diocesano di Napoli. Inventario (1549–1647)* (Naples: Editoriale Comunicazioni Sociali, 2003). The documents that are explicitly labelled as "libri proibiti" (forbidden books) are *c.*74/206, but *c.*30 have other charges beside those that have to deal with forbidden books. This particular catalogue can no longer be used as a guide to locate documents within the archive because, according to the archivists, in the years since it was written the entire collection was moved and rearranged and the state of many documents had further deteriorated. Nevertheless, it remains a useful tool to gain a general idea of what kind of documents are present in this particular collection.

4   Pasqaule Lopez, *Riforma Cattolica e vita religiosa e culturale a Napoli: dalla fine del Cinquecento ai primi del Settecento* (Roma: istituto editoriale del Mezzogiorno, 1964); Id., *Stampa e censura a Napoli nel '600* (Naples: Stabilimento Tip. G. Genovese, 1965); Id., *Inquisizione stampa e censura nel regno di Napoli tra '500 e '600* (Naples: Edizioni del delfino, 1972); Id., *Sul libro a stampa e le origini della censura ecclesiastica* (Naples: edizioni Regina, 1975). Lopez' works are

censorship in a broader context and take into consideration further archival evidence as well as library catalogues the picture that emerges is quite different and more nuanced. I will proceed to illustrate several examples of clashes between printers and censors to illustrate that despite the existence of ecclesiastical censorship the printing of religious books and ephemera was still thriving and also that overall the ecclesiastical censors were pretty lenient towards printers and booksellers.

The first law to be issued in Naples on the subject of religious books was not issued by the Archbishop but rather by the Viceroy. On 25 October 1544, Don Pedro of Toledo issued a proclamation with which he prohibited the printing, selling and even holding of religious books published in the previous thirty years without the written approval of the Cappellano Maggiore. This same law was issued again in 1550 but extended to all kinds of books, not only those on religious topics, and further prohibitions and regulations about the printing and selling of books, both religious and secular, were published in 1586 and 1598. These were the essential *Prammatiche*, the laws, but decrees and reminders were issued almost yearly. In 1562 one of the decrees on this subject tried to enforce the keeping of a customer log by printers and booksellers. This particular requirement did not appear again in any other law or decree, probably because of the impracticality of such a task. However, the frequent repetition of the various regulations addressed to printers and booksellers and the slight changes that can be found between them is indicative of a strong desire from the authorities to regulate the book market and the difficulties that they encountered in establishing an effective strategy to do so. The lack of success from the civil authorities combined with the renewed interest in the topic by ecclesiastical authorities in the second half of the sixteenth century brought a new wave of laws and prohibitions addressed to printers and booksellers, only this time these were not issued by the Viceroy but by the Archbishop.

It is undeniably true that strong ecclesiastical censorship was in place in Naples, and Italy in general, particularly after the Council of Trent (1545–1563), when the different dioceses were called upon to apply the decisions of the Council. The post-Tridentine Church appeared to be a much more controlling structure than before, and this control was applied to several aspects, including the circulation of knowledge. The publication, on 15 March 1564, of the Tridentine Index, a new and updated version of the *Index Librorum Prohibitorum*, is a reflection of this and it is what prompted the dioceses in

---

of the utmost importance because he was able to see and transcribe several documents from the Archivio Storico Diocesano and other smaller ecclesiastical archives that are no longer available to scholars, even if his methodology and his conclusions are now outdated.

PRINT AND RELIGION

Italy to take a keener interest in what was being printed and what books circulated in their territories. It is important to note here, however, that talking about a post-Tridentine Church as it is something that actually existed, a monolithic and cohesive institution, is incorrect. The reality of the application of the Tridentine decrees varied greatly from place to place and it was shaped and influenced by the personal character, experience and inclinations of those who were tasked with the difficult job of making these decrees a reality. In Naples, the brunt of the task of enforcing all of the Tridentine decrees fell upon Archbishop Annibale di Capua, and we will see how his personal experiences affected and shaped his approach to the matter of the circulation of books. Born into a family of strong supporters of the Spanish Crown since the Aragonese period, he was offered the Archbishopal seat in Naples in 1579, with the specific objective of bringing the full force of the Counter-Reformation to the city. Therefore, it should not come as a surprise that the three primary goals of his mandate were: the construction and restoration of churches and monasteries, control over the lives of clergymen and control over the printing industry through censorship. Naples had always been a complex city from a cultural standpoint. The presence of the university and the fact that the city was one of the most important harbours of the Mediterranean created a constant influx of new people and, with them, new ideas and new books. Moreover, the transitory nature of this population made the job of policing them and controlling the kind of ideas that they promoted more challenging. Annibale di Capua was well aware of the difficulties of the task that lay before him, but at the same time, he had first-hand knowledge of what was at stake. He had spent some years in Poland (1586–1591), a place in which religious freedom and the freedom of the printing industry went hand in hand, and there he had the chance of witnessing the peril this brought to the order and strength of the true faith.[5] After his return to Naples, he redoubled his efforts in order to establish strong ecclesiastical control over the printing industry, through several decrees and the institution of yearly book burnings. While all of this is undeniably true, and it clearly indicates the existence of a precise design by the ecclesiastical authorities when it comes to the control of the printing press, whether this strategy was effective, or at least as effective as Lopez indicated, is an entirely different matter.

Annibale issued his first decree on the subject of the circulation of books in 1583. Of all the decrees issued on this subject, this one is the most detailed, dealing not only with printers and booksellers but also with customs officials,

---

5 Jan Wladyslaw Wos, *Annibale di Capua. Nunzio Apostolico e Arcivescovo di Napoli (1544 ca.–1599). Materiali per una biografia* (Rome: Fondazione Giovanni Paolo II, 1984).

convent libraries and readers as well. After his return from Poland, he issued five more decrees in the span of four years, all of them pretty much identical in their wording and provisions to the one cited at the beginning of this chapter, and usually prefaced by an explicit declaration of concern with regard to the difficulties of controlling the circulation of books printed elsewhere and then brought into Naples, as well as the challenges that Neapolitan clandestine print posed to effective control of the printing industry. He reiterated the need for booksellers to provide the Archbishop's office with a catalogue of their wares, under penalty of fines and excommunication. All of these decrees were posted in the city squares and in the main churches, as usual, but the ecclesiastical authorities also took great care to make sure that several copies were affixed in the S. Biagio neighbourhood, where the majority of printers and booksellers had their workshops. The decree published on 21 July 1592, in particular, bore the names of forty booksellers to whom this provision was addressed, along with the location of their shops, all of them between S. Biagio and S. Lorenzo.

The edict published on 26 January 1593 for the first time mentioned pedlars and itinerant printers alongside printers and booksellers. Before Annibale, neither the ecclesiastical nor civil authorities had dedicated much thought to pedlars. The end of the sixteenth century saw an increase in the number of street vendors throughout Europe, and the Kingdom of Naples was not an exception, so much so that it became imperative to specifically address this problem with a decree.

> Since it came to our notice that besides regular booksellers, who have shops and places that can and are often visited by our Reverendi Visitatori, as the Index and the dispositions promoted by the Holy See command us to do, there are in this city and dioceses of Naples numerous sellers of histories, songs, pamphlets and other printed things, published both in Naples and elsewhere, often without a permit, about obscene things that go against the dogmas of our Holy Faith. If these things were to be sold in regular bookshops that are under control and that obey the orders in regard to forbidden books, they would not be sold at all, as we have made clear. Thus, because We have to remedy this situation in obedience to the calling of our Office, in addition to what we have already established and published on this matter, we order, forbid and command, under penalty of excommunication *latae sententia* that no one in this city and dioceses of Naples can sell histories, songs and pamphlets, and particularly that no one can sell those that do not have the name of the printer or the place in which they were published, without showing them first to the Reverend our theologian for approval, or to some other person that we

PRINT AND RELIGION

will indicate, and only after having obtained a written permit from us and our Reverend Vicar. This permit will be granted free of charge. In the same way, it is forbidden to sell books, both new and old, outside of regular bookshops, among the streets and in the city squares, without this permit, under penalty of excommunication and the loss of the books and other punishment, for us to establish if these books are prohibited or do not fall within the terms of the law and Sacred Constitutions on the subject. And so that no one can plead his ignorance on this matter, we order that a copy of this edict will be posted at the door of our most important church, as well as in other public places across this city and dioceses of Naples so that everyone who could think of doing otherwise will feel like he has been already personally warned.

From our Archbishop Palace in Naples on 26 January 1593.[6]

The need to reinforce and reprint some subtle variation of the same decree over and over again, combined with the fact that the authorities began to try to target pedlars as well is a clear sign that their efforts in controlling the printing industry were not as successful as they hoped. They became increasingly aware of the dangers and risks posed by those sellers who did not reside in Naples,

---

6 "Essendo noi informati che oltra i librari ordinarii, che tengono lle loro boteche et librerie publice, le quali spesse volte sogliono essere visitate da i Reverendi Visitatori da noi deputati, conforme all'Indice et ordini della Santa Sede Apostolica et nostri, vi sono anco per questa città et diocesi di Napoli diversi venditori et rivenditori di diverse istoriette, canzoni, libretti ed altre cose stampate, tanto in Napoli come fora Napoli, senza licenza, che trattano non solo di cose oscene et contra bona mores, ma anco alle volte contra i dogmi della nostra Santa Fede Cattolica, le quali cose, si se vendessero nelle librarie solite a visitare e nelle quali si osservano l'ordini sopra ciò dati, non se andrebbero vendendo molte cose indecenti e prohibite, come s'è visto e ritrovato per esperienza. Onde volendo Noi per il debito del nostro pastorale ufficio sopra di ciò provvedere, inherendo all'altri ordini in questa materia fatti e pubblicati, prohibimo, ordinamo e comandamo, sotto pena d'escomunica latae sententiae, che niuna persona possa n'è debba vendere per questa Città e Diocesi di Napoli delle dette Istoriette, canzoni e libretti, et in particolare non si vendino quelle che non hanno il nome del stampatore, né del luogo dove sono stampate, si prima quelle non saranno viste et approbate dal Reverendo nostro theologo o altra persona da noi deputanda, et ottenuta licenza in scriptis da noi e dall Reverendo nostro generale Vicario, quale si darà gratis, né similmente vender fora di dette librarie per le piazze altri libri, né vecchi né novi, senza detta licenza, sotto la detta pena di escomunica e di perdere i libri, et altre pene, iuxta la forma de li Sacri Canoni et Costituzioni sopr cciò fatte, et questo per conoscere si detti libri siano prohibiti o non. Et acciò che niuno possa allegare causa d'ignoranza, comandamo che la copia del presente ordine sia affissa nella porta della nostra maggior Chiesa, et in altri luoghi pubblici di questa Città et Diocesi di Napoli, la quale esecuzione in tale modo fatta vogliamo che avverti ogni contravveniente come si fosse personalmente citato. Dal nostro Arcivescoval Palazzo di Napoli il dì 26 de Gennaro 1593", ASDN, *Carte del card. A. di Capua*, unnumbered ms.

but simply passed through the city and stayed there only long enough to print and sell dangerous, prohibited books.

Speaking of the relationship between ecclesiastical authorities and pedlars, among the documents held in the Sant'Uffizio collection, there is an interesting proceeding against a Roman street performer, Giovanni Pietro Proposito (b. 1567/8), who was arrested together with two Neapolitan colleagues, Giuseppe del Fiore and Leonardo Conte.[7] The charges against them were of having read aloud in one of their spectacles an indulgence by Alessandro VI from 1494 and having sold printed copies of the same. What is particularly fascinating about this is that Giovanni Proposito confessed to having bought 150 copies of this particular indulgence (an engraving of The Virgin Mary and baby Jesus seated on a throne, with Saint Anne beside them, with the text of the indulgence at the bottom) at the printing press of Carlino, by a Domenico Tabanelli. Carlino, who was brought in for questioning, admitted to having rented his printing press to Tabanelli specifically in order for him to print the indulgence.

The indulgence that was printed in Carlino's shop was brought to the attention of the Sant'Uffizio on 28 May by Enrico Bacco, a bookseller who declared that he bought it from a pedlar named Angelo Bentivolo. This however is not the only copy of the indulgence filed with the legal proceedings, but there are three more on the same subject. The first was printed in Rome, the second probably in Venice and the third one does not have any kind of imprimatur but it is probably from the 1580s and 1590s. It is clear that the Sant'Uffizio tried to confiscate as many copies as possible of the indulgence in order to prevent them from being sold. Proposito was sentenced to thirteen months in prison, and his colleagues to nine months. Carlino and his business partner Antonio Pace were both arrested and questioned but the charges against them both had been dropped by June 1599. The printer Domenico Tabanelli had apparently already fled Naples, as is demonstrated by the last page of the proceeding which contains his physical description to be sent to the Roman Curiae. This document is particularly relevant because it is proof of the not-uncommon practice of renting out printing presses to pedlars, charlatans and street performers for them to print their own wares. And, even more important, it proves that the owners of the printing press were not held accountable nor responsible for what was printed by those who rented out their machinery.

---

7 ASDN, Sant'Ufficio, 1138 *Pro Fisco Curiae Archip*[iscopa]*lis Neapolitan*[ae] *contra Ioannem Petrum Propositum Romanum, Joannem Jacobum Carlinum impressorem, Antonium Pacem, Dominicum Tabanelli* (22 May 1599–25 June 1600).

PRINT AND RELIGION

FIGURE 5.1 Forged indulgences attributed to Pope Alexander VI (c.1599) ASDN, Sant'Ufficio, 1138. Naples, Archivio Storico Diocesano

FIGURE 5.2 Forged indulgences attributed to Pope Alexander VI (c.1599) ASDN, Sant'Ufficio, 1138. Naples, Archivio Storico Diocesano

PRINT AND RELIGION

We have seen how the decrees and provisions issued by the ecclesiastical authorities were not the only laws that printers and booksellers had to take into account. Jurisdiction over printed books was nebulous and unclear, with many overlapping areas between civic and ecclesiastical law as well as grey areas that were uncharted territories. Many of the most renowned printers of the time, among which we can find the aforementioned Carlino, Secondino Roncagliolo and even the royal printer Egidio Longo, ended up in front of the ecclesiastical tribunal. On 2 October 1562, for example, Secondino Roncagliolo was arrested for printing and selling a broadsheet with a collection of texts from various indulgences. He did not have permission for it, but he thought that he was doing nothing wrong because he believed the permit that was obtained by his uncle Gio. Domenico Roncagliolo seven years before to be still valid. The ruling was ultimately against him and he was sentenced to four months of excommunication and the seizure of the broadsheet in question. Apparently, the authorities did a thorough job, since the only known copy is the one that is attached to the proceedings.[8] During the questioning, the inquisitors showed a copy of the incriminated broadsheet to Roncagliolo, asking him if he recognised it, to which he replied

> Yes, Sirs. I printed these said excerpts and I took them from other works printed by other printers, and in particular from the said heirs to my father Domenico Roncagliolo. But I did not take any further license to buy them or print them again, because it is known in Naples that things that are printed once in Naples can then be printed again by any other printer without applying for a licence, and in this same way I have printed more of them in the year 1648.[9]

As to who the buyers were, another key point in the interrogation, Roncagliolo replied that he sold around one thousand copies of the broadsheet and most of them to clergymen. After the interrogation, the inquisitors pointed out to Roncagliolo that all the royal and ecclesiastical provisions in regards to print, and in particular those that concerned the ban on printing and

---

8   ASDN, Sant'Ufficio, 3292 *Processus originalis contra Secondinum Roncagliolum Impressorem* (2 Ottobre 1652–8 Febbraio 1653).

9   "R[espondi].ᵗ Sì Sig[no].ʳᵉ che io ho stamp[a].ᵗᵒ li predetti transunti nel così e così, et questi Transunti li ho cavati da altre stampe di altri stampat[o].ʳⁱ, et precise dal q[uonda].ᵐ gli [i.e. dai quondam] heredi di Dom[eni].ᶜᵒ Roncagliolo mio P[ad]re che però non ho pigliato altra lic[enz].ᵃ di ricompirmieli o ristamparmeli, tanto tenevano inciso in Nap[ol].ⁱ che le cose stampate una volta in Nap[ol].ⁱ se possa stampare da ogni altro stampat[or].ᵉ senza pigliare altra lic[enz].ᵃ, come ne ho stampate altre nel anno 1648". ASDN, Sant'Ufficio, 3292 c.5r.

reprinting anything without the proper licence, were always sent to every printer. Furthermore, all of these were regularly printed and posted throughout the entire city. Roncagliolo tried to defend himself, appealing to the tradition rather than the law, stating that in over fifty years of activities he never knew that those particular provisions referred also to reprints and that no one ever questioned him on this matter. As a defence, it was not very effective and he ended up being excommunicated. On 5 February 1653, he wrote a plea to the Archbishop asking for the excommunication to be revoked, since he had every intention of retiring and leaving his business to his nephew, Salvatore Castaldo (who would remain in business until 1688). His absolution was granted on 8 February. The proceedings are straightforward, but some questions remain. It appears that Roncagliolo kept his printing business until 1658 and furthermore it appears that his heir was the same Salvatore who, with the surname Roncagliolo, worked alongside Secondino from 1650 to 1652. It could be that he then chose to change his surname to Castaldo in order to distance himself from the uncle, given his legal trouble. But it could also be that the different surname was used to avoid any mix-up with the Eredi di Secondino (heirs to Secondino), printers who were in business between 1656 and 1682.[10]

Despite the fact that the relatively lenient punishment could suggest otherwise, this was not the first time Roncagliolo found himself in trouble over legal technicalities. In 1623, an anonymous claimant filed charges against him for printing a book written by doctor Francesco Antonio Caserta called *De natura et usu aquarum potabilium*. Roncagliolo had obtained a printing permit for this book from the office of the Viceroy but he had failed to apply for a permit from the Archbishop's court as well. This report was analysed together with another charge, in regard to a book printed in Spanish and written by Giovanni da Salamanca (*Compendio de los beneficios que son reservados, y affectos al Papa*) upon ecclesiastical benefices. Roncagliolo published this book the previous year with a regular permit but, upon reprinting it, new sections were added that were not present in the manuscript that was read and approved by the officials of the Sant'Ufficio. For both of these offences, on 16 March 1623 Archbishop Decio Carafa (1556–1626), sentenced Secondino Roncagliolo to a two month interdict from all editorial activities and to pay an *obligatione untiarum auri viginti quinque* (25 gold *once*). The gold *oncia* was a currency commonly used in Sicily that weighed ca. 4.4 g. In Naples, 1 *oncia* was the equivalent of 30 silver

---

10   See Appendix, chart Q–R.

PRINT AND RELIGION 163

tarì (a coin that weighed ca. 2.45 g). Roncagliolo was sentenced to pay around 100 gr of gold (1.8 kg of silver).[11]

It has been thought that the new rigour of the ecclesiastical authorities, combined with the renewed efforts by the civil authorities, completely stifled the industry, causing a severe economic crisis in the industry whose effects were still visible throughout the seventeenth century. This is simply not true. As we can see in Appendix 1, the first half of the seventeenth century is actually one of the most prolific times for the printing industry, with a great number of new bookshops and printing presses being opened in the city. However, the fact that the industry proved to be strong enough to withstand the wave of religious zealotry does not mean that the sixteenth and seventeenth centuries were not particularly challenging ones for booksellers and printers alike. The few documents that we have analysed serve as proof of the determination with which the authorities carried on with their work and mission. The few examples provided here of instances in which printers came to find themselves in front of Ecclesiastical authorities serve to illustrate what was indeed a common dynamic in the relationship between these two groups. The Catholic Church was aware of the power of printed books and thus was aware of the power that, in a direct or indirect manner, printers had. It was therefore common for Inquisitors and censors to keep a close eye on printers and booksellers and try to bring them to heel with frequent arrest and/or interrogation. This was not something that happened only in Naples. It is said that in Rome, each printer or bookseller was arrested at least once every five years.[12] At the same time, however, the Church needed printers and booksellers to spread books and ideas that the religious authorities approved of. This is why, while it is true that these professionals were often brought before the Inquisitorial tribunals, it is rare that they had severe, career (or even life) ending punishments. Printers and bookseller for their part were aware of the duality of this dynamic and that is why they were not too afraid to push the boundaries a little, if it could gain them a tidy profit.

2 Printing Religious Books

It is important to keep in mind that, despite being the most famous and studied tools, censorship and the threat of excommunication were not the only

---

11 ASDN, Sant'Ufficio, 2139 *Pro Fisco Curiae Archip*[iscopa]*lis Neapolitan*[ae] *contra Secondinum Roncaliolum Impressorem* (13 Gennaio–17 Marzo 1623).

12 Ottavia Niccoli, *Rinascimento* (2005).

weapons that the Church had at its disposal in its fight against the dangers of new ideas and freedom of the press. Almost as important as it was to censor those books deemed dangerous was the effort to publish, print and disseminate those works that were deemed acceptable and painted the church and ecclesiastical authorities in a favourable light. There were various and different ways in which this could be accomplished.

Whereas the civil authorities could grant the title of *Stampatore Regio* to those printers who received a specific royal commission to print official government communications as well as propagandistic works and were compensated for it, there is no evidence of a similar office for religious works before 1640, when the first instances of the title *Stampatore Arcivescovile* (printer of the Archbishop) can be found. Often, religious works could be printed by the Royal Printer, but this is probably more due to the fact that, without a specific and restrictive privilege, the printing of such works was free to all those who could obtain a licence. This is demonstrated by the various printers whose names can be found in many different religious texts. Moreover, the fact that according to Romeo's catalogue, the name of Egidio Longo appears in two different proceedings for forbidden books can be construed as further indication that there was not a strong working relationship between the Royal Printer and the Neapolitan Church.[13] The only one of these documents that are currently available for consultation is a report filed by the Provinciale of the Jesuits of Naples against Egidio Longo for a book that was in the process of being printed. The book, written by a Dominican, was apparently critical of certain papal decrees, particularly those of Gregory XIII. The Vicario of the Sant'Ufficio declared that the printing process should be halted *donec corrigatur* and then gave his permission to resume the print run by 30 June, after the book went through the appropriate amendments. This also proves that although political connections did not mean much when it came to deal with ecclesiastical censorship, the relationship and personal connection between printers and various personalities of the church were something that could work in their favour or even be a disadvantage, depending on the favour that the person or the religious order had at the moment with the local ecclesiastical authorities.

Though it is true that it does not appear that the Church had a designated printer, it is worth mentioning that there is archival evidence pointing to the existence, for a brief period, of a printing press within the hall of the Basilica di San Domenico Maggiore, and it appears that Secondino Roncagliolo even managed it for a brief time. It is particularly challenging to formulate a hypothesis as to when this printing press opened and for how long it was in business.

---

13   ASDNA, Sant'Ufficio, 1415 and 2465.

PRINT AND RELIGION 165

The library and archive of the San Domenico convent were removed from the premises sometime during the nineteenth century, and only recently some of the collections were brought back to the church. Still, the documents and books that were part of their original collection are now scattered between the ASDN, the ASNA and the State Archive in Caserta and there is no telling what was lost in the many relocations. This was particularly the case between 1806 and 1815 when Gioacchino Murat changed the purpose of the building from a convent to a public space, causing major destruction to the artistic and cultural heritage there preserved. Moreover, the church itself went through major remodelling and restoration numerous times throughout the centuries, with the most recent in 1953 to restore the church after the damage it sustained during World War II, thus making it difficult to identify the space in which such business could operate.[14] Research through various catalogues and a conversation with the Head Librarian of San Domenico has led to the identification of seven books with the imprimatur *in aedibus S. Dominici* or *typis regalis Conventus Sancti Dominici* concentrated between 1637 and 1642. These are the books that were printed in San Domenico during that time:

1. Juan Gonzalez de Albeda, *Commentariorum et disputationum in primam partem angelici doctoris divi Thomae* [...] Impressus Compluti in officina Ioannis Gratiani, 1621. Et denuo Neapoli, apud Scipionem Boninum, in aedibus S. Dominici, 1637. Folio, 2 vols., I: pp. [16], 528; II: pp. [12], 328, 176. USTC 4014143

2. Domenico Gravina, *Opusculum de indivisa, & unanimi sacrosancti Evangelii praedicatione* [...] Neapoli, typis Scipionis Bonini, in aedibus S. Dominici, 1637. 4to. pp. [6], 185, [27]. USTC 4044990

3. Domenico Gravina, *Ad discernendas veras a falsis visionibus et revelationibus. Basanites, hoc est, Lapis lydius, theoricam et praxim complectens, ad directionem confessariorum, & qualificatorum S. Inquisitionis* [...] Neapoli, typis Scipionis Bonini in aedibus regal. S. Dominici, 1638. 4to, 2 voll., I: pp. [16], 184, 279 [i.e. 275], [3], 1–56, [2], 57–142, [8]; II: pp. [8], 208, [8]. USTC 4009025

4. Pedro de Ledesma, *Tractatus de divina perfectione, infinitate et magnitudine, circa illa verba, Ego sum, qui sum, &c. Exodi capit. 3. Cui annexus est alius tractatus De perfectione actus essendi creati, circa aliquot quaestiones, quae habentur in principio prima partis D. Thomae, à tertia usque ad quartamdecimam* [...] Salmanticae, apud Ioannem & Andream Renaut

---

14 For a complete history of the Basilica di San Domenico Maggiore and its many restorations, see Orsola Foglia, Ida Maietta (ed), *La fabbrica di San Domenico Maggiore a Napoli. Storia e Restauro* (Naples: Prismi editrice Politecnica, 2016).

166   CHAPTER 5

fratres, 1596. Et iterum Neapoli, in aedibus S. Dominici, apud Scipionem Boninum, 1639. Folio, pp. [8], 554, [6]. USTC 4014146

5.   Luigi da San Severino, *Considerationes devotissimae, respicientes myste-ria incarnationis dominicae ex variis sanctorum patrum coctrinis collectae* [...] Neapoli, typis regalis Conventus Sancti Dominici, apud Franciscum Hieronymum Collignium, 1640. 4to, pp. [16], 290 [i.e. 280], [2]. USTC 4009725

6.   Domenico Paolacci, *Pensieri predicabili sopra tutti gl'Evangelii correnti nella Quaresima* Napoli, per Roberto Mollo, 1640. 4to, 3 voll, 1640 Napoli, nella stampa del reg. Conv. di S. Domen. appresso Francesco Girolamo Colligni, 1640. I: pp. [46], 569, [51]; II: pp. [30], 676 [i.e. 690], [62]; III: pp. [22], 630, [32]. USTC 4009818

7.   Johann Andreas Coppenstein, *Beatus Alanus a Rupe redivivus de psalterio, seu rosari Christi ac Mariae, eiusdemque fraternitate rosaria* Neap[oli]., apud Secondinum Roncagliolum, et denuo typis Reg. Conv. S. Dominici, apud Franc. Hyeronymu Colligniu, 1642. 12mo, pp. [44], 746 [i.e. 696].

It is important to stress the fact that we have no way of knowing if this list is complete for those years, nor for how long the printing press was actually open. However, a couple of things are immediately evident. It was a highly special-ised business dedicated particularly to the printing of large volumes, not only for the library of the convent itself. And it was not run by one printer, but rather various printers could rent the machinery and the space. Despite the very lim-ited number of sources on this particular convent available in the Archivio di Stato I was able to find the ledgers of the convent for most of the seventeenth century.[15] The ledgers appeared to be extremely detailed and well-kept, but there is no mention of the purchase or lease of a printing press (the machine). The question as to when exactly the printing business was established within the halls of the convent remains unsolved, although there are several interest-ing entries including a reference to a *printing* press (*stamperia*). The first note is from February 1640: 'Print of Ledesma: We received ducats 412 which is what we received for the printing of Ledesma'.[16] This entry refers to one of the books that we know was printed *in aedibus Sancti Dominici* (number four on the list above). However, it is not clear whether Scipione Bonino, the printer responsi-ble for this particular book, paid 412 ducats to the convent to rent the printing

---

15   A conversation with Padre Gerardo Imbriani, head archivist in the convent of S. Domenico, suggested that perhaps more documents pertaining to the convent, in particular a regis-ter of all those who took orders and their original name, could be held in the Archivum Generale Ordinis Praedicatorum (AGOP) within the Basilica of Santa Sabina in Rome, however due to COVID restriction I was not able to expand my research in that direction.

16   'Stampa del Ledesma: ricevuti ducati 412 che è quanto si è avuto per la stampa del De Ledesma'. ASNA, Corporazioni religiose soppresse, 471. *Registro di cassa 1638*, leaf 51r.

PRINT AND RELIGION

press or if the entire printing process was done by the Dominicans and Bonino simply paid for having the book printed. A note from September of the same year led me to lean toward the second hypothesis:

> Printing press: we received ducats 10 from those who run the printing press in the convent. It is important to note that this is the first payment that we received for the lease of the printing press.[17]

It would appear probable then, that before September 1640, the printing press was run by the Dominicans, with the occasional printers paying them to print a specific title. As this is the only entry referencing a lease, we do not know for how long the printing press was actually leased to external printers, nor how long this first lease lasted. It is possible that the printing press had its own ledger, and the only entries that we can find in the main ledger are those that required the approval of the Prior himself. This hypothesis is supported by the fact that there are enough entries marked *stamperia* to prove that it was a lucrative business for the convent, one that lasted for a while, but not enough to have a clear picture of how this business was run. What we know is that from 1641 to at least 1644 (this is the last ledger available at the Archivio di Stato) the printing press was strictly connected to a Fra Attanasio Converso, whose name appeared in every entry regarding the *stamperia*. Without the register of ordinations, we have no way of knowing anything about him, but from his name we can easily deduce that he was a former Jew who converted to Christianism, a *converso*.[18] Rather than being a printer, I believe he was a type-founder, given that all entries with his name attached are in reference to the making and selling of printing characters. Despite the fact that we do not have all the answers, the ledgers of San Domenico nevertheless provided some interesting information about their printing press, the most important of which is probably the fact that this was a self-sustaining business. This is demonstrated by the entry from March 1643 in which it is remarked that the money given to Fra Attanasio in order to buy some tin to make printing characters came to the convent from the income of the printing press.[19]

---

17   'Stamperia: ricevuti ducati 10 da quello che tiene la stampa nel Convento. È nota che questo è il primo guadagno che se ne riceve dall'affitto della stamperia' ASNA, Corporazioni religiose soppresse, 472. *Registro di cassa*, leaf 11v.

18   On religious minorities, particularly jews, in Italy see: Emily Michelson, *Catholic spectacle and Rome's Jews: Early Modern Conversion and Resistance* (Princeton: Princeton University Press, 2022).

19   ASNA, Corporazioni religiose soppresse, 474, *Registro di cassa*, leaf 19r.

As interesting as the existence of a printing press within the halls of one of the major churches in Naples is, this cannot be exactly regarded as a tool of religious propaganda, particularly given the nature of the books that were printed there. It is not unreasonable to speculate that the Dominican printing press also printed copies of sermons and orations that were delivered in that church, especially if we consider that after the Tridentine Council the printing of works of this kind both in Latin and the vernacular skyrocketed. However, given that the library of the convent was dismantled in the eighteenth century and that a search within databases produced no results it is not something that can be either confirmed or disproved.

What is certain is that, like the civil authorities, the Church was very much aware of the power of printing as a tool of propaganda, both for counteracting the dissemination of dangerous Protestant ideas and to shift the focus to an approved narrative.[20] It is important to stress once again that the printing of religious books was not a rarity or something that printers engaged with "in their spare time". Rather, in the 15th century breviaries and books of hours were the most common books printed across Europe. These were products that were mainly aimed at the clergy but with the turn of the century and thanks to the contribution and input that a market for religious books aimed at the laity opened up. And it was definitely a big and successful market: by the second half of the 16th century, religious books made up half of the entire output of the printing industry across the peninsula.[21] And the strong connection that exists between orality and printed words is of the utmost importance when it comes to the diffusion of religious text. Already the practice of printing sermons that were given from the pulpit in a pamphlet form and selling them or giving them away at street corners is proof of this increasingly interdependent relationship. Those who did not have the opportunity to listen to the sermon first-hand had the chance to buy a copy, while those who could not read had the opportunity to hear the sermon being recited again and again. Itinerant preachers were masters in this. This is a figure that has always been analyzed in its role of aid in the diffusion and spread of heterodoxies and heretics ideas and while it is undeniably true that these figures played a key role in the diffusion, for example, of Lutheran ideas in the Italian peninsula, reducing the role

---

20   On the propagandistic use of print by the Catholic church see Paolo Sachet, *Publishing for the Popes. The Roman Curia and the Use of Printing (1527–1555)* (Leiden: Brill, 2020).

21   Abigail Broundin, Mary Laven, Deborah Janet Howard, *The sacred home in Renaissance Italy* (Oxford: Oxford University Press, 2018), Michael Millway, 'Fogotten Bestellers from the dawn of the Reformation', in Robert Bast, Andrew Colin Gow (eds), *Continuity and Change: The Harvest of Late-Medieval and Reformation History* (Leiden: Brill, 2000). p. 113–142.

PRINT AND RELIGION 169

of itinerant preachers at only this would be wrong.[22] The strongest preachers in 16th century Italy were Franciscans, Dominicans and Jesuits, instrumental in spreading the "True word".[23]

3 A Harmonious Relationship

Of course, lay publications could and were used as a propagandistic tool by the Church as well, such as the reports of monstrous births, the sighting of comets or even dubious miracles. More often than not, these kinds of stories were used as a symbol by both the Church and the State, either as a warning to keep the people in check or as a positive, favourable sign.

> Between the end of August and the beginning of September 1660, in the lands of Ottaviano, Bosco, Portici, Resina and other nearby castles, the marks of the cross appeared upon some white cloths. These were of a yellowish colour and appeared spontaneously, without a clear cause as to their origin. I can bear witness to the fact that I saw them today, the first Sunday of this month of September, and the sixth day of said month, upon the sleeve of a shirt of a tailor who lived near Santa Sofia. Yesterday, he was hunting near Volla when he spotted the markings and since it appeared to him to be something curious, he told some peasants about them who told him that for some days now they had similar markings upon their white clothes, even those which were stored in their houses. The priest of Resina brought a cassock to the Cardinal Filomarino which was marked with many crosses and which the priest had used that morning while saying Mass and he also said that he had noticed how of the two tablecloths that were displayed on the altar, the lower one was similarly marked. The cassock was shown to the Prior Caracciolo, who lived in his palace in Carbonara street, as well as to other knights and then it was washed but the crosses did not vanish but rather became a light blue colour. The crosses were small, and between them, there were some larger and some more slender. These, as I saw them I am now writing them: ✠ † ✠, some said that they saw them upon the flesh of others, and to this

---

22 Giorgio Caravale, 'Le ambiguità della parola: eresia e ortodossia tra oralità e scrittura nella predicazione italiana del Cinquecento', *The italianist* 34,3 (2014), pp. 478–492.

23 Carlo Delcorno, *Forme della predicazione cattolica fra Cinquecento e Seicento* (Basil: Birkhauser, 1995); Andrew Dell'Antonio, *Listening as Spirtual Practice in Early Modern Italy* (Berkeley: University of California Press, 2011).

day they are still appearing, so much so that we can say that in a short time we have witnessed what some of our ancestors saw in the last century. I remember that in the life of Emperor Charles v, written by Alfonso Ulloa, in the first book fol.7 [it is written] that red and black crosses suddenly appeared in Germany in 1501, and what followed the reader can see for himself.[24]

This account from the diarist Innocenzo Fuidoro is not the only one on the subject. On July 1660 a small Vesuvius eruption took place in Naples, mainly of ash and rocks, without any actual lavic flow. The apparition of the markings of the cross so soon after was regarded as a sign of favour from St Gennaro, with which he wanted to assure the city that he would protect it from the volcano, but also as a sign of displeasure from God, which the city tried to remedy with religious processions, the lighting of lights in the churches after dark and the exhibition of the sacred relics. At least one pamphlet describing the phenomenon was printed in Naples but it is fair to assume that there were actually many of them and that the entire event was widely known, given that Athanasius Kircher (1602–1680) wrote an essay on the subject.[25] He was a celebrated Jesuit natural philosopher, astronomer, geographer and historian. His work on the miracle of the crosses includes one of the first attempts to explain rationally

---

24 "Nella fine d'agosto e principio di Settembre 1660, nelle terre di Ottaiano, Bosco, Portici, Resina et altri castelli convicini, comparvero sopra li panni bianchi alcuni segni di croce, le quali erano di colore d'oglio e naturalmente nascevano, senza vedere da dove venisse l'origine. Io posso testificare d'averle vedute oggi, domenica, prima di questo mese di settembre e sesto giorno di detto mese, sopra una manica di camicia di un sartore, quale abita a Santa Sofia, che essendo stato ieri a caccia alla Volla, si accorse di questi segni, e perché li parve una cosa nuova lo conferì a certi villani, li quali affirmarono che da più giorni erano comparse ancora sopra li panni bianchi loro *etiam* a quelli che rano dentro le case stipati. Il parroco di Resina portò un camise sacerdotale ricciato al cardinale Filomarino arcivescovo, con una quantità di queste croci impresse, che detto parroco se n'era servito la matina nel Santo Sacrificio della Messa, et affrimò che aveva anco osservato che delle due tovaglie, che si mettono su l'altare, in quella di sotto aveva visto impresso dette croci La suddetta camiscia fu fatta vedere al priore Caracciolo, ch'abitava al suo palazzo nella strada di Carbonara et altri cavalieri, e, fattala lavare, le croci non si levarono, però si fecero colore, come dicono le femine, di filo vitriolo; erano piccole assai e fra esse quale più gonfia e qual più sottile. Queste, che come io vidi, come le descrivo: ✠ † ✠, affirmarono alcuni averle viste impresse nelle carni delle persone, né sino a questa giornata sono cessate di comparire, sicchè potemo dire liberamente di aver visto a tempi nostri più assai et in più poco spazio d'anni quello, che in parte viddero li nostri antenati nel secolo passato. Mi ricordo che nella vita di Carlo v Imperatore, scritta d Alfonso Ulloa, nel libro primo, fol. 7 che in Alemagna comparvero nel 1501 le croci rosse e nere, e quello che ne seguì potrò il lettore leggerlo." Fuidoro, *Giornali*, I, pp. 51–52.

25 Athanasius Kircher, *Diatribe de prodigiosis crucibus* (Rome: Blasius Deversin, 1661) USTC 1728408.

PRINT AND RELIGION

a phenomenon that was naturally subject to religious interpretations.[26] The Neapolitan pamphlet on the subject is quite interesting.[27] According to the introduction, it circulated in manuscript form in both Naples and Rome, where it was received with great interest by the public; so much so that the editor decided to print it. This was a common literary trope at the time, often used as a sort of justification for publishing the work in the first place. In the first half, there is a detailed daily account of the happenings around Vesuvius from 26 July 1660 while the second half, *Meraviglie occorse dopo l'incendio* (Marvels that took place after the fire) explains in great detail the miracle of the crosses and provides a list of past occurrences of such prodigies.[28] It was apparently a widespread phenomenon, with the author himself saying that with his own eyes, he counted more than 300. He then went on to recount the scientific and rational explanation that was widely accepted at the time, that of the crosses being a result of the combination of the ashes from the volcano and a particular kind of rain that fell in those days but stressed that he did not believe in this explanation, because it could not account for such a widespread occurrence both in time and places. What is certain is that, despite the apparent rational explanation that was widely accepted, the crosses were still received with anxiety and trepidation:

> It is not easy to decide what such marvels signify. It is true that all those who heard of such happenings took them as a sign of misfortune, and are foreseeing bad things to come. Our crosses, as far as I am aware, did not come with bad omens and therefore we can hold out hope of better things to come.[29]

---

26 Cf. Stephen J. Gould, 'Father Athanasius on the Isthmus of a Middle State. Understanding Kircher's Paleontology', in Paula Findlen (ed), *Athanasius Kircher: The Last Man Who Knew Everything* (New York-London: Routledge, 2004), pp. 207–237: 233–236.

27 Giovanni Battista Zupi, *Continuatione de' successi del prossimo incendio del Vesuuio, con gli effetti della cenere, e pietre da quello vomitate, e con la dichiaratione, & espressione delle croci maravigliose apparse in varij luoghi dopo l'incendio* (Naples: per Gio. Francesco Paci, 1661); SNSP, Sismica 06.E.021. USTC 1729148

28 While none of the Vesuvius eruptions was as popular in the printing world as the one of 1631, it is worth repeating that throughout the seventeenth century the Vesuvius was rarely quiet and at least a couple of pamphlets were printed every time that the volcano came to life.

29 "Quel che tali prodigi pronosticano non è facile stabilire. Vero è che quelli che quelli alle cui orecchie sono arrivate le nove, l'hanno preso per sinistro augurio, e ci pronosticano poco felici successi ... Le nostre croci, per quanto io sappia, non sono state accompagnate da segni infausti, dunque abbiamo occasione di sperare in felici accadimenti", Zupi, *Continuatione*, p. 16.

Much effort was dedicated to creating a portrait of harmony and common goals between Church and State. We have seen in the chapters dedicated to Masaniello's rebellion, the eruption of Vesuvius and the plague, how in the most extreme of the circumstances the predominant narrative was one that celebrated both the strength and resourcefulness of the Viceroy and the mercy of God and the Saints. But even during more placid times, the portrayal of *concordia* (harmony) between the two powers within the city was at the forefront of the propagandistic efforts, through both printed works and public displays. Religious rituals and processions in particular were a tool of propaganda used by both the Spaniards and the ecclesiastical authorities to reinforce their ties with the populace.

Probably the most emblematic example of this is the miracle of St. Gennaro. It is still performed to this day, in an extremely emotional public ceremony. Following a procession guided by the civic authorities, the people of Naples congregate in the Cathedral to witness the display of the relics of St Gennaro (two vials with his blood) and bear witness to the miracle of the blood turning liquid. The ritual is particularly important because the outcome of the miracle itself was, and still is, considered an omen of things to come and a reflection of the favour of God toward the civil and religious authorities. The procession and miracle are performed three times a year, on the Saturday prior to 1 May, on 19 September and on 16 December. Additionally, in times of particular danger for the city, it was common for the relics to be brought out as a sort of shield for the city. The December procession started after 1631 and is a celebration of the miracle performed by the Saint in stopping the flow of lava before it reached the city during the eruption of Vesuvius in 1631. The ceremony in September is to commemorate the date of the saint's martyrdom while the one in May, which is accompanied by a procession, is to commemorate the return of the bones of the saint to Naples after they were stolen and brought to Benevento in 831. Accounts of this ritual were written from the first time it was performed in 1389, long before the beatification of the Saint in 1586, and particularly during the sixteenth and seventeenth centuries printed accounts of the procession and the outcome of the miracle were common and even Fuidoro often reported about it in his *Giornali di Napoli*.

> On the said day [4 July 1660] His Excellency asked Cardinal Filomarino to show the sacred relics, the head and the blood of St Gennaro, in the Tesoro, and so it was done. The Cardinal went to see the relics at [missing text]. His Excellency went to see them at 11 at night and with great devotion, he kissed the blood and went back to his Palace but, before he left, he was told by Carlo Cattaneo how the precious blood had started to turn

PRINT AND RELIGION 173

liquid before it was pulled from his hidden place in the Tesoro and the Archbishop saw the head. It was then put on the altar, the miracle was completed and the blood became liquid and began to boil. This was a sign that the city of Naples had obtained from [St Gennaro's] intercession mercy from some yet unforeseen danger. Monday of the said month the sacred relics were exposed upon the altar of the Tesoro of the Cathedral where many faithful people come to see them and, upon the command of His Holiness, an indulgence was read with which permission was granted to the Dominicans to give absolution for the sins usually reserved to the Archbishop. The blood of St Gennaro remained liquid before the sacred head all day.[30]

Besides the political and religious value that the people of Naples attached to their devotion to their patron Saint and in its miracle, the story of St Gennaro is emblematic of a common dynamic in Neapolitan popular devotion. The city was always extremely devoted to St. Gennaro, and to him, they dedicated processions and prayers. He was the one to whom the city turned in a time of need, with the full support and participation of both civil authorities and the prelates of Naples. This devotion was so embedded in the Neapolitan faith that the Church of Rome decided that it would be better to go along with it, rather than try to censor it, firstly by making Gennaro a Saint of the Church and then by never trying to put a halt to the so-called miracle, even when not acknowledging it as such.[31]

---

30   "Nel detto giorno [4 Luglio 1660] Sua Eccellenza mandò a dire al cardinale Filomarino che avesse fatto esporre le reliquie, cioè il sangue e la testa di San Gennaro al Tesoro, e fu eseguito Scese il cardinale ad ore … e visitò dette reliquie. Sua Eccellenza venne a visitarle ad ore 23, e con molta devotione baciò il sangue e se ne andò in Palazzo; però, prima di partire, li fu fatta relazione da don Carlo Caetano come il prezioso sangue in atto che fu pigliato dalla sua fenestra dove nel tesoro sta serbato, era, prima di veder la testa, cominciato a liquefarsi e che a vista di essa su l'altare si compì il miracolo di liquefarsi e bollire. Dunque era segno che Napoli a sua intercessione aveva da ottenere grazia di qualche imminente pericolo. Lunedì 5 detto, furono esposte le medesime reliquie sull'altare del Tesoro nella Cattedrale, dove fu concorso grande di popolo devoto e, per ordine di Sua Santità, fu pubblicata l'Indulgenza in detta chiesa Cattedrale, concesso alli PP. Domenicani Missionati di poter assolvere tutti casi riservati all'Arcivescovo. Il sangue di San Gennaro si liquefece a vista della testa per tutto questo giorno." Fuidoro, *Gionali*, I, p. 39.

31   For a complete history of the miracle and its relation with the city of Naples and the Catholic church, see Francesco Paolo de Ceglia, *Il segreto di San Gennaro. Storia naturale di un miracolo napoletano* (Turin: Einaudi, 2016).

4 Peculiarities of Neapolitan Devotion

There has often been a distance between popular devotion in Naples and what was approved by the Church, sometimes even a distance between what was approved by the Neapolitan church, with a greater understanding of the feeling of the people, and the Church of Rome. Naples has always been a city with a reputation for heresy, something that was definitely reinforced by the peculiarities of the Neapolitan popular devotion and by the resistance and attachment that the people of Naples showed toward those. On this subject, a fairly unusual document that I found in the Archivio della Congregazione Vaticana in Rome is of particular relevance; it also provides an interesting insight into the topic of religious propaganda.

> Since it has been reported to me that the printed prayer (*oratione*), of which I enclose a copy for Your Lordship, is being sold publicly in Naples, I thought it appropriate to inform you, so that you may tell me what to do about it, since I understood that [i.e. the *oratione*] has been disseminated widely. It has been bought by many people and is supposed to be genuine, so while waiting [for your reply] I will not prevent it from being sold in the best possible way.
> Naples, 21 July 1629.[32]

This letter, sent by the vicar of the Neapolitan Inquisition, Giacomo Terragnolo, to the Secretary of the Congregation of the Holy Office, Giovanni Garsia Mellini (1562–1629), is a clear example of the complexity of establishing a standardised censorship practice during the Counter-Reformation period. Although the enclosed pamphlet mentioned has not been preserved, it is immediately clear that the publication in question must have been some kind of oration of a religious nature, whose content seemed to conform to Catholic orthodoxy, which made its circulation plausibly licit in the eyes of the vicar, who had granted a regular licence to print and sell it. However, in view of the, perhaps unexpected, success in sales, he sought the approval of the Roman authorities as well.

---

32   ACDF, S.O., *Stanza Storica*, HH 1e (*De S. Officio Neapolis. Literae Ministrorum, Nuntiorum, Episcoporum et pro Regum ac Archiepiscoporum illius Regni. Circa Restitutionem Ministri S. Officii*), leaf 377ʳ: "Essendomi stato riferito che per Napoli si vende pubblicamente l'oratione stampata, della quale trasmetto qui accluso un esemplare a Vossignoria, ho giudicato bene significarglielo, affinchè si degni comandar che devo osservare, giacché intendo essersi assai divulgata et che da molti è stata comprata e gli effetti in essa si suppone esser buona, che fra tanto non mancherò di impedirvi che si venda nel miglior modo che sarà possibile. Napoli, 21 luglio 1629."

PRINT AND RELIGION   175

After careful archival examinations, it is possible to hypothesise what the publication in question was. Since it is an *oratione*, a prayer, circulating in the Napolitan area and therefore, in the absence of further specifications, probably printed there, there seems to be only one possible option. This was a small placard, bearing a heading in the form of a title, accompanied by a woodcut by Nicolas Perrey (1596–1661) depicting a couple of angels holding the Holy Shroud and followed by a prayer: *The true portrait of the Holy Shroud in which the body of Our Lord was enveloped once deposed from the cross. A most devoted oration of the Holy Shroud thanks to which a soul is freed from Purgatory every time it is declaimed. Granted by Pope Urban VIII upon a supplication of the most serene Catherine of Austria Duchess of Savoy.*[33] The imprint state as follows: 'Rome, and reprinted in Naples, by Nicolas Perrey, Maccarano [i.e. either Domenico (fl. 1606–56) or Giuseppe (fl. [1627–56)] and Ottavio Beltrano ([fl. 1616–71]), 1629'.[34]

We are therefore dealing with an indulgence in favour of the souls in Purgatory granted for the recitation of a specific prayer. However, here the mystery deepens because it is not possible to clarify whether the supposed original Roman edition of this indulgence ever existed since copies of it are nowhere to be found. Nonetheless, we are led to believe that such an edition must have existed and must itself have had an imprimatur since otherwise, we do not know why the vicar of Naples should have granted a licence for the reprint.

The text of the prayer is a verbatim transcription of the collect (a brief liturgical oration intended to be recited between the Greater Doxology and the Liturgy of the Word) designed for one of the two known orders (*formulae Missae*) of the Mass for the Most Holy Shroud, celebrated on 4 May:

> O God, who has left us a sign of your passion with the Holy Shroud, in which your most holy body was draped by Joseph when taken down from the cross: mercifully grant us that, through your death and burial, we

---

33   *Il vero ritratto del sacro sudario nel quale fu involuto il Corpo di Nostro Signore deposto, che fu dalla Croce. Oratione devotissima del Santissimo Sudario, con la quale si libera un'Anima del Purgatorio, per ogni volta, che si dice, concessa da Papa Clemente Ottavo à preghieri della Sereniss. Infante D. Caterina d'Austria Duchessa di Savoia* On the Neapolitan carreer of Nicolas Perrey, see Ana Minguito Palomares, 'Nicolás Perrey y el uso del grabado en la costrucción de la imagen del virreinato de Nápoles durante el siglo XVII. Compendio y documentación de nuevas obras', *Janus. Estudios sobra el Siglo de Oro* 9 (2020), pp. 221–274.

34   Roma & ristamp. in Napoli, per Nicolò Perrey & per il Maccarano & per Ottavio Beltrano, 1629. Alessandrina University Library in Rome (XIV f.25, 4). None of the printed copies that were attached to the letters in the volume of the ACDF are there because they were removed and end up somewhere else or were probably destroyed during the Napoleonic Wars.

FIGURE 5.3
Holy Shroud indulgence (Roma & ristamp. in Napoli, per Nicolò Perrey & per il Maccarano & per Ottavio Beltrano, 1629). Turin, private collection

may reach the glory of the resurrection. You who live and reign with God Father, in the unity of the Holy Spirit, forever and ever. Amen.[35]

In 1506, upon the request of Charles III Duke of Savoy (1486–1553) and his mother Claudine de Brosse (1450–1513), Pope Julius II (1443–1513) had in fact proclaimed the Bull *Salubria vota*, to receive and confirm throughout the duchy the Divine Office of the Holy Shroud, which came into possession of the House of Savoy in 1453, and its Mass. During the Counter-Reformation, the related liturgy was recodified, probably during the 1590s, to include, among others, the text of the indulgence discussed here.[36]

The importance of the role played by a member of the House of Savoy in the request for the indulgence should be emphasised if one wishes to argue for

---

35 *Deus, qui nobis in sancta Sindone, qua Corpus tuum sacratissimum de Cruce depositum, a Ioseph involutum fuit; passionis tuae vestigia, reliquisti concede propitius: ut per mortem, & sepulturam tuam, ad resurrectionis gloriam perducamur. Qui vivis & regnas cum Deo Patre in unitate Spiritus sancti Deus, per omnia saecula saeculorum. Amen.*

36 Renzo Savarino, 'Lo sviluppo della liturgia ufficiale. Le modalità del culto della sindone nel tempo', in Gian Maria Zaccone, Giuseppe Ghiberti (eds), *Guardare la Sindone. Cinquecento anni di liturgia sindonica* (Cantalupa: Effatà Editrice, 2007), pp. 205–226 (indulgence quoted on p. 215).

PRINT AND RELIGION

its authenticity. Considering the already well-established connection between the ducal family and the relic in question, it can be speculated that this *oratione* may have originated thanks to private communication between Catalina Micaela (1567–1597), Infanta of Spain and Duchess of Savoy by marriage, and Pope Clement VIII (1536–1605) between 1592 and 1597, after the enthronement of the Pope and before the demise of the Catalina Micaela. However, just as there are no documents in the Vatican archives to confirm this hypothesis, we have no evidence to confirm or exclude the possibility that the entire indulgence may be a forgery, crafted somewhere in the Duchy of Savoy, Rome or (less plausibly) Naples. One thing is for certain: the vicar of the Neapolitan Inquisition must have received a favourable response from Rome, although the reply to the letter of 21 July 1629 is now lost. This is confirmed by the inclusion of the prayer's text, along with a clear reference to the fact that it was an indulgence, in a devotional manual intended for the private teaching of *humanae litterae*. This *Arte di profittare nelle lettere*, by the Campanian man of letters Altobello Gagliaro (fl. 1631–45) was published in Naples with the required imprimatur in 1634 and reprinted there ten years later.[37] Meanwhile, in 1638, the indulgence had reached such a broad circulation that it was mentioned, in an appreciative tone, in one of the most comprehensive theological treatises dedicated to Purgatory published during the Baroque period, *Legatio Ecclesiae triumphantis ad militantem*, by the Antwerpian Discalced Carmelite Elias a Sancta Theresia, known only through this work.[38]

Problems concerning the authenticity and lawfulness of indulgences continued to arise well into the seventeenth century, reaching such a degree that the Roman authorities felt the need to regulate their control through the establishment of a dedicated institution. Thus, Pope Clement IX (1600–1669), after having appointed a dedicated commission of cardinals in 1667, two years later gave it a permanent form with the creation, sanctioned by the papal brief *In ipsis pontificatus nostri primordiis*, of the Congregation for Indulgences and Sacred Relics, which operated until 1904. Before the turning point brought about by Clement IX, assessing the authenticity of indulgences and relics was among the many tasks of the Congregation of the Holy Office, which from time to time devoted sessions to this purpose. As a further demonstration of how delicate and difficult these issues were to resolve, besides being

---

37   *Arte di profittare nelle lettere, e nelle virtù. A' padri di famiglia, & a' maestri di scuola* (Naples: per Gio. Domenico Montanaro, 1634), p. 138 (second edition, Naples: per Ettore Cicconio, 1644, pp. 135–136).

38   Elias a Sancta Theresia, *Legatio Ecclesiae triumphantis ad militantem, pro liberandis animabus Purgatorii communibus concivibus, libris tribus solide luculenterque explicata ...* (Antwerp: apud Jacobum Meseum, 1638), p. 393.

often subject to partial scholarly evaluations due to the lack of documentary sources, it suffices to recall that indulgences previously authorised by Rome could be subsequently condemned as forgeries or apocrypha. This would seem to be exactly the case with our indulgence. Thanks to an excerpt published in 1670 in an authoritative treatise on canon law by the French Jesuit theologian George Gobat (1600–1679), taken from the account of the Congregation of the Holy Office's gathering of 18 May 1657 (the original of which should be preserved in the volumes of the *Decreta* series at the ACDF), we know that on this date the 1629 indulgence was condemned as apocryphal.[39] While this turn of events drastically reduced the circulation of the indulgence, it did not cause its total disappearance.[40] The circulation in the territories of the empire must have remained indeed rather wide if one considers that, even at the end of the eighteenth century, a Spanish version of the prayer was included in a manual intended for the novices of the Hospitaller Order of the Brothers of Saint John of God.[41]

Besides the complex editorial journey of the text of the indulgence and its importance as proof that the ecclesiastical authorities took on an active role in the promotion and distribution of those publications that they felt were useful to their agenda, this story is important because it sheds light on one of the most peculiar and famous aspects of popular devotion. Usually, an indulgence is something that could be granted exclusively by members of the clergy and, particularly after the Council of Trent, the practice was monitored very closely. This, however, was something that was being sold publicly, which presumably meant not only by the clergy but also by booksellers and possibly pedlars, and was therefore widely known and popular in the streets of Naples. The reason for this popularity is probably the same reason that prompted Terragnolo to ask for advice from his superiors in Rome rather than simply shut down the entire business, and it is due to the content of the indulgence. It was, as we have established, a prayer designed to free a soul from Purgatory, and the devotion around the souls trapped in Purgatory was particularly popular in Naples. Known as *culto delle anime pezzentelle* (devotion to the poor unfortunate

---

39   George Gobat, *Quinarius tractatuum theologo-iuridicorum* ... (Constance: typis Joannis Jacobi Straub, 1670), p. 340.

40   Only three copies of this indulgence are known, preserved in the collections of the Alessandrina University Library in Rome (XIV f.25, 4), the Vatican Library (Stamp.Barb. X.I.96, 46b) and the Royal Library of Turin (unrecorded).

41   Augustín de Victoria, *Instrución de nobicios del Orden de la Hospitalidad* ... ([S.l.n., 1799]), p. 162.

souls) it is an aspect of popular piety that is specific to Naples, with ancient roots and still alive to this day.[42]

It is unclear when, exactly, this devotion began, although archaeological evidence points to some form of worship of the dead having taken place in the paleo-Christian basilica of St Pietro ad Aram. The crypt, with its skulls and bones, is still open to visitors. The first evidence of this devotion being popular enough to attract notice from the authorities, and presumably one of the first attempts to harness it and bring it within the orthodox practice, can be found in 1616 when the construction of the church of Santa Maria delle Anime del Purgatorio ad Arco began. This was a church that was specifically dedicated to the care and devotion of souls in purgatory, which in itself is not particularly unusual given that the matter was of particular interest to the Counter-Reformation Church. In Naples, however, this devotion was already established, and it had a very particular connotation. What was, or rather, what is, the devotion to the *anime pezzentelle*? These are the unnamed souls, the poor and derelict of the city, who died with no one left to pray for them. The people of Naples, therefore, decided to adopt one of these souls, to pray for their salvation, in exchange for small favours and protection. Always popular and deeply felt within the city, the practice grew and strengthened in times of plagues and crisis, when the unnamed dead grew in number. The adoption of the soul was often manifested through the adoption of one of the skulls held in the church, which the devotees polished and to which they left small offerings.

Despite the almost pagan nature of this devotion, the church never attempted to stifle it. On the contrary, it appears that whenever possible the ecclesiastical authorities tried to encourage it and gave their seal of approval, as with the indulgence discussed earlier. Throughout the centuries this practice had its highs and lows but was always present in the background of popular devotion, so much so that to this day this and the miracle of St Gennaro are the best-known aspects of popular religion in Naples. When, in the nineteenth century Napoleon declared that burial sites needed to be moved outside the city walls, the mass grave known as Cimitero delle Fontanelle was born. Located in a former turf mine, turf being a yellowish porous volcanic rock extremely common in Naples used for construction since Roman times, it is now the most famous location tied to the devotion to the *anime pezzentelle*. The practice of adopting the skull became more and more common through the centuries, with certain skulls becoming famous for granting a particular

---

42   There is some speculation that the word *pezzentelle* could come from the latin word *puto*, which means ask. Therefore it should not be translated as "poor" but as "those who ask". Personally I stand by the first meaning.

180 CHAPTER 5

kind of favour – the skull known as Donna Lucia in the church of Santa Maria delle Anime del Purgatorio ad Arco for example is famous for bringing forth marriage proposals. This practice became so widespread that in 1969 the Bishop of Naples became concerned that the people of the city paid more attention to these souls than to the Catholic saints, and he intervened to put an end to it. However, it survived as local folklore and, judging by the offerings that can be found while visiting the Cimitero delle Fontanelle, it is still a practice that the people of Naples cherish.

This brief glimpse into one of the most peculiar devotions of Naples is by no means a complete study of the phenomenon but serves to highlight the complexity of Neapolitan spirituality. It is further proof of the willingness of the ecclesiastical authorities to work alongside both Rome and the people of Naples, to encourage what was already popular rather than trying to stifle it in an effort to gain popularity within the city, thus reducing the possibilities for the people of the city to stray. Alongside what could be considered a more political propagandistic effort, the attention of the ecclesiastical authorities was also dedicated to spiritual matters, particularly to the dissemination of orthodoxy to all social strata through popular print. The most common of such publications were sermons in the vernacular and the lives and miracles of important saints of the city, particularly St. Gennaro.[43] Printed copies of the religious ceremonies performed for the ruling elite on the occasions of births, marriages, deaths and other noteworthy anniversaries, also provided good business for the print shops.[44]

The willingness of the ecclesiastical authorities to concede the point when it came to this particular devotion is not, however, an indicator that things always went this way or that the Roman Church was content to leave carte blanche to the people of Naples, but rather proof of a deep knowledge of their audience and a willingness on the part of the Church to pick its battle carefully. Coming back to the pamphlet discussed by the Inquisitor of Bologna that we mentioned in the introduction, this is an example of the Church coming down hard on the attempt at manipulation put forth by the Neapolitan people.

In particular, in regard to the pamphlet that was printed in Rome and reprinted in Bologna, it is evident that the decision of the Inquisition to suppress it was a successful one, given the scarcity of surviving copies. Of the edition printed in Bologna, there is only a single surviving copy, which is the one in the ACDF. Of the one printed in Rome only 3 known copies survived (USTC

---

43   BNN SQ.25.K.44 (1), SNSP, Capasso 02.AA.8(2).

44   We have already mentioned several of such publications in the course of the book. Other examples can be found in Banco Napoli 01.D.30.

PRINT AND RELIGION

1728396). It is impossible to know how this pamphlet came to be printed, though it is interesting and worth mentioning that Igazio de' Lazari was trialled by the Inquisition the following year, for reasons as of yet unknown but that I hypothesise are related to this particular work. But since I cannot elaborate further on this at the moment, and even if I could it would lead us off track, let me go back to the content of the pamphlet, which originated for sure in Naples. It is a supplication put forth by the citizens of Naples and addressed to the Pope asking for the canonization of Gaetano of Tiene. In it, several members of the Sedili of the city as well as doctors wrote sworn testimonies of the miracles performed by Gaetano in the lazzeretto of Naples during the plague of 1656, citing those as the evidence needed to support their request. Furthermore, they state that Gaetano is already being regarded as Blessed (Beato) and among the protectors and patrons of the city, despite knowing that a decree by Urbano VIII forbade such devotions.[45] Basically what they are doing with this is asking the Church for the stamp of approval upon a popular devotion that already existed in Naples, and that became even more strongly felt and popular after the plague epidemic. In this instance, however, it seems that the people of Naples went too far. Not only did they explicitly acknowledge that they were carrying on with what could be deemed a forbidden practice, which was something that could have worked in their favour as well as against them. They also went about it in the wrong way, because from 1634 the possibility of putting forth someone for Beatification was reserved exclusively for members of the Church. This means that what the citizens of Naples should have done was present their case to the Archbishop in Naples, who would have reviewed the evidence and then if he deemed them valid, would have proceeded to send a request to the Office in Rome. We do not have news of when this very inappropriate and dangerous request was received in Rome and how they responded, but given the fact that the pamphlets were condemned by the Inquisition, the printer stood trial and the Beatification of Gaetano of Thiene happened only in 1671 it is safe to say that the outcome of the Neapolitan plea was not a positive one.

The approach to the business of print by the ecclesiastical authorities was multifaceted. Through censorship and a conscious effort to encourage the dissemination of certain kinds of publications, and also by working with the civic authorities, the church of Naples tried to shape a communications strategy that aimed to maintain control of the Neapolitan souls and keep them far away from the dangers of the Protestant and heretical ideas that, despite their best efforts, circulated widely in the city.

---

45   In the letter *Coelestis Hierusalem cives.*

Conclusions

Conventionally, the end of the Spanish Viceroyalty in Naples is dated to 1707, when the first of the so-called Austrian Viceroys entered Naples. However, already by 1700, with the death of Charles II of Spain and the beginning of the Spanish War of Succession, the conflict involved the Neapolitan realm and its printing industry.

It seems fitting to close this book with one last look at two of the most famous and prolific printers of the Spanish Viceroyalty, whose journey is a perfect mirror for what was happening in Naples immediately after the death of Charles II. We met Antonio Bulifon in Chapter 1, when he led a group of his colleagues in presenting a petition to the Real Giurisdizione against the exclusive licence held by Giuseppe Abbate for the *Ordinario Romano*. We met Domenico Antonio Parrino in Chapter 2, when he was battling against none other than Bulifon for the privilege to print the Neapolitan newspaper. These two printers had a long-standing rivalry. Both of them ran extremely prolific printing presses and were responsible for some of the most prestigious editions published during the Spanish Viceroyalty; both of them vied for the privilege of being the editor of the *Gazzette* and both of them had the ambition of writing the official, comprehensive history of Spanish Naples.[1] Given such fierce competition, it should come as no surprise that even their political views were vastly different. United in their unwavering support for the Spanish rulers, once the last of the Spanish Habsburg died and the Kingdom of Naples became one of the many territories involved in the Spanish war of Succession, Parrino and Bulifon found themselves on opposite sides of the barricades. Bulifon, perhaps unsurprisingly given that he was born in France himself, became a strong supporter of the claim of the Bourbon Philip V, while Parrino maintained his loyalty to the Habsburg family, offering his support to Archduke Charles VI.

In the beginning, the tide seemed to be in favour of Bulifon and the French party. When Philip V was crowned King of Spain he immediately rewarded the loyalty of the French printer by stripping Parrino of his rights to the *Gazzette* and granting the privilege to Bulifon, despite the fact that Parrino's contract had yet to expire. Moreover, while Parrino had been paying a steep price of 800 ducats per year for this privilege, it was granted to his rival for less than half the price at 300 ducats.

---

1 On the rivalry between Bulifon and Parrino see Nino Cortese, "Introduzione." In Antonio Bulifon, *Giornali di Napoli*, pp. xx–xxv.

CONCLUSIONS 183

> With a royal decree on 30 June 1702 [the Viceroy] grants Nicola Bulifone the Privilegio to print the Gazzette in this Realm ... We grant to said Bulifone the privilege of the said task for the price of only 300 ducats per year.[2]

Bulifon was of course extremely grateful for this and repaid the sovereign by printing several propagandistic pamphlets in Italian and French in favour of the French party, besides of course ensuring that any Austrian victory was kept far away from the pages of the newspaper.[3] There are no archival testimonies as to Parrino's reaction to the loss of the privilege but we can assume that, even if he did not fight back, he was less than pleased about it. He remained steadfast in his loyalty to the Austrian party and was vocal in his contempt for Bulifon and his exaggerated servility to the French party.[4]

It is interesting to note that, even though the *Gazzette* had always been a political and propagandistic tool, apparently Parrino was more capable of subtlety than his rival. The majority of the Neapolitan people held the same political allegiance as Parrino since the obviously partial accounts published by Bulifon in his *Gazzette* were widely criticised. The criticism against him went so far that, according to a chronicle of the time, several rhymes against him were printed and spread throughout the city, calling him a 'Buffone' and harshly criticising anyone who could be so foolish and dumb as to believe the French.[5] Parrino did not have to wait long for his revenge against the rival. In 1704, Bulifon left his printing press to his son Nicola, who held the same political view as his father, but the tide was already turning in favour of the

---

2   "Con carta reale del 30 Giugno 1702 concede a Nicola Bulifone il Privileggio di poter imprimere le Gazzette in questo regno ... si dia a detto Bulifone il carico di detta incombenza pagando solamente ducati 300 l'anno" Biase Giuliano, *Libri di regali ordini di Sua Maestà*. SNSP, MS. XXV. A. 3, p. 29.

3   Antonio Bulifon, *Relation de ce qui s'est passé dans la ville de Naples en 1701*. USTC 1752426 This is a lost book, but was mentioned by Bulifon himself in his Giornali. Antonio Bulifon, Nino Cortese (ed), *I giornali di Napoli dal 1547 al 1706*. (Naples: Società Napoletana di Storia Patria, 1932); Antonio Bulifon, *Lettera di N.N. ad N.N. in cui gli dà ragguaglio distinto delle feste fatte in questa fedelissima città di Napoli per l'acclamazione del nuovo monarca delle Spagne Filippo V* (Naples: Felice Mosca, 1701), USTC 1752425; Antonio Bulifon, *Lettera scritta ad un suo amico in Francia, dove gli dà ragguaglio delle feste fatte in Napoli coll'occasione della pubblica entrata fatta in essa città da Filippo V, monarca delle Spagne Scritta prima in franzese e poi tradotta nell'Italiano* (Naples: Felice Mosca, 1701); Antonio Bulifon, *Altra lettera scritta da A.B. a un suo amico, nella quale gli dà ragguaglio della seconda cavalcata fatta in Napoli per la solenne entrata dell'eminentissimo signor cardinale Carlo Barberini, mandato da Sua Santità in qualità di suo legato a latere a Filippo V monarca delle Spagne* (Naples: Felice Mosca, 1702).

4   Bulifon, *Giornali*, vol. 1, pp. XVI–XVI.

5   *Ibid.*

Austrian party. In 1707, when they finally entered Naples, the privilege for the *Gazzette* reverted back to Parrino who exacted the ultimate vengeance against his long-time rival, inciting a mob to torch his shop, an incident in which Bulifon's son apparently lost his life.

> Royal Decree of 4 August 1707 ... with which we granted back to Giuseppe Antonio Parrino the task of composing, printing and selling the *Gazzette* and the *Avvisi*, which are published every week, as well as other writings of such nature that are deemed worthy of being printed and divulged, and that he will hold [this privilege] for the rest of his life.[6]

Less than thirty years later, Naples ended up once again in the hands of the Bourbons. However, the most significant change was that, from 1759 and still under the rule of the same Bourbons, Naples became an independent kingdom, not subject to some other ruler or nation. At the time, despite being French in origin, the Bourbon family was ruling Spain and it was only when the newly crowned Charles III renounced his claims to the territory of Southern Italy in favour of keeping the Spanish crown and left them to his third son Ferdinand of Bourbon that the kingdom of Naples became a separate entity, independent from the Spanish crown.

Traditionally, the Bourbon period, which lasted until the proclamation of the Kingdom of Italy in 1861, albeit with a brief break during the Napoleonic period (1806–1815), has always been celebrated as the heyday of Neapolitan history. As is always the case in the human experience, what better way to celebrate and idealise something than to disparage and demonise what came before? This is precisely what happened to the historiography of the Kingdom of Naples, where already by the end of the eighteenth century the Spanish Viceroyalty was characterised as some sort of dark age for Southern Italy. Things only got worse after 1861 when faced with incorporation into the new Kingdom of Italy, nostalgia for a perceived golden age under Bourbon rule bled through into the making of history. Some efforts were made at the beginning of the twentieth century toward a complete history of the Kingdom of Naples, a history that would re-evaluate even the Spanish Viceroyalty. However, even in the best-case scenario, that particular time period was only looked at through the lens of

---

6 "Carta reale delli 4 Agosto 1707 ... con la quale si fa mercede a' Giuseppe Antonio Parrino che se reintegri nell'incumbenza di formare, imprimere, e vendere le Gazzette, et avvisi, che si pubblicano tutte le settimane, et l'altri scritture di questa qualità, che fussero degne di darsi alla stampa, e divulgarsi, a ciò le goda durante la sua vita" Biase Giuliano, *Libri di regali ordini di Sua Maestà*. SNSP, MS. XXV. A. 3, p. 141.

a continuous and bitter conflict between the brave people of Naples and the foreign, oppressive and suffocating Spanish rule.

During the course of this book, I have highlighted several examples of the ways in which the Spanish authorities used the printed word, particularly in the form of popular print, to build a relationship with their Neapolitan subjects. The work undertaken, although by no means exhaustive, provided nonetheless proof of a different dynamic between the people of Naples and the Spanish authorities, one less centred around conflict and more geared toward a pacific co-existence that worked well for both parties. This was possible thanks to extensive archival research and the use of primary sources of different kinds. A methodology that combined the practical aspects of book history studies with the hermeneutic approach to primary sources typical of Anglophone cultural and social history, allowed me to analyse sources newly discovered or integrated for the first time into the study of the book trade.

This has allowed us to paint a picture of the state of popular printing in Naples, specifically in relation to the political engagement of the people of Naples. But having proven that this is an effective methodology when it comes to Neapolitan history, despite the obstacles that are provided by the nature of the Neapolitan archives themselves, I cannot help but reflect on the different research possibilities that are now available. We could envisage an in-depth analysis of Spanish culture in Naples, not only through the lenses of the acts of patronage provided by the Spanish crown but focusing on occasions for the Spanish and Neapolitan common folk to share the same cultural experiences. This is a largely unresearched subject, one that I would have liked to be able to include in my book but that I was forced to put on the back burner due to the difficulties of archival access and research brought on by the Covid pandemic. However, even if we focus our attention on aspects of the Spanish Viceroyalty that have already been studied, like for example the history of heresy and Protestantism in Naples, there is still so much potential for further research and new approaches. Because while it is true that there have been books published on Naples and heresy, it is also true they still rely on premises that I have proved to be obsolete during the course of this book. That the assumption that the Neapolitan cultural environment was hostile and repressive has led to work using partial sources, relying heavily on inquisition papers and often without using actual Neapolitan sources.

Even if we want to focus our attention on more practical research, leaning more toward book history, the possibilities are endless. Of course, what better place to start than with a bibliography of the popular print of the Spanish Viceroyalty? While similar works were undertaken for other parts of Europe in the 1970s, they did not involve Southern Italy and are of course less than complete due to the limited technology available at the time.[7] However, just looking at the number of printed materials mentioned in the book should provide an idea of the richness of popular print in Naples at the time as well as the usefulness of such a bibliography. For now, I have concentrated my efforts on compiling an exhaustive list of all printers, publishers and booksellers who worked in Naples during the Spanish Viceroyalty and when they were in business, which can be found in the Appendix.

---

7 Arnaldo Segarizzi, *Bibliografia delle stampe popolari italiane della Reale biblioteca Nazionale di San Marco di Venezia* (Bergamo: Istituto Italiano d'Arti Grafiche, 1913); Carlo Angeleri, *Bibliografia delle stampe popolari a carattere profano dei secoli XVI e XVII conservate nella Biblioteca Nazionale di Firenze* (Florence: Sansoni Antiquariato, 1953); Pietro Manzi, *La tipografia Napoletana nel '500* (7 vols., Florence: Olschki, 1968–1975).

APPENDIX

People of the Book Trade in Seventeenth-Century Naples

∴

© KONINKLIJKE BRILL BV, LEIDEN, 2025 | DOI:10.1163/9789004549401_009

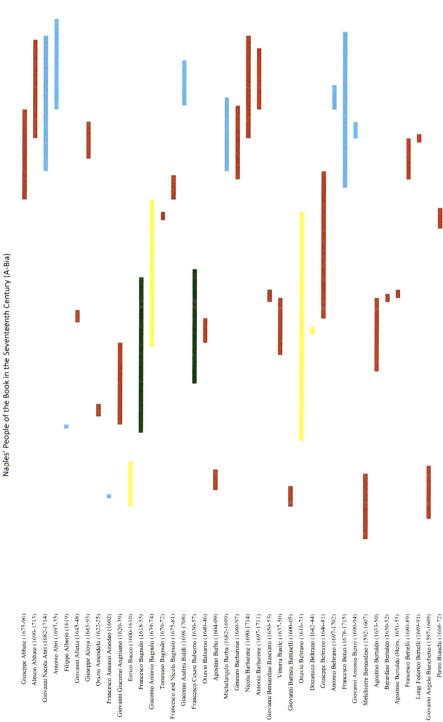

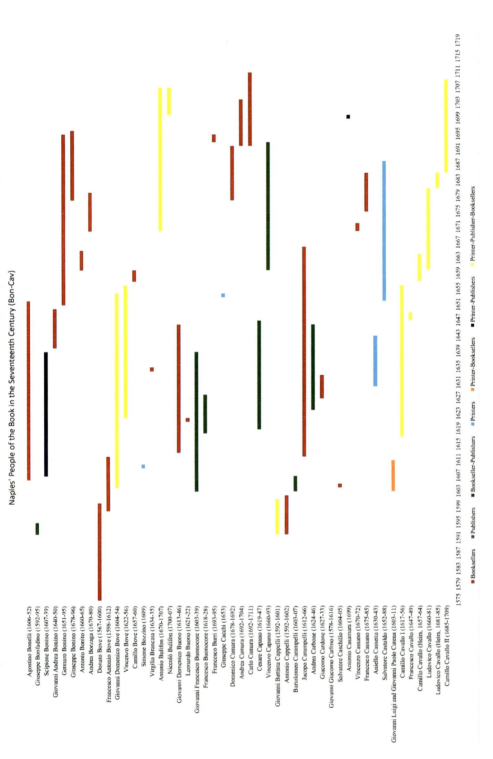

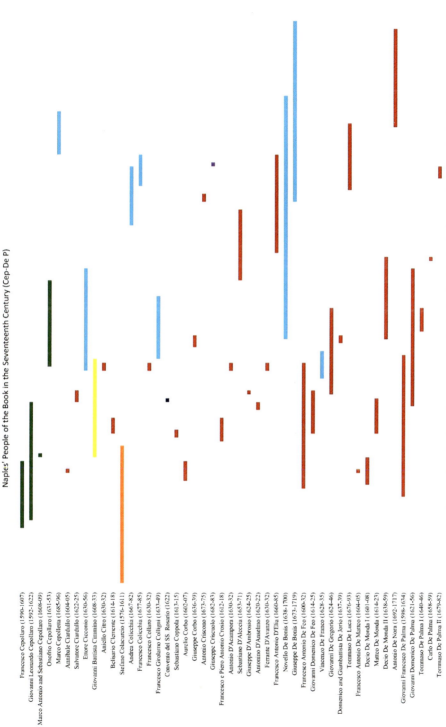

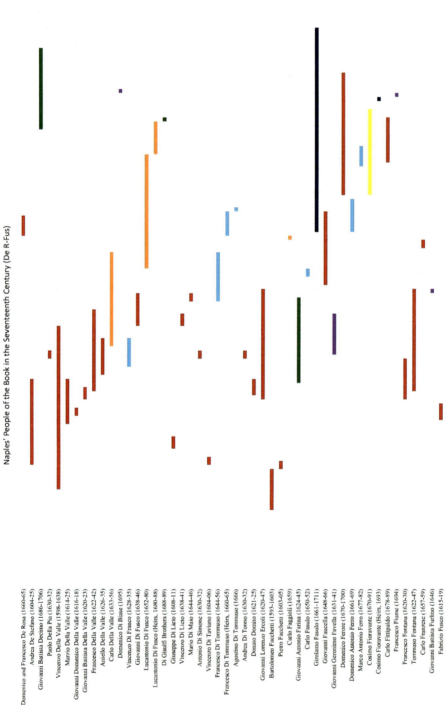

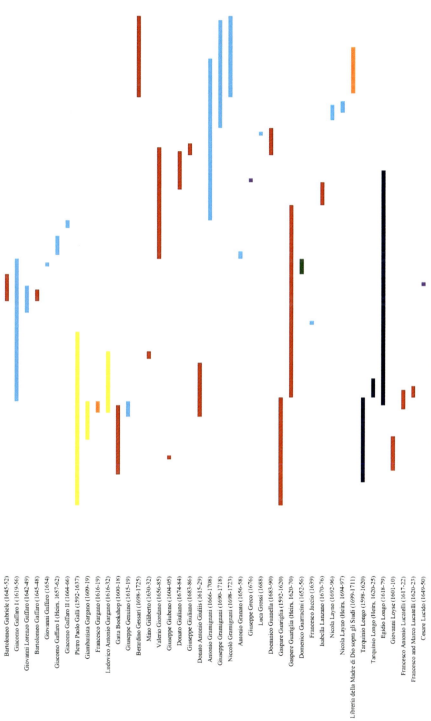

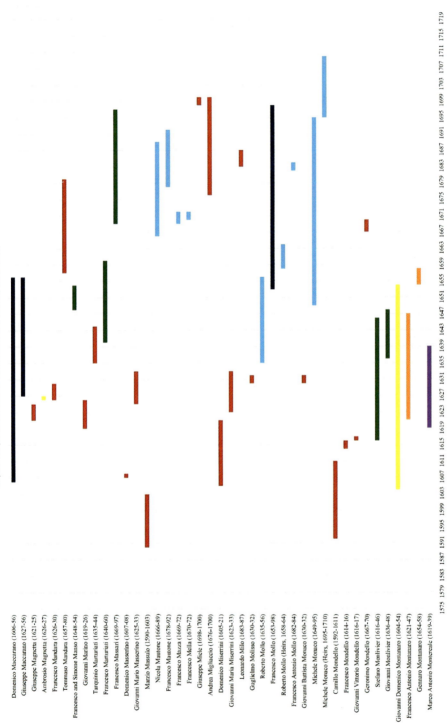

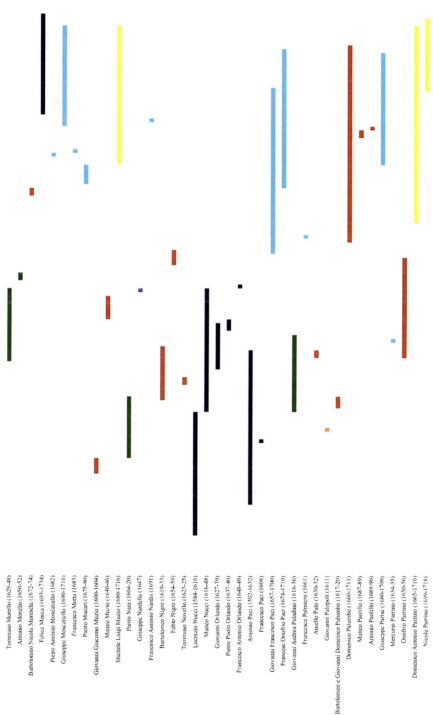

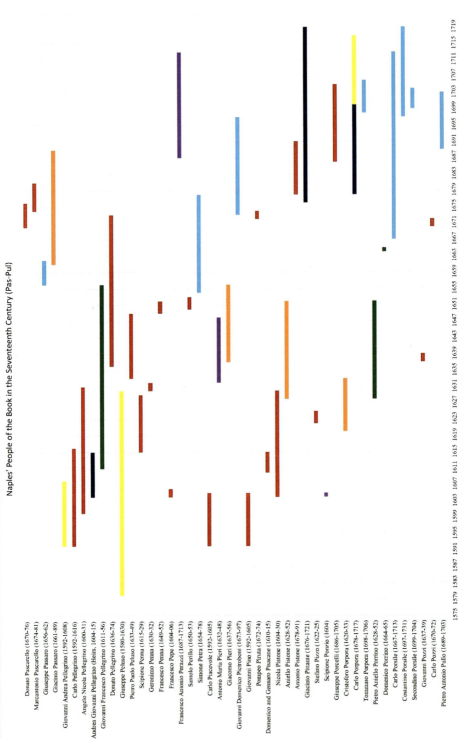

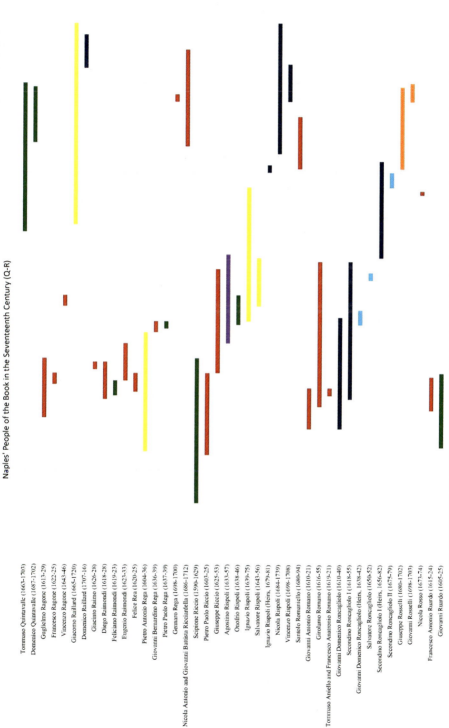

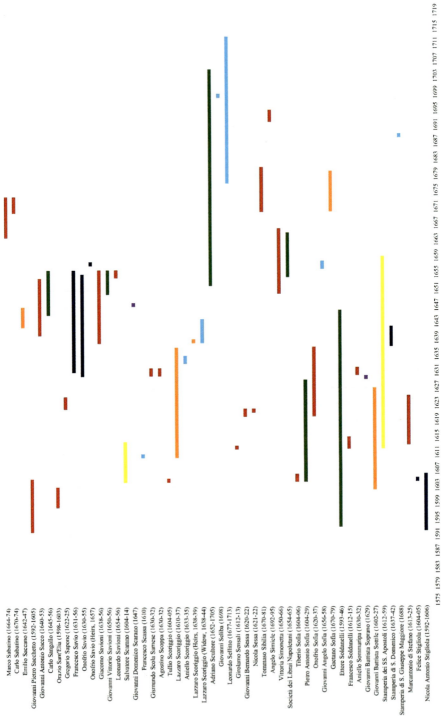

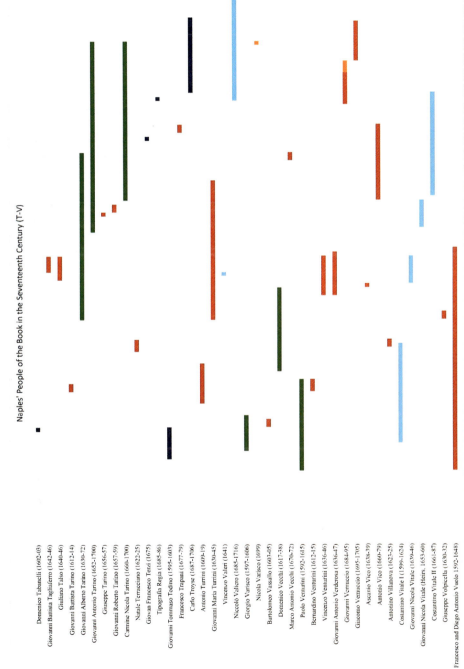

Selected Bibliography

Primary Sources

Manuscript

[Anonymous], *Sante visite di A. Filomarino* ADSN, IV.

[Anonymous], *Pro Fisco Curiae Archip[iscopa]lis Neapolitan[ae] contra Ioannem Petrum Propositum Romanum, Joannem Jacobum Carlinum impressorem, Antonium Pacem, Dominicum Tabanelli* ASDN, Sant'Ufficio 1138.

[Anonymous], *Processus originalis contra Secondinum Roncagliolum Impressorem* ASDN, Sant'Ufficio 3292.

[Anonymous], *Librari St. Biasij.* ASN, ms 176/2.

[Anonymous], *S. Biagio Maggiore, Governo* ASN, CM, Statuti e Corporazioni, fs. 1205/115.

[Anonymous], *Patronato della S. Casa sulla Chiesa di S. Biagio Maggiore* ASN, Cart. Culto 2, Reale Stabilimento dell'Annunziata di Napoli, Fasc. 8 bis.

[Anonymous], *Manifetso ritrovato di mattina affiso in una piazza di Napoli stampato in Aix et risposta*, (1648). BNN, Bib. San Martino, ms 253 (ex 244).

[Anonymous], *Sollevazioni dell'anno 1647*, [Naples, XVIII.] SNSP, ms XXII.C.6.

[Annibale di Capua], *Carte del Cardinale A. di Capua.* ASDN, ms. s.n.

Biase Giuliano, *Libri di regali ordini di Sua Maestà.* SNSP, MS. XXV. A. 3.

Bucca d'Aragona, Ferrante. *Giornali historici* (1629–37). BNN, X B.51.

Follieri de' Torrenteros, Antonio. *Quattrocento anni di vita operaia napoletana* (1882–84). SNSP, XXXIV A 42.

[San Domenico's Convent], *Registro di cassa.* ASN, Corporazioni religiose soppresse, 472.

Printed

a Sancta Theresia, Elias. *Legatio Ecclesiae triumphantis ad militantem, pro liberandis animabus Purgatorii communibus concivibus, libris tribus solide luculenterque explicata* [...] (Antwerp: apud Jacobum Meseum, 1638), USTC 1511421.

[Anonymous]. *Il vero ritratto del sacro sudario nel quale fu involuto il Corpo di Nostro Signore deposto, che fu dalla Croce. Oratione devotissima del Santissimo Sudario, con la quale si libera un'Anima del Purgatorio, per ogni volta, che si dice, concessa da Papa Clemente Ottavo à preghieri della Sereniss. Infante D. Caterina d'Austria Duchessa di Savoia* (Naples: per Nicolo Perrey, & per il Maccarano, & per Ottavio Beltrano, 1629), USTC 4002683.

[Anonymous]. *L'afflitta Partenope per l'incendio del Vesuvio al suo Glorioso Protettore Gennaro. Dell'Insensato Accademico Furioso* (Naples: nella stampa di Secondino Roncagliolo, 1632), USTC 4010884.

SELECTED BIBLIOGRAPHY

Lotti, Giovanni. *L'incendio del Vesuvio in ottava rima di Giovanni Lotti Accademico Errante* (Naples: per Gio. Domenico Roncagliolo, 1632), USTC 4010881.

[Anonymous]. *Nuove Osservationi fatte sopra gli effetti dell'incendio del Monte Vesuvio* (Naples: per Lazzaro Scoriggio, 1632), USTC 4011046.

[Anonymous]. *Novissima Relatione dell'incendio successo nel monte di Somma a 16 Decembre 1631. Con un'avviso di quello che è successo nell'istesso dì nella città di Cattaro, nelle parti d'Albania* (Naples: per Egidio Longo, 1632), USTC 4011031.

[Anonymous]. *La strage di Vesuvio* (Naples: per Egidio Longo, 1632), USTC 4011559.

[Anonymous]. *Manifesto delle giustificate ationi della corona di Spagna, e delle violenze della corona di Francia. Tradotto dalla lingua castigliana all'italiano* (Naples: per Egidio Longo stampatore regio, 1636), USTC 4011105.

[Anonymous]. *Discorso sincerissimo fatto da un'umile e affettuoso servitore della Corona di Francia al (per se stesso) Pio, Giusto, Magnanimo e Cristianissimo Ludovico XIII re di Francia* (Macerata and Naples: s.n., 1636), USTC 4011106.

[Anonymous]. *Risposta al manifesto del Christianissimo Re di Francia, nel quale espone le ragioni dell'armi sue incamminate al Regno di Napoli, impresso in Parigi a 26 Aprile 1648* (Naples: per Domenico Maccarano, 1648), USTC 4020306.

[Annymous]. *Relatione del tumulto seditioso di Parigi e regno di Francia. Principiato nel mese di Maggio 1648* (Naples: per Egidio Longo stampatore regio, 1649), USTC 4019539.

[Anonymous]. [Letter sent to the Neapolitan city government]. S.l.n.d. (dated 27 November 1654). USTC 1752427.

[Anonymous]. [Letter sent to the Neapolitan city government]. S.l.n.d. (dated 3 December 1654), USTC 1752428.

[Anonymous]. *Copia del decreto pubblicato in Napoli dall'illustrissima deputazione di questa Fedelissima Città, in riconoscenza del singolar beneficio ricevuto nella liberatione dal Contagio da suoi Santi Patroni e Nostra Gloriosa Cittadina Santa Rosalia* (In Palermo e in Bologna: Gio Battista Ferroni, 1657), USTC 1752419.

[Anonymous]. *Supplica della città di Napoli alla Santità di N.S. Alessandro VII. Con attestazioni pubbliche della liberatione della medesima dal contagio, per l'intercessione del S. Gaetano Tiene, fondatore dei Clerici regolari. Per ottenerlo Protettore* (In Roma e in Bologna: per gli HH del Dozza, 1657), USTC 1731477.

[Anonymous]. *Raggioni per la fedelissima città di Napoli negli affari della Santa Inquisizione* (Pesaro: Gio. Battista Giotti, 1661), USTC 1752420.

[Anonymous]. *Relatione dello spaventoso incendio seguito nella Gran Città di Costantinopoli, metropoli dell'impero orientale a 5 settembre di quest'anno 1693* (Naples: appresso Domenico Antonio Parrino e Camillo Cavallo, 1693), USTC 1752421.

[Anonymous]. *Nova e distinta relatione della Vittoria ottenuta dall'armi cesaree nel combattimento seguito sotto Giula, con fuga e rotta data a' Turchi [...]* (Naples: appresso Domenico Antonio Parrino e Camillo Cavallo, 1693), USTC 1752422.

202   SELECTED BIBLIOGRAPHY

[Anonymous]. *Vera e distinta relatione del terremoto accaduto in Napoli e parte del suo regno il giorno 8 di Settembre 1694. Dove si dà ragguaglio delli danni che il medesimo ha cagionato in molte parti del medesimo Regno e in particolare nelle tre province di Principato, Citra, Ultra e Basilicata. Con il numero di morti e feriti che nelle medesime sono restati sotto le pietre* (Naples: per Dom. Ant. Parrino, e Camillo Cavallo, 1694), USTC 1728338.

[Anonymous]. *Nuova distinta relazione della considerabilissima Vittoria, riportata dal Regio Esercito, comandato in persona dal glorioso nostro monarca Carlo Terzo Sopra quella de' Gallispani fortemente trincierato nelle vicinanze di Saragoza il dì 20 d'Agosto 1710 con la totale disfatta del medesimo. La cui nuova in cinque giorni è capitata qua a S. Em. Il Cardinal Grimani nostro Vice.Rè, e capitan Generale, la notte di giovedì 4 del corrente Settembre* (Naples: per Domenico-Antonio Parrino e Camillo Cavallo, 1710), USTC 1752423.

Apolloni, Giovanni. *Il Vesuvio ardente di Giovanni Apolloni all'Illustrissimo Signor Conte Mario Carpegna* (Naples: per Egidio Longo, 1632), USTC 4011033.

Bagatta, Giovanni Bonifacio. *Vita della Ven. Serva di Dio Orsola Benincasa* (Rome: per Francesco de Lazzeri, 1696), USTC 1723970.

Benigno, Domenico. *La strage di Vesuvio* (Naples: per Egidio Longo, 1632), USTC 4011559.

Bonadonna, Orazio. *Tesoro di sanità, nel quale si contengono secreti mirabilissimi, per sanare quanti mali possono venire alle persone & stroppiar quanti sani siano al mondo* (Naples: per Domenico Maccarano 1628), USTC 4004695.

Bove, Vincenzo. *Nuove Osservationi fatte sopra gli effetti dell'incendio del Monte Vesuvio, Aggiunte alla Decima Relatione dello stesso incendio già data in luce. Di nuovo rivista, e ristampata per Vincenzo Bove* (Naples: per Lazaro Scoriggio, 1632), USTC 4011940.

Bove, Vincenzo. *Il Vesuvio acceso. Descritto da Vincenzo Bove per l'Illustrissimo Signore Gio. Battista Valenzuela Velazquez, Primo Reggente per la Maestà Cath. nel Conseg. Supremo d'Italia* (Naples: per Secondino Roncagliolo, 1632), USTC 4011047.

Braccini, Giulio Cesare. *Relatione dell'incendio fattosi nel Vesuvio alle 16 di Dicembre 1631. Scritta dal Signor Abbate Giulio Cesare Braccini da Gioviano di Lucca in una lettera diretta all'Eminentissimo e Reverendissimo Signore il sig. Girolamo Colonna* (Naples: per Secondino Roncagliolo, 1631), USTC 4011032.

Bulifon, Antonio. *Cronicamerone overo Annali, e giornali historici delle cose notabili accadute nella città, e Regno di Napoli, dalla natività di N.S. sino all'anno 1690* (Naples: a spese dell'autore, presso Giuseppe Roselli, 1690), USTC 1752424.

Bulifon, Antonio. *Lettera di N.N. ad N.N. in cui gli dà ragguaglio distinto delle feste fatte in questa fedelissima città di Napoli per l'acclamazione del nuovo monarca delle Spagne Filippo V* (Naples: Felice Mosca, 1701), USTC 1752425.

Bulifon, Antonio. *Lettera scritta ad un suo amico in Francia, dove gli dà ragguaglio delle feste fatte in Napoli coll'occasione della pubblica entrata fatta in essa città da Filippo V, monarca delle Spagne Scritta prima in franzese e poi tradotta nell'Italiano* (Naples: Felice Mosca, 1701), USTC 1752429.

SELECTED BIBLIOGRAPHY

Bulifon, Antonio. *Altra lettera scritta da A.B. a un suo amico, nella quale gli dà ragguaglio della seconda cavalcata fatta in Napoli per la solenne entrata dell'eminentissimo signor cardinale Carlo Barberini, mandato da Sua Santità in qualità di suo legato a latere a Filippo V monarca delle Spagne* (Naples: Felice Mosca, 1702), USTC 1752430.

Bulifon, Antonio. *I giornali di Napoli dal 1547 al 1706*, edited by Nino Cortese (Naples: Società Napoletana di Storia Patria, 1932).

Capaccio, Giulio Cesare. *Il forastiero dialogi di Giulio Cesare Capaccio academico otioso. Ne i quali, oltre a quel che si ragiona dell'origine di Napoli, governo antico della sua Republica, duchi che sotto gli imperadori greci vi hebbero dominio, religione, guerre che con varie nationi successero, si tratta anche de i re* [...](Naples: per Gio. Domenico Roncagliolo, 1634), USTC 4011531.

Cavallo, Camillo, ed. *Avvisi di Napoli* (Naples: per Camillo Cavallo, Domenico Antonio Parrino, 1675–1703).

Celano, Carlo. *Notitie del bello, dell'antico, e del curioso della città di Napoli, per i signori forastieri, date dal canonico Carlo Celano napoletano. Divise in diece giornate* 10 vols (Naples: nella stamperia di Giacomo Raillard, 1692), USTC 1752431.

Cortese, Isabella. *I secreti della Signora Isabella Cortese, ne' quali si contengono cose minerali, medicinali, artificiose e alchemiche, e molte dell'arte profumatoria, appartenenemti a ogni gran signora* (Venice: appresso Giovanni Bariletto, 1561), USTC 824295.

Costo, Tommaso. *Giunta, overo Terza parte del Compendio dell'istoria del regno di Napoli scritta da Tomaso Costo cittadino napoletano. Nella quale si contiene quanto di notabile, e ad esso regno appartenente è accaduto dal principio dell'anno 1563 insino al fine dell'Ottantasei* (Naples: appresso Horazio Salviani, 1590²), USTC 824416.

d'Amato, Cinzio. *Nuova, et utilissima prattica di tutto quello ch'al diligente barbiero s'appartiene, cioè di cavar sangue medicar ferite, et balsamar corpi humani. Con altri mirabili secreti, e figure* (Naples: per Ottavio Beltrano, 1632), USTC 4011020.

[de Eugeni, Angelo]. *Il maraviglioso e tremendo incendio del monte Vesuvio; detto a Napoli la montagna di Somma nel 1631* (Naples: per Ottavio Beltrano, 1632), USTC 4011023.

[Deputati della Conservazione della Salute], *Appartenendosi a noi* ... (Naples: per Carlo Porsile, 1691), USTC 1752418.

De Sariis, Alessio, ed. *Codice delle leggi del Regno di Napoli* 13 vols (Naples: presso Vincenzo Orsini e dal medesimo si associa nella sua stamperia dirimpetto il Divino Amore, 1792–97).

[de Toledo y Zúñiga, Pedro Álvarez]. *Bando et comandamento da parte dell'Illustrissimo signor Don Pietro de Toledo Marchese de Villa Franca Viceré Locotenente et Capitaneo generale de la Maesta Cesarea nel presente Regno* (Naples: datus in Castro Novo, 1551), USTC 844173.

de Victoria, Augustín. *Instrución de nobicios del Orden de la Hospitalidad* [...] S.l.n., [1799].

204 SELECTED BIBLIOGRAPHY

Donzelli, Giuseppe. *Partenope liberata overo Racconto dell' heroica risolutione fatta dal Popolo di Napoli per sottrarsi con tutto il Regno all'insopportabil Giogo delli Spagnuoli* (Naples: appresso Ottavio Beltrano, 1647), USTC 4020291.

Favella, Giovanni Geronimo. *Abbozzo delle ruine fatte dal Monte di Somma, con il seguito infino ad hoggi 23 di Gennaro 1632. All'infinita cortesia, rara gentilezza & unica generosità del Sig. Paolo Ruschi Gio Gieronimo Favella offerisce, dedica e dona* (Naples: nella stampa di Secondino Roncagliolo, 1632), USTC 4011050.

[Finella, Filippo]. *Incendio del Vesuvio del Lanelfi* (Naples: appresso Ottavio Beltrano, 1632), USTC 4011026.

Forleo, Giovanni. *Meteorico discorso sopra i segni, cause, effetti, tempi & luoghi generalmente di tutti i Terremoti & incendi di diverse parti della terra* (Naples: per Secondino Roncagliolo, si vendono all'insegna del Bove, 1632), USTC 4014038.

Fuidoro, Innocenzo (born Vincenzo D'Onofrio). *I giornali di Napoli dal 1660 al 1680*, edited by Franco Schlitzer, Antonio Padula and Vittoria Omodeo. 4 vols (Naples: Società Napoletana di Storia Patria, 1934–43).

Gagliaro, Altobello. *Arte di profittare nelle lettere, e nelle virtù. A' padri di famiglia, & a' maestri di scuola* (Naples: per Gio. Domenico Montanaro, 1634), USTC 4014141.

Gagliaro, Altobello. *Arte di profittare nelle lettere, e nelle virtù. A' padri di famiglia, & a' maestri di scuola* (Naples: per Ettorre Cicconio, 1644), USTC 4016594.

Gatta, Geronimo. *Di una gravissima peste che nella passata primavera e estate dell'anno 1656 depopulò la città di Napoli* (Naples: per Luc'Antonio Fusco, 1659), USTC 1752432.

[Giannetti, Giovanni]. *La vera relatione del prodigio novamente successo nel Monte Vesuvio, con la nota di quante volte è successo ne' tempi antichi, con una breve dichiarazione di quel che significa* (Naples: per Gio. Domenico Roncagliolo, 1632), USTC 1752433.

Giraffi, Alessandro. *Le rivolutioni di Napoli descritte dal signor Alessandro Giraffi. Con pienissimo ragguaglio d'ogni successo, e trattati secreti e palesi.* (S.l.n., [1647]), USTC 4020365.

Gobat, Georges. *Quinarius tractatuum theologo-iuridicorum* [...] (Constance: typis Joannis Jacobi Straub, 1670), USTC 2627997.

[Kingdom of Naples], *Bando e comandamento da parte dell' Illustrissimo signor Don Pietro de Toledo* (Naples: 1551), USTC 1752437.

[Kingdom of Naples], *Carolus Dei cratia* [!] *rex, &c* (Naples: per Carlo Porsile 1696), USTC 1706591.

[Kingdom of Naples], *Carolus Dei gratia rex* (Naples: per Carlo Porsile stampatore della Regia Corte, 1699), USTC 1706589.

[Kingdom of Naples], *Philippis Dei Gratia Rex ...* (Naples: per Carlo Porsile regio stampatore, 1702), USTC 1752439.

Kircher, Athanasius. *Diatribe de progidiosis crucibus* (Rome: Blasius Deversin, 1661), USTC 1728408.

SELECTED BIBLIOGRAPHY

[Martorella, Felice, and Marco Aurelio Severino], *Consultatio medicorum praevia sectione cadaverum pro praeservatione et curatione pestis* (Naples: per Egidio Longo, 1656), USTC 1752434.

[Masino, Michelangelo], *Distinta relatione dell'incendio del Vesuvio, Alli 16 di Decembre 1631 successo. Con la relatione dell'incendio della città di Pozzuoli, e cause delli terremoti, al tempo di Don Pietro da Toledo Vicerè in questo regno nell'anno 1534* (Naples: per Gio Domenico Roncagliolo, 1632), USTC 4012327.

Morexano, Carlo. *Torchio di osservationi della peste di Napoli dal Dottor Carlo Morexano Messinese* (Naples: per Sebastiano di Alecci, 1659), USTC 1728624.

[Navarrete, Antonio], *Breve relaciòn de los servicios hechos a su Magestad por el Doctor D. Antonio Navarrete, Cavallero del Avito de Sant Tiago, Decano y Propresidente del Sacro Consejo de Napolès* (S.l.n., [1601]), USTC 1752435.

Normile, Giuseppe. *L'incedij del Monte Vesuvio, e delle stragi e rovine, ch'ha fatto ne' tempi antichi e moderni, infino a 3 di Marzo 1632* (Naples: per Egidio Longo. Si vende all'insegna del Bove, 1632), USTC 4011052.

Orlando, Giovanni. *Dell'incendio del monte di Somma. Compita relazione di quanto è successo infino ad hoggi. Pubblicato per Giovanni Orlando Romano alla Pietà* (Naples: per Lazzaro Scoriggio, 1632), USTC 1752436.

[Orlando, Giovanni]. *Nuova, e compita relatione del spaventevole incendio del Monte di Somma detto il Vesuvio, dove s'intende minutamente tutto quello che e successo fin'al presente giorno, con la nota di quante volte detto Monte si sia abbrugiato [...] aggiuntovi un remedio devotissimo contro il terremoto* (Naples: per Lazzaro Scoriggio, 1632), USTC 4011083.

[Padavino, Marc'Antonio]. *Lettera narratoria a pieno la verità dei successi del Monte Vesuvio detto di Somma, seguiti alli 16 di Dicembre fin alli 22 dello istesso mese. Scritta da un gentilhuomo dimorante in Napoli a uno di questa corte* (Rome: appresso Francesco Cavalli, 1632), USTC 4011030.

Pandolfi, Giuseppe. *La povertà arrichita ovvero l'hospitio de' poveri mendicanti fondato dall'eccellentissimo signor Don Pietro Antonio Raymondo Folch de Cardona* (Naples: Egidio Longo, 1671), USTC 1728276.

Parrino, Domenico. *Teatro eroico, e politico dei governi de' Vicerè del Regno di Napoli dal tempo del Re Ferdinando il Cattolico fino al presente* 3 vols (Naples: nella nuova stampa del Parrino e del Mutii, 1692–94), USTC 1734907.

Pasquale, Nicolò. *A' posteri della peste di Napoli e suo Regno nell'anno 1656, dalla redentione del mondo* (Naples: per Luc'Antonio di Fusco, 1668), USTC 1734919.

Pelliccia, Alessio Aurelio. *Raccolta di varie croniche, diarj, ed altri opuscoli così italiani, come latini appartenenti alla storia del Regno di Napoli* 5 vols (Naples: presso Bernardo Perger, 1780–82).

[Regio consiglio collaterale], *Essendosi ricevuto ordine di S.M. con sue regali lettere ...* (Naples: 1702), USTC 1752438.

Riaco, Carlo Francesco. *Il giudicio di Napoli. Discorso del passato contagio rassomigliato al Giudicio Universale* (Perugia: per Pietro di Tommaso, 1658), USTC 1715251.

Ruffo, Flavio. *La ristampata lettera con aggiunta di molte cose notabili, del Signor Abbate D. Flavio Ruffo. Nella quale dià vera & minuta relatione delli Segni, terremoti e incendi del Monte Vesuvio, cominciando dalli 10 del mese di Dicembre 1631 per infino alli 16 Gennaio 1632* (Naples: appresso Lazzaro Scoriggio, 1632), USTC 4011043.

Summonte, Giovanni Antonio. *Historia della città e Regno di Napoli di Gio. Antonio Summonte napolitano. Ove si trattano le cose più notabili accadute dalla sua edificatione sin'a tempi nostri; con l'origine, sito, forma, religione […] oltre gli imperatori greci, duci, e prencipi* 4 vols (Naples: a spese di Antonio Bulifon libraro all'insegna della Sirena, 1675), USTC 1735048.

Toppi, Niccolò. *Biblioteca napoletana et apparato a gli huomini illustri in lettere di Napoli, e del Regno* (Naples: appresso Antonio Bulifon all'insegna della Sirena, 1678), USTC 1736385.

Tutini, Camillo. *Racconto della sollevatione di Napoli accaduta nell'anno MDCXLVII*, edited by Marino Verde (Rome: Istituto storico italiano per l'età moderna e contemporanea, 1997).

Vario, Domenico Alfeno, ed. *Pragmaticae edicta decreta interdicta regiaeque sanctiones regni neapolitani olim viri consultissimi collegerunt suisque titulis tribuerunt Prosper Caravita* […] 4 vols (Naples: Sumptibus Antonii Cervoni, 1772).

Zupi, Giovanni Battista. *Continuatione de' successi del prossimo incendio del Vesuvio, con gli effetti della cenere, e pietre da quello vomitate, e con la dichiaratione, & espressione delle croci maravigliose apparse in varij luoghi dopo l'incendio* (Naples: per Gio. Francesco Paci, 1661), USTC 1729148.

Literature

Amabile, Luigi. *Il Santo Officio della Inquisizione in Napoli: narrazione storica con molti documenti inediti.* 2 vols (Città di Castello: S. Lapi Tipografo-Editore, 1892).

Ambrasi, Domenico. 'Società e vita religiosa a Napoli nell'Età Moderna', *Asprenas*, 18, 4 (1971), pp. 494–504.

Amendola, Nadia. *La poesia di Giovanni Pietro Monesio, Giovanni Lotti e Lelio Orsini nella cantata da camera del XVII secolo.* PhD book, Università di Roma "Tor Vergata", Johannes Gutenberg-Universität Mainz, 2016/2017.

Angeleri, Carlo. *Bibliografia delle stampe popolari a carattere profano dei secoli XVI e XVII conservate nella Biblioteca Nazionale di Firenze* (Florence: Sansoni Antiquariato, 1953).

[Anonymous]. 'La morte di Gio. Vincenzo Starace Eletto del popolo di Napoli, nel maggio 1585; racconto tratto da un ms. del secolo XVIII', *Archivio Storico per le Province Napoletane* 1, 1 (1876), pp. 131–138.

SELECTED BIBLIOGRAPHY

Antonelli, Attilio, ed. *Cerimoniale del viceregno spagnolo e austriaco di Napoli, 1650–1717* (Soveria Mannelli (CZ): Rubbettino; Crotone: V&V, 2012).

Antonelli, Attilio, and Miguel Diez de Aux, eds. *Cerimoniale del viceregno spagnolo di Napoli 1503–1622* (Naples: Arte'm, 2015).

Arblaster, Paul, *From Ghent to Aix* (Leiden: Brill, 2014).

Arrieta Alberdi, Jon. 'La dimensión institucional y jurídica de las cortes virreinales en la monarquías hispánica', in Cardim, Pedro and Palos, Joan Lluís (eds), *El mundo de los virreyes en las monarquías de España y Portugal* (Madrid: Vuervert, 2012), pp. 33–70.

Associazione Professori di Liturgia, ed. *Liturgia e religiosità popolare: proposte di analisi e orientamenti. Atti della VII settimana di studio dell'associazione professori di liturgia. Seiano di Vico Equense (Napoli), 4–8 settembre 1978* (Bologna: EDB, 1979).

Astarita, Tommaso. *The Continuity of Feudal Power: The Caracciolo di Brienza in Spanish Naples* (Cambridge and New York: Cambridge University Press, 2002).

Astarita, Tommaso. *Between Salt Water and Holy Water: A History of Southern Italy* (New York: W.W. Norton, 2005).

Astarita, Tommaso, ed. *A Companion to Early Modern Naples* (Leiden and Boston: Brill, 2013).

Baker-Bates, Piers, and Miles Pattenden, eds. *The Spanish Presence in Sixteenth-Century Italy. Images of Iberia* (Farnham: Ashgate, 2015).

Benigno, Francesco. *Parole nel tempo: un lessico per pensare la storia* (Rome: Viella, 2013).

Bentley, Jerry Harrell. *Politics and Culture in Renaissance Naples* (Princeton: Princeton University Press, 1987).

Bianco, Furio. *Storie raccontate, storie disegnate. Cerimonie di giustizia capitale e cronaca nera nelle stampe popolari e nelle memorie cittadine tra '500 e '800* (Udine: E. & C., 2001).

Black, Christopher F. *Storia dell'Inquisizione in Italia. Tribunali, eretici, censura* (Rome: Carocci, 2013).

Boccadamo, Giulia. 'Prime indagini sull'organizzazione della Confraternita napoletana della Redenzione dei Cattivi', *Campania Sacra*, 8, 9 (1977), pp. 121–158.

Boldan, Kamil. 'Lamentatio Nigropontis: An Unknown Print of Sixtus Riessinger, a Prototypographer of Naples', *Acta Musei Nationalis Pragae – Historia litterarum* 67, 1–2 (2022), pp. 5–12.

Borrelli, Raffaele. *Memorie storiche della chiesa di San Giacomo dei Nobili Spagnuoli e sue dipendenze* (Naples: R. Tipografia Francesco Giannini & Figli, 1903).

Bosse, Monika, and Andrè Stoll, eds. *Napoli Viceregno spagnolo. Una capitale della cultura alle origini dell'Europa moderna, secc. XVI–XVII* (Naples: La scuola di Pitagora, 2013²).

Bouvier, Renè, and Andrè Laffargue. *Vita napoletana nel XVIII secolo* (Naples: Treves, 2006²).

Braida, Lodovica, and Mario Infelise, eds. *Libri per tutti: generi editoriali di larga circolazione tra antico regime ed età contemporanea*. (Turin: UTET, 2010).

Bruni, Flavia, and Andrew Pettegree, eds. *Lost Books. Reconstructing the Print World of Pre-Industrial Europe* (Leiden and Boston: Brill, 2016).

Burke, Peter. *Popular Culture in Early Modern Europe* (London: Temple Smith, 1978).

Burke, Peter 'The Virgin of the Carmine and the Revolt of Masaniello', *Past & Present* 99, 1 (1983), pp. 3–21.

Burke, Peter. 'Masaniello: A Response', *Past & Present* 114, 1 (1987), pp. 197–199.

Burke, Peter. *The Historical Anthropology of Early Modern Italy: Essays on Perception and Communication* (Cambridge and New York: Cambridge University Press, 1987).

Burke, Peter. *A Social History of Knowledge* 2 vols (Cambridge: Polity, 2012).

Burke, Peter. *Identity, Culture & Communications in the Early Modern World* (Brighton: Edward Everett Root, 2018).

Burke, Peter. *What is Cultural History* (Cambridge: Polity, 2019³).

Bury, Michael, ed. *The Print in Italy, 1550–1620* (London: British Museum Press, 2001).

Caiazza, Pietro. 'Nunziatura di Napoli e problemi religiosi nel Viceregno post-tridentino', *Rivista di Storia della Chiesa in Italia*, 42 (1988), pp. 24–69.

Calabria, Antonio. *The Cost of Empire. The Finances of the Kingdom of Naples in the Time of the Spanish Rule* (Cambridge and New York: Cambridge University Press, 1991).

Calabria, Antonio, and John A. Marino, eds. *Good Government in Spanish Naples* (New York: Peter Lang, 1990).

Calaresu, Melissa, Filippo De Vivo, and Joan Pau Rubiés, eds. *Exploring Cultural History: Essays in Honour of Peter Burke* (London: Routledge, 2010).

Calaresu, Melissa, and Helen Hills, eds. *New Approaches to Naples c.1500–1800: The Power of Place* (Burlington: Ashgate, 2013).

Calvi, Giulia. 'L'oro, il fuoco, le forche: la peste napoletana del 1656', *Archivio storico italiano* 139, 3 (1981), pp. 405–458.

Camporesi, Piero. 'Cultura popolare e cultura d'élite fra Medioevo ed età moderna', in Romano Ruggiero, Vivanti Corrado (eds), *Storia d'Italia: Annali. 4: Intellettuali e potere* (Turin: Einaudi, 1981), pp. 81–157.

Camporesi, Piero. *Rustici e buffoni: cultura popolare e cultura d'élite fra Medioevo ed età moderna* (Turin. Einaudi, 1991).

Camporesi, Piero, ed. *Il libro dei vagabondi. Lo Speculum cerretanorum di Teseo Pini, Il vagabondo di Rafaele Frianoro e altri testi di furfanteria* (Turin: Einaudi, 1973).

Cantù, Francesca, ed. *Las cortes virreinales de la monarquía española: América e Italia* (Rome: Viella, 2008).

SELECTED BIBLIOGRAPHY

Cantù, Francesca, and Maria Antonietta Visceglia, eds. *L'Italia di Carlo V. Guerra, religione e politica nel primo Cinquecento* (Rome: Viella, 2003).

Capaccio, Giulio Cesare. 'Napoli descritta ne' principii del secolo XVII', *Archivio Storico per le Province Napoletane* 7, 1 pp. 68–103, 7, 3 pp. 531–554, 7, 4 (1882), pp. 776–797.

Capasso, Bartolomeo. 'Breve cronica dai 2 Giugno 1543 a 25 Maggio 1547 di Geronimo de Spenis da Frattamaggiore', *Archivio Storico per Le Province Napoletane* 2, 3 (1877), pp. 511–531.

Capasso, Bartolomeo. *Sulla circoscrizione civile ed ecclesiastica e sulla popolazione della città di Napoli dalla fine del sec. XIII fino al 1809* (Naples: Tipografia della regia università, 1892).

Capasso, Bartolomeo. *Catalogo ragionato dei libri registri e scritture esistenti nella sezione antica, o prima serie dell'Archivio municipale di Napoli (1387–1806)* (Naples: stab. Tip. F. Giannini, 1899).

Caputo, Vincenzo, Gianfrancesco, Lorenza, Palmieri Pasquale eds, *Tales of two cities. News, Stories and Media Events in Early Modern Florence and Naples* (Rome: Viella, 2023).

Caracciolo, Carlos H. 'Natural disasters and European Printed News Network', in Raymond Joad and Moxham Noah (eds), *News Networks in Early Modern Europe* (Leiden and Boston: Brill, 2016), pp. 756–778.

Carrió-Invernizzi, Diana. *El gobierno de las imágenes. Ceremonial y mecenazgo en la Italia española de la segunda mitad del siglo XVII* (Vervuert: Iberoamericana, 2008).

Carrió-Invernizzi, Diana. 'The Viceregal Court of Naples: Ceremony and Representation of the Spanish Viceroy in the Second Half of the Seventeenth Century', in Piotr Salwa (ed) *Polish Baroque, European Contexts. Proceedings of an International Seminar held at The Institute for Interdisciplinary Studies "Artes Liberales", University of Warsaw, June 27–28, 2011* (Warszawa: [s. n.], 2012), pp. 77–93.

Caserta, Aldo ed. *Archivi Ecclesiastici Di Napoli* (Naples: G. D'Agostino, 1961).

Castaldo, Marianna. 'L'editoria nel Regno di Napoli e la circolazione del libro francese nel XVIII secolo.' *Rivista di Terra di Lavoro-Bollettino on-line dell'Archivio di Stato di Caserta* 9, 1 (2015), pp. 37–48.

Cecere, Domenico, Chiara De Caprio, Lorenza Gianfrancesco, and Pasquale Palmieri, eds. *Disaster Narratives in Early Modern Naples. Politics, Communication and Culture* (Rome: Viella, 2018).

Ceglia, Francesco Paolo de. *Souls of Naples. Corporeal Ghosts and Spiritual Bodies in Early Modern Naples* (Rome: Viella, 2023).

Cestaro, Antonio, ed. *Geronimo Seripando e la chiesa del suo tempo nel V centenario della nascita. Atti del convegno di Salerno, 14–16 Ottobre 1994* (Rome: Edizioni di Storia e Letteratura, 1997).

Ceva Grimaldi, Francesco. *Memorie storiche della città di Napoli* (Naples: Arnaldo Forni, 1976).

Chartier, Roger. 'Loisir et sociabilité: lire à haute voix dans l'Europe moderne.' *Littératures classiques* 12 (1990), pp. 127–147.

Chartier, Roger. *L'ordre des livres: lecteurs, auteurs, bibliothèques en Europe entre XIV e et XVIII e siècle* (Aix-en-Provence: Alinea, 1992).

Chartier, Roger, ed. *Les usages de l'imprime: XV e–XIX e siècle* (Paris: Fayard, 1987).

Cherchi, Paolo. 'Juan de Garnica: Un memoriale sul cerimoniale della corte napoletana', *Archivio Storico per le Province Napoletane* 92 (1975), pp. 213–24.

Cirese, Alberto Mario. *Cultura egemonica e culture subalterne: rassegna degli studi sul mondo popolare tradizionale* (Palermo: Palumbo 1973).

Cirillo Mastrocinque, Adelaide. *Usi e costumi popolari a Napoli nel Seicento* (Naples: Edizioni del Mezzogiorno, 1978).

Civil, Pierre, Antonio Gargano, Matteo Palumbo, and Encarnación Sánchez García, eds. *Fra Italia e Spagna: Napoli crocevia di culture durante il vicereame* (Naples: Liguori, 2011).

Cocco, Sean. *Watching Vesuvius: A History of Science and Culture in Early Modern Italy* (Chicago: Chicago University Press, 2012).

Cochrane, Eric. 'Southern Italy in the Age of the Spanish Viceroys: Some Recent Titles', *The Journal of Modern History* 58, 1 (1986), pp. 194–217.

Cohn Jr., Samuel K. *Cultures of Plague: Medical Thinking at The End of the Renaissance* (Oxford and New York: Oxford University Press, 2011).

Cohn Jr, Samuel K., Marcello Fantoni, Franco Franceschi, and Fabrizio Ricciardelli, eds. *Late Medieval and Early Modern Ritual: Studies in Italian Urban Culture* (Turnhout: Brepols, 2013).

Colapietra, Raffaele. *Vita pubblica e classi politiche del Viceregno napoletano: 1656–1734* (Rome: Edizioni di Storia e Letteratura, 1961).

Coniglio, Giuseppe. *Il regno di Napoli al tempo di Carlo V* (Naples: Edizioni scientifiche italiane, 1951).

Coniglio, Giuseppe. 'Fonti per la storia del Viceregno nell'Archivio di Stato di Napoli', *Notizie degli Archivi di Stato* 13, 2 (1953), pp. 87–92.

Coniglio, Giuseppe. *Il viceregno di Napoli nel secolo XVII* (Rome: Edizioni di Storia e Letteratura, 1955).

Coniglio, Giuseppe. *I viceré spagnoli di Napoli* (Naples: Fausto Fiorentio, 1967).

Coniglio, Giuseppe. *Consulte e bilanci del Viceregno di Napoli dal 1507 al 1533* (Rome: Istituto storico italiano per l'età moderna e contemporanea, 1983).

Coniglio, Giuseppe. *Il viceregno di Don Pietro di Toledo, 1532–53* (Naples: Giannini, 1984).

Conti, Vittorio. *Le leggi di una rivoluzione. I bandi della Repubblica Napoletana dall'Ottobre 1647 all'aprile 1648* (Naples: Jovene, 1983).

Conti, Vittorio. *La rivoluzione repubblicana a Napoli e le strutture rappresentative (1647–1648)* (Florence: Centro Editoriale Toscano, 1984).

SELECTED BIBLIOGRAPHY

Cortese, Nino. *Cultura e politica a Napoli dal Cinque al Settecento* (Naples: Edizioni Scientifiche Italiane, 1965).

Crivelli, Benedetta, and Gaetano Sabatino. 'La carrera de un mercader judeoconverso en el Nápoles español. Negocios y relaciones políticas de Miguel Vaaz (1590–1616)', *Hispania* 76, 253 (2016), pp. 323–354.

Croce, Benedetto. *Storia del Regno di Napoli* (Milan: Adelphi, 1992²).

D'Addosio, Giambattista. *Sommario dei testamenti e legati a favore della Santa Casa dell'Annunziata di Napoli che si conservano nell'archivio de' Pio Luogo, compilato da D'Addosio Giambattista Segretario Capo dello Stabilimento, dal 1466 a 1680* (Naples: pei Tipi Barnaba Cons di Antonio, 1895).

D'Alessio, Silvana. 'Un'esemplare cronologia. *Le rivoluzioni di Napoli* di Alessandro Giraffi (1647)', *Annali dell'Istituto Italiano per gli Studi Storici* 15 (1998), pp. 287–340.

D'Alessio, Silvana. 'Una nuova aurora. Su un manoscritto de *Le rivoluzioni di Napoli* di Alessandro Giraffi,' *Il pensiero politico: rivista di storia delle idee politiche e sociali* 32, 3 (1999), pp. 383–403.

D'Alessio, Silvana. 'Un'ultima punizione. Napoli, 1656', *Il pensiero politico: rivista di storia delle idee politiche e sociali* 36, 2 (2003), pp. 325–334.

D'Alessio, Silvana. *Masaniello. La sua vita e il suo mito in Europa* (Rome: Salerno, 2007).

D'Elia, Renata. *Vita popolare nella Napoli spagnuola* (Naples: Luigi Regina Editore, 1971).

Dandelet, Thomas James. *Spanish Rome 1500–1700* (New Haven: Yale University Press, 2001).

Dandelet, Thomas James, and John A. Marino, eds. *Spain in Italy. Politics, Society and Religion 1500–1700* (Leiden and Boston: Brill, 2007).

Darnton, Robert. 'First Steps Toward a History of Reading', *Australian Journal of French Studies*, 23, 1 (1986), pp. 5–30.

Dauverd, Céline. *Church and State in Spanish Italy: Rituals and Legitimacy in the Kingdom of Naples* (Cambridge and New York: Cambridge University Press, 2020).

De Blasiis, Giuseppe. 'Relazione della pestilenza accaduta in Napoli l'anno 1656', *Archivio Storico per le Province Napoletane* 1, 3 (1876), pp. 323–357.

De Caprio, Chiara. *Scrivere la storia a Napoli tra Medioevo e prima età moderna* (Rome: Salerno, 2012).

De Ceglia, Francesco Paolo. *Il segreto di San Gennaro. Storia naturale di un miracolo napoletano* (Turin: Einaudi, 2016).

De Frede, Carlo. 'La stampa a Napoli nel Cinquecento e la diffusione delle idee riformate', in Santoro Marco (ed). *La stampa in Italia nel Cinquecento. Atti del convegno: Roma, 17–21 ottobre 1989* (Rome: Bulzoni Editore, 1992), pp. 754–775.

De Frede, Carlo. 'Tipografi, editori e librai italiani del Cinquecento coinvolti in processi di eresia', *Rivista di storia della Chiesa in Italia* 23, 1 (1969), pp. 21–53.

212   SELECTED BIBLIOGRAPHY

De Lisio, Pasquale Alberto. *Gli anni della svolta. Tradizione umanistica e Viceregno nel primo Cinquecento Napoletano* (Salerno: Società editrice salernitana, 1976).

De Maio, Romeo. 'Storiografia dell'Ottocento ed Archivi Ecclesiastici di Napoli in riferimento alla storia delle istituzioni sociali e della cultura popolare', *Archivia Ecclesiae. Bollettino dell'Associazione Archivistica Ecclesiastica* 3–4 (1960–61), pp. 126–131.

De Maio, Romeo. 'Il problema del quietismo napoletano', *Rivista storica italiana* 81, 4 (1969), pp. 722–744.

De Maio, Romeo. 'Privilegi e criminalità nel Viceregno di Napoli', *Archivio storico per la Calabria e la Lucania* 42 (1975), pp. 43–49.

De Maio, Romeo. *Religiosità a Napoli: 1656–1799* (Napoli: Edizioni scientifiche italiane, 1997).

De Martino, Ernesto. *Il mondo magico: prolegomeni a una storia del magismo* (Turin: Einaudi, 1948).

De Martino, Ernesto. *Sud e magia* (Milan: Feltrinelli, 1959).

De Renzi, Salvatore. *Napoli nell'anno 1656. Ovvero documenti della pestilenza che desolò Napoli nell'anno 1656, preceduti dalla storia di questa tremenda sventura narrata* (Naples: tipografia di Domenico de Pascale, 1867).

De Robertis, Francesco M., and Mauro Spagnoletti, eds. *Atti del congresso internazionale di studi sull'età del Viceregno* (Bari: Grafica BGM, 1977).

De Rosa, Gabriele. *La vita religiosa nel Seicento nel Regno* (Naples: Edizioni scientifiche italiane, 1989).

De Vivo, Filippo. *Information and Communication in Venice* (Oxford and New York: Oxford University Press, 2007).

De Vivo, Filippo. *Patrizi, informatori, barbieri: politica e comunicazione a Venezia nella prima età moderna* (Milan: Feltrinelli, 2012).

Del Giudice, Giuseppe. 'Un processo di stato al tempo dei tumulti avvenuti in Napoli nel 1547 pel Tribunale della Inquisizione', *Archivio Storico per le Province Napoletane* 2, 2 (1877), pp. 205–264.

Di Franco, Saverio. 'Le rivolte del Regno di Napoli del 1647–1648 nei manoscritti napoletani', *Archivio Storico per le Province Napoletane* 125 (2007), pp. 326–457.

Di Marco, Giampiero. 'Librai, Editori e Tipografi a Napoli Nel XVII Secolo', *La Bibliofilia* 112 (2010), pp. 21–60, 141–184.

Donsì Gentile, Jolanda, et al., eds. *Archivi privati: inventario sommario* 2 vols (Naples: Arte tipografica, 1967).

Dooley, Brendan. *The Social History of Skepticism. Experience and Doubt in Early Modern Culture* (Baltimore and London: The Johns Hopkins University Press, 1999).

Dooley, Brendan, ed. *The Dissemination of News and the Emergence of Contemporaneity in Early Modern Europe* (Farnham: Ashgate, 2011).

Dooley, Brendan, ed. *A Companion to Astrology in the Renaissance* (Leiden and Boston: Brill, 2014).

SELECTED BIBLIOGRAPHY

Dooley, Brendan, and Sabrina A. Baron, eds. *The Politics of Information in Early Modern Europe* (London and New York: Routledge, 2001).

Eamon, William. 'Science and Popular Culture in Sixteenth Century Italy: the Professors of Secrets and Their Books', *The Sixteenth Century Journal*, 16, 4 (1985), pp. 471–485.

Eamon, William. *Science and the Secrets of Nature. Books of Secrets in Medieval and Early Modern Culture* (Princeton: Princeton University Press, 1994).

Edelmayer, Friedrich. 'The 'Leyenda Negra' and the Circulation of Anti-Catholic and Anti-Spanish Prejudices', *European History Online* (*2011*): http://ieg-ego.eu/en/threads /models-and-stereotypes/the-spanish-century/friedrich-edelmayer-the-ley enda-negra-and-the-circulation-of-anti-catholic-and-anti-spanish-prejudices (last accessed 15 July 2022).

Esposito, Loredana. 'Il fondo Sismico della Società Napoletana di Storia Patria', *Archivio storico per le Province napoletane* 125 (2004), pp. 597–601.

Everson, Jane E. 'The Melting Pot of Science and Belief. Studying Vesuvius in Seventeenth-century Naples', *Renaissance Studies*, 26, 5 (2012), pp. 691–727.

Faraglia, Nunzio Federigo, ed. 'Il tumulto napolitano dell'anno 1585. Relazione contemporanea', *Archivio Storico per le Province Napoletane* 11, 3 (1886), pp. 433–441.

Faraglia, Nunzio Federigo. 'Le ottine ed il reggimento popolare in Napoli', *Atti della Accademia Pontaniana* 28 (1898), pp. 1–38.

Finkelstein, David, and Alistair McCleary. *An Introduction to Book History* (London and New York: Routledge, 2013).

Firpo, Massimo. *Riforma protestante ed eresie nell'Italia del Cinquecento: un profilo storico* (Rome and Bari: Laterza, 1993).

Foglia, Orsola, and Ida Maietta, eds. *La fabbrica di San Domenico Maggiore a Napoli. Storia e Restauro* (Naples: Prismi editrice politecnica, 2016).

Forgione, Mario. *I viccrè, 1503–1707: cronache irriverenti di due secoli di dominazione spagnola a Napoli* (Naples: ESC, 1998).

Fragnito, Gigliola, and Adrian Belton, eds. *Church, Censorship and Culture in Early Modern Italy* (Cambridge and New York: Cambridge University Press, 2001).

Furchheim, Federigo. *Bibliografia del Vesuvio. Compilata e corredata di note critiche estratte dai più autorevoli scrittori vesuviani* (Naples: ditta F. Furhheim di Emilio Prass editore, 1897).

Fusco, Idamaria. *La grande epidemia: potere e corpi sociali di fronte all'emergenza nella Napoli spagnola* (Naples: Guida, 2017).

Fusco, Idamaria. 'The Importance of Prevention and Institutions. Governing the Emergency in the 1690–92 Plague Epidemic in the Kingdom of Naples', *Annales de démographie historique* 134 (2017), pp. 95–123.

Fùrnari, Mario. *Li ditti antichi de lo popolo napoletano: la tradizione popolare in Campania* (Naples: Fausto Fiorentino Editrice, 1986[5]).

Galandra, Irene Cooper. 'Unlocking pious homes: revealing devotional exchanges and religious materiality in early modern Naples', *Renaissance Studies* 33.5 (2019), pp. 832–853.

Galasso, Giuseppe. *Momenti e problemi di storia napoletana nell'età di Carlo V* (Naples: Società Napoletana di Storia Patria, 1962).

Galasso, Giuseppe. Napoli spagnola dopo Masaniello (Florence: Sansoni, 1982).

Galasso, Giuseppe. L'altra Europa. Per un'antologia storica del Mezzogiorno d'Italia (Milan: Mondadori, 1982).

Galasso, Giuseppe. *Alla periferia dell'impero: Il Regno di Napoli nel periodo spagnolo (secoli XVI–XVII)* (Turin: Einaudi, 1994).

Galasso, Giuseppe. *Napoli capitale. Identità politica e identità cittadina: studi e ricerche, 1266–1860* (Naples: Electa, 1998).

Galasso, Giuseppe, and Adriana Valerio, eds. *Donne e religione a Napoli: secoli XVI–XVIII* (Milano: Franco Angeli, 2001).

Garzya, Antonio, ed. *Per la storia della tipografia napoletana nei Secoli XV–XVIII. Atti del Convegno Internazionale – Napoli 16–17 dicembre 2005* (Naples: Accademia Pontaniana, 2006).

Gentilcore, David. *Healers and Healing in Early Modern Italy* (Manchester: Manchester University Press, 1998).

Gentilcore, David. 'Tutti i modi che adoprano i ceretani per far bezzi: Towards a database of Italian charlatans', *Ludica. Annali di storia e civiltà del gioco* 5–6 (2000), pp. 201–215.

Gentilcore, David. *Medical Charlatanism in Early Modern Italy* (Oxford and New York: Oxford University Press, 2006).

Gentilcore, David. 'Negoziare rimedi in tempo di peste: alchimisti, ciarlatani, protomedici', *Roma moderna e contemporanea*, 14 (2006), pp. 75–91.

Ginzburg, Carlo. *I Benandanti: stregoneria e culti agrari tra Cinquecento e Seicento* (Turin: Einaudi, 1972²).

Ginzburg, Carlo. *Il formaggio e i vermi: il cosmo di un mugnaio del '500* (Turin: Einaudi, 1999²).

Ginzburg, Carlo. *Storia notturna: una decifrazione del sabba* (Turin: Einaudi, 2008²).

Giustiniani, Lorenzo. *Saggio storico-critico sulla tipografia del Regno di Napoli* (Naples: nella stamperia di Vincenzo Orsini: a spese del libraio Vincenzo Altobelli, 1793).

Giustiniani, Lorenzo, ed. *Nuova collezione delle prammatiche del Regno di Napoli* 15 vols (Naples: Stamperia Simoniana, 1803–08).

Godard, Gaston, Giuseppe Guzzetta and Giuliana Frati. 'Manuscript on the Vesuvius Eruption of 1631 by the Carthusian Dom Saverio Tarfaglione', *Analecta Cartusiana* 291 (2017), pp. 16–66.

Gould, Stephen J. 'Father Athanasius on the Isthmus of a Middle State. Understanding Kircher's Paleontology', in Findlen Paula (ed), *Athanasius Kircher: The Last Man Who Knew Everything* (New York and London: Routledge, 2004: 207–237).

SELECTED BIBLIOGRAPHY

Grendler, Paul F. *Schooling in Renaissance Italy. Literacy and Learning, 1300–1600* (Baltimore and London: The Johns Hopkins University Press, 1989).

Guarino, Gabriel. 'Spanish Celebrations in Seventeenth-century Naples', *The Sixteenth Century Journal*, 37, 1 (2006), pp. 25–41.

Guarino, Gabriel. *Representing the King's Splendor: Communication and Reception of Symbolic Forms of Power in Viceregal Naples* (Manchester and New York: Manchester University Press, 2010).

Guarino, Gabriel. 'Taming Transgression and Violence in the Carnivals of Early Modern Naples', *The Historical Journal* 60, 1 (2017), pp. 1–20.

Harms, Roeland, Joad Raymond, and Jeroen Salman, eds. *Not Dead Things. The Dissemination of Popular Print in England and Wales, Italy, and the Low Countries* (Leiden and Boston: Brill, 2013).

Haug, Hélène. 'Relecture critique de l'histoire de la lecture. Régularités discursives chez les historiens modernes', *Le Moyen Âge* 120, 1 (2014), pp. 123–133.

Hernando Sánchez, Carlos José. *Castilla y Nápoles en el siglo XVI. El Virrey Pedro de Toledo: linaje, estrado y cultura (1532–1553)* (Valladolid: Junta di Castilla y León Consejería de Cultura y Turismo, 1994).

Hillgarth, Jocelyn Nigel. 'Spanish Historiography and Iberian Reality', *History and Theory, 24, 1 (1985), pp. 23–43.*

Houston, Robert Allan. *Literacy in Early Modern Europe* (London and New York: Routledge, 2022[2]).

Houston, Robert Allan. 'Literacy', *European History Online* (2011): http://ieg-ego.eu/en/threads/backgrounds/literacy (last accessed 15 July 2022).

Hugon, Alain. *Naples insurgée, 1647–1648. De l'événement à la mémoire* (Rennes: Presses Universitaires de Rennes, 2011).

Infelise, Mario. *Prima dei giornali: alle origini della pubblica informazione, secoli XVI e XVII* (Rome and Bari: Laterza, 2002).

Keen, Benjamin. 'The Black Legend Revisited: Assumptions and Realities', *Hispanic American Historical Review* 49, 4 (1969), pp. 703–719.

Kelly, Gary, ed. *The Oxford History of Popular Print Culture* 3 vols (Oxford and New York: Oxford University Press, 2011).

Kelly, Samantha. *The Cronaca di Partenope: An Introduction to and Critical Edition of the First Vernacular History of Naples* (Leiden and Boston: Brill, 2011).

Koopmans, Joop W., ed. *News and Politics in Early Modern Europe (1500–1800)* (Leuven and Dudley (MA): Peeters, 2005).

Lamal, Nina, Cumby, Jamie Helmers, J. Helmer (eds), *Print and power in Early Modern Europe (1500–1800)* (Leiden: Brill, 2021).

Lamal, Nina. 'The first Advertisements in Italian Newspapers (1683–1700)', in Weduwen, Arthur der, Walsby, Malcolm, *The book world of Early Modern Europe* (Leiden and Boston: Brill, 2022), pp. 455–480.

Lancaster, Jordan. *In the Shadow of Vesuvius: A Cultural History of Naples* (London and New York: Palgrave Macmillan, 2005).

Lombardi, Giovanni. 'Tipografia e Commercio Cartolibrario a Napoli Nel Seicento', *Studi Storici*, 39, 1 (1998), pp. 137–159.

Lombardi, Giovanni. 'Note archivistiche sulla storia dell'editoria napoletana', in Tortorelli Gianfranco (ed), *Gli archivi degli editori: studi e prospettive di ricerca* (Bologna: Pàtron, 1998), pp. 45–58.

Lombardi, Giovanni. *Tra le pagine di San Biagio. L'economia della stampa a Napoli in età moderna* (Napoli, Edizioni Scientifiche Italiane, 2000).

Lopez, Pasquale. *Riforma cattolica e vita religiosa e culturale a Napoli: dalla fine del Cinquecento ai primi del Settecento* (Naples and Rome: Istituto editoriale del Mezzogiorno, 1964).

Lopez, Pasquale. *Stampa e censura a Napoli nel '600* (Naples: Stabilimento Tip. G. Genovese, 1965).

Lopez, Pasquale. *Inquisizione, stampa e censura nel Regno di Napoli tra '500 e '600* (Naples: Edizioni del Delfino, 1974).

Lopez, Pasquale. *Sul libro a stampa e le origini della censura ecclesiastica* (Naples: Edizioni Regina, 1975).

Lopez, Pasquale. *Clero, eresia e magia nella Napoli del Viceregno* (Naples: Adriano Gallina Editore, 1984).

Lopez, Pasquale. *Napoli e la peste, 1464–1530: politica, istituzioni, problemi sanitari* (Naples: Jovene, 1989).

Lumsden, Audrey. 'A Spanish Viceroy of Naples in the Sixteenth Century', *Bulletin of Spanish Studies* 23, 89 (1946), pp. 30–37.

Macchiavelli, Gianni. *Dizionario dei librai di Napoli nel Rinascimento* (Naples: M. D'Auria Editore, 2012).

Magnanini, Suzanne. 'Postulated Routes from Naples to Paris: The Printer Antonio Bulifon and Giambattista Basile's Fairy Tales in Seventeenth-Century France', *Marvels & Tales* 21, 1 (2007), pp. 78–92.

Maiorini, Maria Grazia. *Il Viceregno di Napoli. Introduzione alla raccolta di documenti curata da Giuseppe Coniglio* (Naples: Giannini, 1992).

Mancini, Franco. *Feste ed apparati civili e religiosi in Napoli dal Viceregno alla capitale* (Naples: Edizioni scientifiche italiane, 1968).

Manzi, Pietro. *Annali della stamperia Stigliola a Porta Reale in Napoli (1593–1606)* (Florence: Olschki, 1968).

Manzi, Pietro. *Annali di Giovanni Sultzbach (Napoli, 1529–1544 – Capua, 1547)* (Florence: Olschki, 1970).

Manzi, Pietro. *La tipografia napoletana del '500. Annali di Sigismondo Mayr, Giovanni A. de Caneto, Antonio de Frizis, Giovanni Pasquet de Sallo, 1503–1535* (Florence: Olschki, 1971).

SELECTED BIBLIOGRAPHY

Manzi, Pietro. *La tipografia napoletana del '500. Annali di Mattia Cancer ed eredi, 1529–1595* (Florence: Olschki, 1972).

Manzi, Pietro. *La tipografia napoletana del '500. Annali di Giovanni Paolo Suganappo, Raimondo Amato, Giovanni de Boy, Giovanni Maria Scotto e tipografi minori (1533–1570)* (Florence: Olschki, 1973).

Manzi, Pietro. *La tipografia napoletana del '500. Annali di Giuseppe Cacchi, Giovanni Battista Cappelli e tipografi minori (1566–1600)* (Florence: Olschki, 1974).

Manzi, Pietro. *La tipografia napoletana del '500. Annali di Orazio Salviani (1566–1594)* (Florence: Olschki, 1974).

Manzi, Pietro. *La tipografia napoletana del '500. Annali di Giovanni Giacomo Carlino e di Tarquino Longo (1593–1620)* (Florence: Olschki, 1975).

Marino, John A. *Becoming Neapolitan: Citizen Culture in Baroque Naples* (Baltimore: Johns Hopkins University Press, 2011).

Mazzoleni, Jole. *Le fonti documentarie e bibliografiche dal sec. X al XX conservate presso l'Archivio di Stato di Napoli* (Naples: Arte Tipografica, 1974).

McElligot, Jason, 'Advertising and Selling in Cromwellian Newsbooks', in Shanti Graeli (ed), *Buying and Selling. The Business of Books in Early Modern Europe* (Leiden: Brill, 2019), pp. 467–488.

Messina, Pietro. 'Giuseppe Donzelli e la rivoluzione napoletana del 1647–1648', *Studi storici* 28, 1 (1987), pp. 185–202.

Michelson, Emily. *The Pulpit and the Press in Reformation Italy* (Cambridge (MA): Harvard University Press, 2013).

Midura, Rachel. 'Policing in Print: Social Control in Spanish and Borromean Milan (1535–1584)', in Lamal Nina, Cumby Jamie, Helmers J. Helmer (eds), *Print and Power in Early Modern Europe (1500–1800)* (Leiden and Boston: Brill, 2021), pp. 21–47.

Miele, Michele. 'La penetrazione protestante a Salerno verso la metà del '500 secondo un documento dell'Inquisizione', *Italia Sacra*, 15–16 (1970), pp. 829–840.

Miletti, Mario Nicola. 'Per scuotersi il giogo ispano. La nobiltà napoletana chiamata alla rivolta da un memoriale del 1688', *Frontiere d'Europa* 2, 2 (1996), pp. 151–242.

Minguito Palomares, Ana. 'Nicolás Perrey y el uso del grabado en la costrucción de la imagen del virreinato de Nápoles durante el siglo XVII. Compendio y documentación de nuevas obras', *Janus. Estudios sobra el Siglo de Oro* 9 (2020), pp. 221–274.

Mongelli, Nicola. 'Diffusione di un medicamento popolare nel Regno di Napoli: la teriaca di Andromaco', *Lares. Quadrimestrale di studi demoetnoantropologici* 42, 3–4 (1976), pp. 308–344.

Monti, Gaetano Maria. *Dal Duecento al Settecento: studi storico-giuridici* (Naples: I.T.E.A., 1925).

Mrozek Eliszezynski, Giuseppe. 'Il destino del cardinal Filomarino. Dibattito sulla rivolta, conclave e peste negli anni del viceré Castrillo (1653–1658)', *Studi storici 57, 3 (2016), pp. 605–637.*

Mrozek Eliszezynski, Giuseppe. 'Le responsabilità della rivolta. Le accuse del vicerè Oñate e le risposte del cardinal Filomarino (1648–1653)', *Studi storici 58, 1 (2017)*, pp. 119–151.

Mrozek Eliszezynski, Giuseppe. *Ascanio Filomarino: nobiltà, Chiesa e potere nell'Italia del Seicento* (Rome: Viella, 2017).

Mrozek Eliszezynski, Giuseppe. *Una fedeltà sempre in bilico: favoriti e aristocratici tra Madrid e Napoli (secoli XVI–XVII)* (Rome: Aracne, 2021).

Musi, Aurelio. 'Monumenti del dibattito politico a Napoli nella prima metà del secolo XVII', *Archivio Storico per le Province Napoletane* 90 (1973), pp. 345–372.

Musi, Aurelio. 'Integration and Resistance in Spanish Italy, 1500–1800', in Blickle Peter (ed) *Resistance, Representation, and Community* (Oxford: Clarendon Press; Strasbourg: European Science Foundation, 1977), pp. 305–319.

Musi, Aurelio. *La rivolta di Masaniello nella scena politica barocca* (Naples: Guida, 1989).

Musi, Aurelio. 'Le élites internazionali a Napoli dal primo Cinquecento alla guerra dei Trent'anni', in Del Treppo Mario (ed), *Sistema di rapporti ed élites economiche in Europa (secoli XII–XVII)* (Treppo. Naples: Liguori, 1994), pp. 133–161.

Musi, Aurelio. 'Napoli e la Spagna tra XVI e XVII secolo: studi e orientamenti storiografici recenti', *Clio* 31, 3 (1995), pp. 449–468.

Musi, Aurelio, and Saverio Di Franco, eds. *Mondo antico in rivolta (Napoli 1647–48)* (Manduria: Lacaita, 2006).

Mussell, James. 'The Passing of Print', *Media History* 18, 1 (2012), pp. 77–92.

Mutinelli, Fabio, ed. *Storia arcana ed aneddotica d'Italia raccontata dai veneti ambasciatori* 4 vols (Venice: Tip. di Pietro Naratovich, 1855–58).

Muto, Giovanni. 'Forme e contenuti economici dell'assistenza nel Mezzogiorno moderno: il caso di Napoli', in Politi Giorgio, Rosa Mario, Della Peruta Franco (eds), *Timore e carità: i poveri nell'Italia moderna. Atti del convegno 'Pauperismo e assistenza negli antichi stati italiani': Cremona, 28–30 marzo 1980* (Cremona: Biblioteca Statale di Cremona, 1982), pp. 237–258.

Muto, Giovanni. *Le finanze pubbliche napoletane tra riforme e restaurazione (1520–1634)* (Naples: Edizioni scientifiche italiane, 1980).

Napoli, Maria Consiglia. 'Lettura e circolazione del libro tra le classi popolari a Napoli tra '500 e '600', in Pellizzari Maria Rosaria (ed), *Sulle vie della scrittura. Alfabetizzazione, cultura scritta e istituzioni in età moderna* (Naples: Edizioni Scienfiche Italiane, 1989), pp. 375–390.

Napolitano, Nicola. *Masaniello e Genoino. Mito e coscienza di una rivolta* (Naples: Fausto Fiorentino Editore, 1962).

Niccoli, Ottavia. *Prophecy and People in Renaissance Italy* (Princeton: Princeton University Press, 1990).

Niccoli, Ottavia. *Rinascimento anticlericale: infamia, propaganda e satira in Italia tra Quattro e Cinquecento* (Rome and Bari: Laterza, 2005).

SELECTED BIBLIOGRAPHY

Niccoli, Ottavia. 'Cultura popolare: un relitto abbandonato?', *Studi storici* 56, 4 (2015), pp. 997–1010.

Nestola, Paola. 'Incorporati tra i confini della monarchia cattolica. Vescovi portoghesi, spagnoli e italiani nel Viceregno di Napoli durante l'unione dinastica', *Revista de História das Ideias* 33 (2012), pp. 101–163.

Notari, Francesco. 'La compagnia dei Bianchi della Giustizia: l'assistenza ai condannati a morte nella Napoli moderna', in Russo Carla (ed), *Chiesa e comunità nella Diocesi di Napoli tra Cinque e Settecento* (Naples: Guida, 1984), pp. 281–371.

Novati, Francesco, Edoardo Barbieri, and Alberto Brambilla, eds. *Scritti sull'editoria popolare nell'Italia di Antico Regime* (Rome: Archivio Guido Izzi, 2004).

Nuovo, Angela. *Il commercio librario nell'Italia del Rinascimento* (Milan: Franco Angeli, 2003).

Nuovo, Angela. *The Book Trade in the Italian Renaissance* (Leiden and Boston, Brill, 2013).

Olschki, Leo Samuele. *Choix de livres anciens rares et curieux* 13 vols (Florence: Olschki, 1907–66).

Padiglione, Carlo. *La Biblioteca del Museo Nazionale nella Certosa di S. Martino in Napoli ed i suoi manoscritti esposti e catalogati* (Naples: Stabilimento tipografico di F. Giannini, 1876).

Palmieri, Pasquale. 'Dal terremoto aretino alle eruzioni vesuviane: letture religiose della catastrofe in età rivoluzionaria', *Dimensioni e problemi della ricerca sotrica* 9, 2 (2013), pp. 225–250.

Panico, Guido. *Il carnefice e la piazza: crudeltà di Stato e violenza popolare a Napoli in età moderna* (Naples: Edizioni Scientifiche Italiane, 1985).

Petrucci, Armando, ed. *Libri, editori e pubblico nell'Europa moderna. Guida storica e critica* (Rome and Bari: Laterza, 1977).

Pettegree, Andrew. *The Book in the Renaissance* (New Haven and London: Yale University Press, 2010).

Pettegree, Andrew. *The Invention of News. How the World Came to Know About Itself* (New Haven and London: Yale University Press, 2014).

Pettegree, Andrew, ed. *Broadsheets: Single-Sheet Publishing in the First Age of Print* (Leiden and Boston: Brill, 2017).

Piedimonte, Antonio Emanuele. *Alchimia e medicina a Napoli. Viaggio alle origini delle arti sanitarie tra antichi ospedali, spezierie, curiosità e grandi personaggi* (Naples: Intra Moenia, 2014).

Pollmann, Judith. *Memory in Early Modern Europe, 1500–1800* (London and New York: Oxford University Press, 2017).

Pontieri, Ernesto. 'Sulle origini della compagnia dei Bianchi della Giustizia in Napoli e sui suoi statuti del 1525', *Campania Sacra* 3 (1972), pp. 1–26.

SELECTED BIBLIOGRAPHY

Pontieri, Ernesto. 'Le origini della Riforma cattolico-tridentina a Napoli (note ed appunti)', in Rivista di Storia della Chiesa in Italia (ed) *Problemi di vita religiosa in Italia nel Cinquecento. Atti del convegno di storia della Chiesa in Italia: Bologna, 2–6 Settembre 1958* (Padua: Antenore, 1960), pp. 289–313.

Rak, Michele. *A dismisura d'uomo: feste e spettacolo del Barocco tra Napoli e Roma* (Palermo: Duepunti, 2012).

Randall, David. *Credibility in Elizabethan and Early Stuart Military News* (London: Pickering & Chatto, 2008).

Raymond, Joad. 'Exporting Impartiality', in Murphy, Kathryn, Traininger, Anita (eds) *The Emergence of Impartiality* (Leiden: Brill, 2014). pp. 141–167.

Raymond, Joad, ed. *Cheap print in Britain and Ireland to 1660* (Oxford and New York: Oxford University Press, 2011).

Raymond, Joad, and Moxham, Noah eds. *News Networks in Early Modern Europe* (Leiden and Boston: Brill, 2016).

Ricci, Saverio. *Il sommo inquisitore: Giulio Antonio Santori tra autobiografia e storia (1532–1602)* (Roma: Salerno, 2002).

Ricciardi, Emilio. *Appunti per una storia dell'urbanistica napoletana* (Viterbo: Betagamma, 2002).

Riccio, Luigi. 'Nuovi documenti sull'incendio vesuviano dell'anno 1631 e bibliografia di quella eruzione', *Archivio Storico per le Province Napoletane* 14, 3 (1889), pp. 489–555.

Risolo, Maria. 'Stampatori e librai della parrocchia di san Gennaro all'Olmo ai primi del '700', in Rao Anna Maria (ed), *Editoria e cultura a Napoli nel XVIII secolo. Atti del Convegno organizzato dall'Istituto Universitario Orientale, dalla Società Italiana di Studi sul Secolo XVIII e dall'Istituto Italiano per gli Studi Filosofici, Napoli, 5–7 dicembre 1996* (Naples: Liguori, 1998), pp. 97–115.

Ritchie, Neil. 'Genoino, Masaniello and the 1647 Revolution in Naples', *History Today*, 30, 6 (1980), pp. 27–32.

Rivera, Annamaria. *Il mago, il santo, la morte, la festa: forme religiose nella cultura popolare* (Bari: Dedalo, 1988).

Romeo, Giovanni. *Aspettando il boia: condannati a morte, confortatori e inquisitori nella Napoli della Controriforma* (Florence: Sansoni, 1993).

Romeo, Giovanni. *Il fondo Sant'Ufficio dell'Archivio Diocesano di Napoli. Inventario (1549–1647)* (Naples: Editoriale Comunicazioni Sociali, 2003).

Rosa, Mario. 'Vita religiosa e pietà eucaristica nella Napoli del Cinquecento', *Rivista di Storia e Letteratura Religiosa* 4, 1 (1968), pp. 38–54.

Rovito, Pier Luigi, *Il Viceregno spagnolo di Napoli: ordinamento, istituzioni, culture di governo* (Naples: Arte tipografica, 2003).

Rozzo, Ugo. *La strage ignorata. I fogli volanti a stampa nell'Italia dei secoli XV e XVI* (Udine: Forum, 2008).

SELECTED BIBLIOGRAPHY

Russell, Camilla. *Giulia Gonzaga and the Religious Controversies of Sixteenth-Century Italy* (Turnhout: Brepols, 2006).

Russo, Piera, Sara D'Amico, and Ivana Rocco, eds. *Le miscellanee del Fondo Villarosa della Biblioteca Nazionale di Napoli: vita sociale e civile nella Napoli del Settecento* (Napoli: Arte'm, 2017).

Sabato, Milena. *Il sapere che brucia. Libri, censure e rapporti Stato-Chiesa nel Regno di Napoli fra '500 e '600* (Galatina (LE): Congedo, 2009).

Sachet, Paolo. *Publishing for the popes. The Roman Curia and the Use of Printing (1527–1555)* (Leiden, Boston: Brill, 2020).

Salman, Jeroen. *Pedlars and the Popular Press: Itinerant Distribution Networks in England and the Netherlands 1600–1850* (Leiden and Boston: Brill, 2014).

Salzberg, Rosa. *Ephemeral City. Cheap Print and Urban Culture in Renaissance Venice* (Manchester: Manchester University Press, 2014).

Sánchez García, Encarnación. *Imprenta y cultura en la Napoles virreinal: los signos de la presencia espanola* (Florence: Alinea, 2007).

Sánchez García, Encarnación. 'Cultura hispánica impresa en Nápoles hacia 1630', In Wood Noble Oliver, Roe Jeremy, Lawrance Jeremy (eds), *Poder y saber: bibliotecas y bibliofilia en la época del conde-duque de Olivares* (Madrid: Centro de Estudios Europa Hispánica, 2011), pp. 455–478.

Sánchez García, Encarnación. 'Genero historico y recepcion de modelos clasicos en la Napoles del siglo XVI: algunos ejemplos', In Bravo Paloma, Iglesias Cècile and Sangirardi Giuseppe (eds), *La renaissance des genres: pratiques et théories des genres littéraires entre Italie et Espagne (XV–XVII siècles)* (Dijon: Éditions universitaires de Dijon, 2012), pp. 166–179.

Sánchez García, Encarnación. 'Producción impresa hispánica en el Reino de Nápoles (1503–1707)', in Puga Marìa Luisa Cerròn (ed), *Siglo de Oro (prosa y poesía)* (Rome: Bagatto, 2012), pp. 338–346.

Sánchez García, Encarnación, ed. *Lingua spagnola e cultura ispanica a Napoli fra Rinascimento e barocco: testimonianze a stampa* (Naples: Pironti, 2013).

Sánchez García, Encarnación, ed. *Rinascimento meridionale: Napoli e il viceré Pedro de Toledo (1532–1553)* (Naples: Pironti, 2016).

Savarino, Renzo. 'Lo sviluppo della liturgia ufficiale. Le modalità del culto della sindone nel tempo', in Zaccone Gian Maria, Ghiberti Giuseppe (eds), *Guardare la Sindone. Cinquecento anni di liturgia sindonica* (Cantalupa (TO): Effatà Editrice, 2007), pp. 205–226.

Sbordone, Silvia. *Editori e tipografi a Napoli nel '600* (Naples: Accademia Pontaniana, 1990).

Scaduto, Francesco. *Censura della stampa negli ex regni di Sicilia e di Napoli* (Palermo: Stab. Tip. Virzì, 1886).

Scaramella, Pierroberto. *Le lettere della Congregazione del Sant'Ufficio ai tribunali di fede di Napoli, 1563–1625* (Trieste: Edizioni Università di Trieste; Naples: Istituto Italiano per gli Studi Filosofici, 2002).

Scaramella, Pierroberto. "Inquisizione, eresia e poteri feudali nel Viceregno napoletano alla metà del Cinquecento." in *Per il Cinquecento religioso italiano: clero, cultura, società. Atti del convegno internazionale di studi, Siena, 27–30 Giugno 2001* 2 vols (Rome: Edizioni dell'Ateneo, 2003), pp. 513–521.

Scarth, Alwyn. *Vesuvius: A biography* (Princeton and Oxford: Oxford University Press, 2009).

Segarizzi, Arnaldo. *Bibliografia delle stampe popolari italiane della Reale biblioteca Nazionale di San Marco di Venezia* (Bergamo: Istituto Italiano d'Arti Grafiche, 1913).

Shepard, Leslie. *The History of Street Literature: The Story of Broadside Ballads, Chapbooks, Proclamations, News-Sheets, Election Bills, Tracts, Pamphlets, Cocks, Catchpennies and Other Ephemera* (Newton Abbot: David and Charles, 1973).

Silletti, Costanza. 'Alle radici dell'editoria nel Regno di Napoli. I capitoli statutari della Confraternita di S. Biagio dei librai a Napoli', *Bollettino Storico della Basilicata*, 18 (2002), pp. 255–263.

Silvestri, Alfonso. 'Sui banchieri pubblici napoletani nella prima metà del Cinquecento. Notizie e documenti', *Bollettino dell'Archivio Storico del Banco di Napoli*, 2 (1950), pp. 22–34.

Strazzullo, Franco. *I diari dei cerimonieri della Cattedrale di Napoli: una fonte per la storia napoletana* (Naples: Agar, 1961).

Tedeschi, John A. *The Prosecution of Heresy: Collected Studies on the Inquisition in Early Modern Italy* (Binghamton (NY): Medieval & Renaissance Texts & Studies, 1991).

Thorndike, Lynn. *History of Magic and Experimental Science* 8 vols (New York: Columbia University Press, 1923–58).

Tortora, Alfonso. *L'eruzione vesuviana del 1631. Una storia moderna* (Rome: Carocci, 2014).

Ventura, Piero. *La capitale dei privilegi. Governo spagnolo, burocrazia e cittadinanza a Napoli nel Cinquecento* (Naples: Federico II University Press, 2018).

Villani, Pasquale. *Nunziature di Napoli* (Rome: Istituto storico italiano, 1962).

Villari, Rosario. *La rivolta antispagnola a Napoli: le origini (1585–1647)* (Rome and Bari: Laterza, 1976).

Villari, Rosario. *Ribelli e riformatori: dal XVI al XVIII secolo* (Rome: Editori Riuniti, 1979).

Villari, Rosario. 'Masaniello: Contemporary and Recent Interpretations', *Past & Present* 108, 1 (1985), pp. 117–132.

Villari, Rosario. *Elogio della dissimulazione: la lotta politica nel Seicento* (Rome and Bari: Laterza, 1987).

Villari, Rosario. *Per il re o per la patria: la fedeltà nel Seicento* (Rome and Bari: Laterza, 1994).

SELECTED BIBLIOGRAPHY

Villari, Rosario. *Politica barocca: inquietudini, mutamento e prudenza* (Rome and Bari: Laterza, 2010).

Villari, Rosario. *Un sogno di libertà. Napoli nel declino di un impero* (Milan: Mondadori, 2012).

Vitale, Giuliana. 'Ricerche sulla vita religiosa e caritativa a Napoli tra Medioevo ed Età Moderna', *Archivio Storico per le Province Napoletane* 86–87 (1970), pp. 207–291.

Wassyng Roworth, Wendy. 'The Evolution of History Painting: Masaniello's Revolt and Other Disasters in Seventeenth-Century Naples', *The Art Bulletin* 75, 2 (1993), pp. 219–234.

Weduwen, Arthur der, Pettegree, Andrew, *The Dutch Republic and the Birth of Modern Advertising* (Leiden: Brill, 2020).

Weduwen, Arthur der, Pettegree, Andrew, Kemp, Graeme eds. *Book Trade Catalogues in Early Modern Europe* (Leiden and Boston: Brill, 2021) https://doi.org/10.1163/9789004422247.

Wos, Jan Wladyslaw. *Annibale di Capua. Nunzio Apostolico e Arcivescovo di Napoli (1544 ca.–1599) Materiali per una biografia.* (Rome: Fondazione Giovanni Paolo II, 1984).

Zappella, Giuseppina. *Tipografia campana del Cinquecento: centri e stampatori. Dizionario storico-bibliografico* (Naples: Accademia Pontaniana, 1984).

Index of Modern Authors

Burke, Peter   10–11

Cecere, Domenico   150
Croce, Benedetto   15

Darnton, Robert   13
De Vivo, Filippo   5, 6
Di Marco, Giampiero   26
Di Martino, Ernesto   10
Dooley, Brendan   5

Gentilcore, David   140
Ginzburg, Carlo   10–11

Infelise, Mario   5

Lopez, Pasquale   153

Manzi, Pietro   35, 53

Niccoli, Ottavia   6, 7

Raymond, Joad   7
Romeo, Giovanni   21, 153, 164

Salzberg, Rosa   6

Thornidike, Lynn   117

Index of Names and Subjects

Abbate, Giuseppe 50–51
accademia degli Erranti 125
accademia degli Incauti 129*n*26
accademia degli Insensati 125*n*17
accademia degli Investiganti 121
accademia degli Oziosi 121
accademia de' Segreti 121
Aguiar, Emanuel 141
Alba, Fernando Álvarez de Toledo y Mendoza Duke of 51*n*33
Alecci, Sebastiano 137*n*41
Alexander VI (pope) 158–159
Alfonso V of Aragon 2
Angelis, Alonso 140*n*48
Aniello, Tommaso 93–97
See also Masaniello
Annese, Gennaro 93*n*9, 94–97, 107
Apolloni, Giovanni 126
Arpaia, Francesco Antonio 106
Austria, Juan José de 95, 112

Bacco, Enrico 158
Bacon, Francis 117
Bagatta, Giovanni Bonifacio 147*n*65
Baratto, Agostino 138
Baronio, Cesare (cardinal) 132
Beltramo (family) 35
Beltramo, Ottavio 121*n*10, 123, 129*n*26, 135*n*33, 137*n*39, 175
Benavides Dávila y Corella, Francisco de 52
Benigno, Domenico 25*n*
Benincasa, Orsola 140, 147
Bentivolo, Angelo 158
Biase, Giuliano 183*n*2
Bonadonna, Orazio 121*n*10
Bonino, Scipione 166
Bovarini, Leandro 125*n*17
Bove, Vincenzo 122*n*12, 123, 126*n*20, 129*n*26
Bozzuti, Giuseppe 140*n*48
Braccini, Giulio Cesare 135*n*32
Brancaccio, Carlo 87
Brancaccio, Francesco Maria (cardinal) 23
Bucca, Ferrante 136
Bulifon, Antonio 5*n*9, 35, 43–45, 50–53, 53*n*36, 55, 56*n*, 83, 125*n*18, 182–184
Bulifon, Nicola 55, 183

Campanile, Giuseppe 51
Capaccio, Giulio Cesare 90*n*5
Capocefalo, Giuseppe 118
Caracciolo (prior) 169
Carafa, Decio 162
Carlino, Giovanni Giacomo 158–161
Caserta, Francesco Antonio 162
Castaldo, Salvatore 162
Castriglio [i.e. Castrillo], García de Avellaneda y Haro Count of 141, 147
Catalina Micaela Infanta of Spain and Duchess of Savoy 177
Cattaneo, Carlo 172
Cavalli, Francesco 127*n*22
Cavallo, Camillo 20, 67–69, 69*n*21, 70–73, 76–79, 80*n*34, 83–85
Cavallo, Ludovico 67–68, 74*n*, 76, 83
Celano, Carlo 53, 55*n*, 147, 148*n*68
Charles II of Spain 182
Charles III, Duke of Savoy 176
Charles V of Habsburg 170
Charles VI of Habsburg 182
Cicconio, Ettore 177*n*37
Clement VIIII (pope) 177
Clement IX (pope) 177
Consiglio Collaterale 46, 51–53, 61
Conte, Leonardo 158
Converso, Attanasio 167
Córdoba, Gonzalo Fernández de 1, 32, 66
Cortese, Isabella 120
Costo, Tommaso 90*n*5
Criscuolo, Maddalena 55
Cuomo, Vincenzo 123

d'Andrea, Giovanni Antonio 118
d'Avalos, Alfonso Francesco 33, 34*n*
de Brosse, Claudine 176
de David, Franciscus Antonius 34
De Fusco, Luca Antonio 53*n*36, 116*n*1, 145*n*60
de' Lazari, Ignazio 181
Delegazione della Real Giurisdizione 19, 49*n*29
See also Real Giurisdizione
del Fiore, Giuseppe 158
Della Porta, Giovan Battista 54, 55, 118, 121

INDEX OF NAMES AND SUBJECTS

del Negro, Gasparino   144
deputati della Salute   140–144
De Renzi, Salvatore   118, 139, 141n51, 146n62,
   149n
de Ulloa, Alfonso   170
Di Capua, Annibale   21, 151, 155–156
Di Fusco, Pietro   51n33
d'Onofrio, Vincenzo   52n
   See also Fuidoro, Innocenzo
Donzelli, Giuseppe   104n19, 105

Eugeni, Frat'Angelo   135n33

Favella, Geronimo   67, 128n23
Filomarino, Ascanio (cardinal)   169, 172
Finella, Filippo   129
   See also Lanelfi
Forleo, Giovanni   129
Forment, Juad   91
Fuidoro, Innocenzo   51n33, 52, 120n, 170,
   173n30
   See also Vincenzo d'Onofrio
Furchheim, Federigo   124n16

Gaffaro, Lorenzo   55, 105n21, 108n
Gagliaro, Altobello   177
Galilei, Galileo   117
Garzia Mellini, Giovanni (cardinal)   174
Gatta, Geronimo   145
gazzette   20–24, 53, 56, 61, 68–79, 83
Giannetti, Giovanni   129n25
Genoino, Giulio   94
Giotti, Giovanni Battista   51n33
Giraffi, Alessandro   92n
Giuliano, Donato   78, 79n
Giunta (family)   43, 45
Giunta, Luca Antonio   43
Giustiniani, Lorenzo   46n26
Giustiniani, Lucio   35
Gobat, George   178
Gondi, Giovan Battista   146n61
Grande de Lorenzana, Francisco   137n39
Grassi, Pietro Andrea   44
Grimaldi, Donato   140n48
Guise, Henry II de Lorraine Duke of   55,
   95–99, 101–108, 108n

Julius II (pope)   176

Kircher, Athanasius   170

Lanelfi   129n26
Lazzeri, Francesco   147n65
Ledesma, Pedro de   166
Leo, Luise   43
Liotti, Francesco   141
Longo, Egidio   25, 51, 52, 54, 58, 85, 109,
   110n31, 114, 122n12, 123, 126n20, 135,
   141–143, 147, 161, 164
Longo, Tarquinio   54
Lopez, Miguel   70
los Vélez, Pedro Fajardo de Zúñiga y
   Requeséns, Marquess of   92n
Lotti, Giovanni   125

Maccaramo, Domenico Ferrante   35, 85,
   110n30, 121n10, 123, 175
Maffuccio, Andrea   64n11
Magliabechi, Antonio   5n9
Manuzio (family)   43
Maria Anna of Habsburg Infanta of Spain
   136
Masaniello   93–95, 115, 137
   rebellion/revolt   1, 22, 24, 26, 54, 55, 59,
      60, 82, 88, 93–97, 102, 104, 110, 138, 172
   See also Aniello, Tommaso
Masino, Michel'angelo   134
Martorella, Felice   143n57
Moccia, Luigi   14
Monlivet, Stefano   35
Monterrey, Manuel de Acevedo y Zúñiga
   Count of   67, 128n23, 135
Morexano, Carlo   137–138, 141n49, 144–145,
   148n67
Mosca, Felice   183n3
Murat, Gioacchino   165

Navarrete, Antonio Pérez   91
Normile, Gioseffo   122n12

Ognatte [i.e. Oñate] Íñigo Vélez de Guevara,
   Count of   114n36
Orlandi, Francesco Antonio   112, 114n36
Orlandi, Giovanni   132–134, 137n39
Osuna, Pedro Téllez-Girón, Duke of   90

Pace, Antonio   158
Paci, Giovanni Francesco   171n27
Padavino, Marc'Antonio   127n22, 136
Parrino, Domenico Antonio   43, 52–53, 56,
   57n1, 67–76, 80n34, 85, 140n48, 145, 182

INDEX OF NAMES AND SUBJECTS

Pepe, Filippo Giacomo   69
Peretti (abbot)   25
Perrey, Alexis   122
Perrey, Nicolas   175
Philip V of Spain   182
Pignoranda [i.e. Peñaranda], Gaspar de
    Bracamonte, Count of   120
plague   1, 24, 117, 137–150, 172
Porsile, Carlo   64n12, 65n17, 66n
Prezioso, Giovanni Camillo   151
Proposito, Giovanni Pietro   158

Raillard, Giacomo   35, 55
Real Cancelleria   46
Real Giurisdizione   47–51
    See also Delegazione della Real
    Giurisdizione
Regia Camera della Sommaria   125
Riaco, Carlo Francesco   137
Riessenger, Sixtus   2
Romano, Giovanni Orlando   126n21
Roncagliolo (family)   123
Roncagliolo, Domenico   125n18, 126n19,
    129n25, 134n28, 137n39, 161
Roncagliolo, Secondino   35, 44, 55, 58, 106n,
    107n24, 125n17, 127n21, 128n23, 129n25,
    135n32, 161–164
Rosano, Giovan Giacomo   36
Rosselli, Giuseppe   55
Ruffo, Carlo   128n23
Ruffo, Flavio   127, 128n23

Salamanca, Juan de   162
Salviani, Orazio   33

San Domenico Maggiore (convent)   20,
    164–168
San Gennaro   124–129, 134, 135, 136, 146, 170,
    172, 179, 180
Santa Rosalia   21
Savio, Francesco   123
Scoriggio, Lazzaro   116n1, 123, 126n21, 128n23,
    132n
Severino, Marco Aurelio   143n57
Spadaro, Micco   93n9, 127, 139
Spatafora, Antonia   128n23
Speyer, Johann of   2
Spinola, Giulio   141
Starace, Vincenzo   88–91
Summonte, Giovanni Antonio   53n36, 90n5

Tabanelli, Domenico   158
Terragnolo, Giacomo   174
Thiene, Gaetano (saint)   21, 181
Toledo y Zúñiga, Pedro Álvarez de   12, 26,
    33, 57n1, 154
Tommaso, Pietro   137n40
Toppi, Niccolò   125

Urban VIII (pope)   175, 181

Venderosa, Gio[vanni] Antonio   45
Vesuvius   24, 66, 96, 122, 131, 134, 137, 170, 171
    See also volcanic eruption
volcanic eruption   1, 27, 117, 122–137, 172

Zupi, Giovanni Battista   171n27